Andrew M. Scott

The Dynamics of Interdependence

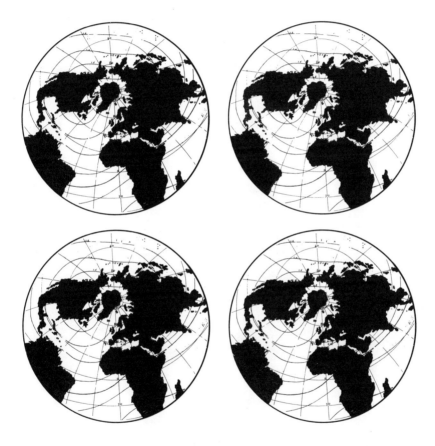

The University of North Carolina Press

Chapel Hill and London

© 1982 The University of North Carolina Press

All rights reserved

Manufactured in the United States of America

Library of Congress Cataloging in Publication Data

Scott, Andrew MacKay.
   The dynamics of interdependence.

   Bibliography: p.
   Includes index.
   I. International relations. I. Title.
JX1395.S349   327.1   82-2023
ISBN 0-8078-1527-6   AACR2
ISBN 0-8078-4092-0 (pbk.)

Contents

Introduction

Since humankind's knowledge and physical capacities have never been as great as they now are, how does it happen that there are so many difficult international problems? How does it happen that nations, even the most powerful, have difficulty achieving the ends they desire and avoiding the ills they want to avoid? Why is it that the global scene is littered with major and persistent problems for the existence of which no actor can be held clearly responsible—inflation, pollution, energy crises, emerging resource shortages, food and population problems, the great gap between rich and poor nations, an unstable international economic system, problems with multinational corporations, and so on? Where do such problems spring from and why are they proving so hard to deal with?

Despite the fact that they have been studying the subject for several millennia, scholars and statesmen have not achieved an adequate understanding of international politics. Principally this is because the world keeps changing while they are striving to describe and understand it. The conditions Thucydides depicted in *The Peloponnesian Wars*, or those that Machiavelli advised a prince about, have a good deal in common with contemporary conditions but are also different in important respects.

A body of knowledge, insight, and theory concerning international politics has developed over time but it has not kept pace with the profound transformations taking place in the international system. Individuals perceive the world in terms of the mental constructs with which their minds are furnished, but many of the concepts being used today in an effort to comprehend the global system are tired leftovers from an earlier era. Reality has outrun theory. Humankind is trying to understand and manage a highly interactive and interdependent world while relying upon assumptions and concepts developed for a preinterdependent world. Thucydides and Machiavelli may have had a better grip on the international scene in their respective times than contemporaries do today, because the fit between ideas and reality may have been closer then.

The traditional issues of world politics in the preinterdependent era normally revolved around matters of domination and subordination, power and control. They had to do with the way in which relationships among actors were established, managed, and changed, with the capabilities of actors, and with the strategies and tactics that they might utilize. These issues had to do, often, with relationships between actors in special subsystems. The contemporary scene abounds with examples of that kind of relationship—Soviet-American relations, relations between the USSR and the nations of Eastern Europe, Arab-Israeli differences, relationships within the NATO alliance, and so on. These are problems of a kind that Alexander, Caesar, Napoleon, or Metternich would have understood. Issues of this kind have probably existed since the beginning of relations between organized geographic units. Their emergence did not depend on a particular level of technology and required only enough interaction to allow contending parties to come into contact with one another. It is not surprising, then, to find such issues analyzed in a perceptive way by Thucydides. In the preinterdependent era there was little concern for global problems because there were few of them and it was too early for observers to think globally. Thucydides could, and did, think in what we would now call "systems" terms about the problems of the Greek city-states, but global thinking lay several thousand years in the future.

With technological advances and a rise in the level of interaction among actors, however, the situation began to change rapidly in the twentieth century. Issues arose the very existence of which would have astonished a Caesar or Napoleon: issues involving global inflation, recession, unemployment, currency instabilities; environmental issues involving pollution of the atmosphere, the seas, oceans, and lakes, inadvertent weather modification, purposeful weather modification, the elimination of entire species; global resource issues relating to energy, minerals, over-fishing of the seas, the mining of the ocean depths, the proper way to utilize the Antarctic continent; issues involving the creation of global organizations to promote peace, development, and improvement in the quality of life around the world; issues relating to global population, total world food production, the carrying capacity of the globe and the nature of limits to growth. We find little nourishment in Thucydides concerning such matters.

Problems of this kind cut across national boundaries and the lines of various subsystems and may be global in extent. A polluted atmosphere circulates alike over western and eastern European countries. If the oxygen-producing capabilities of the oceans should be damaged, the problem would affect both developed and developing nations. If the climate should be radically changed, the ozone layer seriously damaged, fossil fuel resources exhausted, or if world population should not be brought under control, the effects would be felt by socialist and nonsocialist nations alike.

Humankind has long had the capacity to fashion global problems but the means by which it formerly did so were so slow-moving that the problems were scarcely conceived of as involving human agency. For that reason they went largely unrecognized. Deforestation of the lands around the Mediterranean began early, as did desertification of once-fertile lands in the Near East. Unplanned cultural diffusion has also been a powerful force for centuries (Braudel, 1973, 2:757–75; Wallerstein, 1974, chaps. 5 and 6).

Although global processes existed in earlier epochs they were then far fewer in number. In the twentieth century the rate of production of global processes and problems has turned sharply upward, and for reasons that are apparent. The number of actors on the world scene has increased greatly, the level of interaction among them has increased, and the impact of the technologies at their disposal has increased markedly. Global processes, therefore, are both more numerous and ripen faster than they once did. Humankind can do in a decade that which, earlier, might have taken centuries.

Because global problems were uncommon in earlier centuries, and then usually went unrecognized, analysts have had little experience in thinking about them. Now, however, they must devote attention to such problems. Conceptually, analysts are caught between two different worlds. On the one hand, there is the relatively simple world that existed before World War I and that was explained fairly well by the traditional notions of power politics. On the other hand, there is the vastly more complex world of the present that is, thus far, very inadequately comprehended. Unless humankind can come to understand what is happening to it and why, it will be powerless to shape events and will drift with the tide. Needed, therefore, is a vastly improved understanding of the dynamics of interaction and interdependence. What combination of processes moved the global system from what it was to what it now is? And what processes are now at work that will give it the configuration it will have in years to come? Can we see through events, and beneath them, and discern emerging patterns? Can we understand the way in which the newer kind of global problems are tied in with the more traditional issues of power politics?

This book will seek to answer some of those questions. It is organized into four parts. Part I will deal with the evolutionary dynamics of the global system and the state of our understanding of them. Part II will examine "constraint systems" and some of the problems of traditional power politics. Part III will treat relationships between constraint systems and global processes. Part IV will deal with a range of problems associated with the management of global change. How are sovereign nations, caught up in power politics and preoccupied with questions of the national interest, to achieve the collective foresight and the degree of consensus needed for the management of contemporary global processes?

Abbreviations

EEC   European Economic Community

GATT   General Agreement on Tariffs and Trade

GEMS   Global Environmental Monitoring System

IBRD   International Bank for Reconstruction and Development
          (World Bank)

IGO   international governmental organization

IMF   International Monetary Fund

NATO   North Atlantic Treaty Organization

NGO   international nongovernmental organization

NIEO   New International Economic Order

NIIO   New International Information Order

OPEC   Organization of Petroleum-Exporting Countries

PLO   Palestinian Liberation Organization

SALT II   Strategic Arms Limitation Treaty II

SEATO   Southeast Asia Treaty Organization

TNE   transnational enterprise

UNCTAD   United Nations Conference on Trade and Development

UNEP   United Nations Environmental Program

Part I.
Evolutionary Dynamics
of the Global System

1. A World in Transition

An Interaction/Technology Continuum

In the distant past civilizations often existed without being aware of one another. One of the by-products of the travels of a Marco Polo, a Columbus, or a Cortez was the introduction of these civilizations to one another. During the fifteenth century most societies touched each other only occasionally and what happened in one society was apt to be little influenced by what happened in other parts of the globe. In the sixteenth century the tempo of interaction around the Mediterranean basin picked up and, as a consequence of the great explorations, developments in the New World and Asia began to influence European nations (Braudel, 1973).

The Seven Years War (1756–63) afflicted almost all of Europe and North America, and its consequences reached to India. The nineteenth century opened with the far-reaching Napoleonic Wars, and the twentieth century brought the first conflict to be called a world war. When it was resumed in 1939, it was, of course, another world war. Over a period of centuries the geographical extent of the global system expanded and the intensity of interaction within it increased manyfold.

Signs of the increase as well as reasons for it are not hard to find. The single most important factor contributing to the growth of interaction has doubtless been the economic. A global economy took shape in the eighteenth century and became more closely knit in the nineteenth and twentieth centuries.[1] The web of markets grew more dense, increased in number, expanded in scope, and· became linked with one another (Gilpin, 1977). By the middle of the nineteenth century Karl Marx, in the *Communist Manifesto*, was able to depict the impact of some market processes quite clearly.

> The bourgeoisie, by the rapid movement of all instruments of production, by the immensely facilitated means of communication, draws all, even the most barbarian, nations into civilization. The cheap prices

of its commodities are the heavy artillery with which it batters down all Chinese walls, with which it forces the barbarians' intensely obstinate hatred of foreigners to capitulate. It compels all nations, on pain of extinction, to adopt the bourgeois mode of production; it compels them to introduce what it calls civilization into their midst, i.e., to become bourgeois themselves. In one word, it creates a world after its own image. [Marx and Engels, 1959, p. 11]

Technological advances have also been important contributors to the growth of interaction. With the arrival of the new energy base represented by the fossil fuels—coal, gas, oil—humans began to draw on the capital accumulation of millions of years and the tempo of interaction accelerated markedly. These energy sources came to drive factories and to propel ships and trains and, in time, planes. Metallurgy and technology made rapid strides, thousands of new products were drawn into existence, mass production appeared on the scene and was followed by mass distribution as well.

Speed of movement has also accelerated sharply. Through most of history man's movement could not exceed the speed of a running horse. In the nineteenth century, with the steam locomotive, speeds started climbing and in the 1890s the speed of one hundred miles per hour was first exceeded. People, products, mail, and communications in general were on an upward curve. By the 1960s velocities had been achieved that allowed an escape from the gravitational pull of the earth, and the exploration of the solar system could begin. So swift has been this development that a single life can easily extend from the first powered flight in 1903 to intercontinental supersonic passenger flight.

To be sure, not everything can be done at once. Some things cannot be done until appropriate technologies are at hand. As Arthur C. Clarke has reminded us: "You cannot bridge the Golden Gate with wood—you have to wait until the steel age arrives; you cannot operate a TV system with ropes and pulleys—you have to wait until electronics come along" (1965, p. 50). By the same token, however, as the number of available technologies increases—steel, electronics, hydraulics, etc.—the ways in which those technologies can be imaginatively coupled increases sharply and the rate of technological innovation, in consequence, climbs rapidly. With millions of scientists and technicians in thousands of factories and laboratories in dozens of countries all working actively, important technological innovations are no longer separated by centuries or even decades but seem to appear in a more or less continuous flow. So closely do advanced technologies come on the heels of one another

—computers, nuclear energy, television, microelectronics, communications satellites, lasers—that they are created almost simultaneously, for all practical purposes, and coexist and combine with one another in scores of ways.

Another factor contributing to the growth of interaction has been the increase in the number of actors on the global scene. There is now almost no region that remains outside the global system. Scores of new nations have come into existence since 1945, and the aggregate of resources devoted to international activities of all kinds by governments has grown exponentially. The repertoire of actions available to these actors has also expanded as a result of technological and social innovation. In addition, whole new categories of actors have become important: regional organizations, international governmental organizations, multinational corporations, and transnational organizations such as the Organization of Petroleum-Exporting Countries and the Palestinian Liberation Organization.

As the global system became more interactive, there was an increase in the number of issues and wants being agitated that, in turn, led to a rapid rise in the number of international organizations in existence. The sixteenth edition of the *Yearbook of International Organizations* (Brussels: Union of International Associations, 1977) lists over 4,600 organizations, governmental and nongovernmental, and the number climbs each year. The resources devoted to international activities by these organizations also appear to be increasing. This means that the institutional environment continues to change and that the actions poured into the global arena by international organizations are multiplying.

Each of these factors—economic development and commerce, technological advance, the increase in the number of actors and actions—had profound international implications. As the global system developed, it became clear that any important new process or product would soon be internationalized wherever it might originate. John Maynard Keynes was struck by the way in which technology and economic organization had combined to produce a tightly knit world economy by 1914.

> The inhabitant of London could order by telephone, sipping his morning tea in bed, the various products of the whole earth, in such quantity as he might see fit, and reasonably expect their early delivery upon his doorstep; he could at the same moment and by the same means adventure his wealth in the natural resources and new enterprises of any quarter of the world, and share, without exertion or even trouble, in their pro-

> spective fruits and advantages. . . . He could secure forthwith, if he
> wished it, cheap and comfortable means of transit to any country or
> climate without passport or other formality. [1920, p. 11]

When that world economy broke down in the 1930s, the Great Depression
was unavoidably worldwide.

The development of a world economy moved forward again rapidly after
World War II. The Bretton Woods arrangements were set up to foster trade
and encourage development, and they succeeded in doing so. Transnational
enterprises grew in number and size and became important agents of international interaction. Investment, resource use, research, production, distribution, the provision of services—all of them were significantly internationalized.

The direction of movement of these processes is interesting but so, too, is
their evident acceleration. Perception of this acceleration is not new. Henry
Adams, in his *The Education of Henry Adams*, dwelt at length on the acceleration of scientific and technological innovation and formulated a general Law
of Acceleration, which has been little remarked. Alfred North Whitehead
commented on it during the 1930s:

> If we compare the technologies of civilization west of Mesopotamia
> at the epochs 100 A.D., the culmination of the Roman Empire, and 1400
> A.D., the close of the Middle Ages, we find practically no advance in
> technology. There was some gain in metallurgy, some elaboration of
> clockwork, the recent invention of gunpowder with its influence all in
> the future, some advance in the art of navigation, also with its influence
> in the future. If we compare 1400 A.D. with 1700 A.D., there is a great
> advance; gunpowder, and printing, and navigation, and the technique of
> commerce, had produced their effect. But even then, the analogy
> between life in the eighteenth century and life in the great period of
> ancient Rome was singularly close. . . . In the fifty years between 1780
> and 1830, a number of inventions came with a rush into effective
> operation. The age of steam power and of machinery was introduced.
> [1933, pp. 116–17]

One indicator after another shows the same thing: gradual change over a
long period of time and sharply accelerating change during recent decades
(Appendix 1). One observer, after examining eight indicators, concluded,
"With some variation according to the specific indicator used, recent decades

reveal a general tendency for many forms of human interconnectedness across national boundaries to be doubling every ten years" (Inkeles, 1975, p. 479). To be sure, some forms of interaction have declined, such as the slave trade and passenger travel by ship, but the general trend is powerfully upward. A world in which sailing ships move across vast oceans at five knots is different from one in which satellites course through the heavens and man reaches out beyond the solar system. A world in which the ultimate weapon of war is a mounted knight is different from one in which scientists hurry from neutron warheads to lasers to particle beam weapons and beyond.

It is helpful, therefore, to conceive of the global system as having moved along a continuum, over a long period of time, from a condition characterized by relatively low levels of interaction and technology to one characterized by high, and rapidly rising, levels.

At relatively low levels of complexity, interaction is seldom a dominant factor in a social system. As a sytem becomes larger and more complex, and as the rate of interaction doubles, and doubles, and doubles again, quantitative change begins to produce qualitative change. The dynamics of the system begin to shift with each significant increase in the level of interaction. A family with one child will have different dynamics from one with five children; a town of one hundred thousand operates differently from a metropolis of several million. With an increase in size and complexity a minor problem may quickly become important and then critical. So it is with the global system. Rate of movement on the interaction/technology continuum is the single most important variable influencing system change.[2]

Interaction, Interconnectedness, Interdependence

In their discussion of interdependence as an analytic concept, Robert Keohane and Joseph Nye make this simple but helpful observation: "In common parlance *dependence* means a state of being determined or significantly affected by external forces. *Interdependence*, most simply defined, means *mutual* dependence. Interdependence in world politics refers to situations characterized by reciprocal effects among countries or among actors in different countries" (1977, p. 8). They then go on to distinguish interdependence (high-cost, important) from interconnectedness (low-cost, unimportant). In these pages, however, no distinction will be made between interdependence and interconnectedness. Indeed, the three terms (interdependence, interconnectedness, interaction) will be used interchangeably to help prevent the ennui a reader might feel from encountering a single term many times. If there is interaction or interconnectedness, then there is some degree of interdependence, even if the degree is slight and the mutual dependence somewhat asymmetrical. In international affairs dependency is a scalar variable and it would probably not be useful to try to draw a sharp distinction between effects that are costly or not costly.

The passage quoted above is highly general since it refers only to "reciprocal effects among countries or among actors in different countries." That language is interpreted here to include transnational actors such as international governmental organizations (IMF, GATT, IBRD, etc.), international nongovernmental organizations (Red Cross), transnational enterprises (Shell, Exxon, IBM), and supranational institutions such as the European Common Market.

It hardly need be pointed out that actors may affect one another without intending to do so. A government may take actions to deal with domestic economic and political situations which have ramifications affecting other actors. It may wish to deal with unemployment, inflation, declining productivity, balance-of-payments difficulties, the penetration of its markets by foreign companies, investment flows, and the like.

System Change

Evolution of the global system along the interaction/technology continuum has brought many changes since 1900. New forms of cooperation have emerged and so have new forms of conflict. War, in 1900, was largely the business of soldiers, and fighting was likely to take place away from most of the civilian population. Land warfare had not yet been mechanized and the concept of blitzkrieg and total war were still in the future. In the era before aircraft and missiles it was not yet possible to strike at a distance. A surprise attack was difficult to organize, and, in the prenuclear era, initial blows could not be truly devastating. Development of the peculiar logic of deterrence, and first and second strikes, lay in the future.

Save for an occasional dynastic war, domestic conflict was rarely internationalized. Now internal conflict is quite commonly internationalized. In 1900 observers assumed that there was war and there was peace and that those two options exhausted the possibilities. Since then, attention has come to be focused on guerrilla warfare, including "wars of national liberation," proxy wars, limited wars of various kinds, cold war, and covert operations.

Such changes in conflict and cooperation are closely associated with the increasing porosity of national borders. The fact that borders were relatively impermeable in 1900 affected the forms of conflict and cooperation that were then used, and the sharp increase in porosity since then has also affected them. Satellites wheel overhead, watching and listening. Aircraft and missiles have little trouble crossing political boundaries, and the same holds for radio transmissions and television signals bounced off satellites. Telephone lines, newspapers, magazines, books, pipelines, power lines, and people all cross borders with ease. In 1900 national economies were also, to a vastly greater extent than at present, self-contained. National actors were far less dependent on one another and on developments in the international system as a whole.

Since borders were more effective insulators then than now, a higher proportion of the problems that arose had their origins in internal affairs. Foreign policy was, therefore, less important than it now is. Furthermore, because of the relative impermeability of borders in 1900, relations between nations were largely formal and external. When nation X wanted to influence nation Y, it had to rely upon external pressure because it was incapable of reaching inside the borders of Y to exercise direct or indirect influence on decision processes in Y.

Today, however, many of the instruments of statecraft involve the crossing of national borders, with agencies of one society reaching inside another to shape its policies or processes: foreign aid, technical assistance, cultural exchange programs, information programs, military assistance and training missions, covert operations, the stationing of military forces in other countries, maintenance of foreign bases, and the like (Scott, 1965).

Another consequence of increasing interaction within the global system and increasing porosity of national borders has been an undermining of the juridical basis of the nation-state. National sovereignty is the foundation on which the nation-state rests. A necessary corollary of that principle is the doctrine of nonintervention. If each nation is a supreme legal entity, owing obedience to no higher authority, then, obviously, no nation is justified in intervening in the internal affairs of another. These twin principles—sovereignty and nonintervention—emerged as the nation-state system took shape following the Treaty of Westphalia in 1648. They were probably quite appropriate and useful at the time, for nation-states were entering an era of relative impermeability, and therefore sovereignty and nonintervention could seem like workable concepts.

As the global system continued to evolve along the interaction/technology continuum, however, these principles less and less fitted emerging realities. Today, the assistance that small nations seek from great powers is often grounded on intervention rather than nonintervention. Conversely, when the great powers exercise their leading roles, they do so increasingly by means of purposeful intervention in other societies. Great and small nations alike continue to give lip service to the principle of nonintervention, but neither can afford to see it observed in practice. The routine intervention of one nation in the affairs of another fundamentally weakens the idea of sovereignty.

Another important change in the dynamics of the global system resulting from a higher level of interaction has to do with the kinds of problems produced, their complexity, and their scope. At the turn of the century, international problems were usually of a politico-military nature and were likely to be associated with the formation, operation, or decline of particular subsystems. There were relatively few system-wide problems. Now, however, because of the increase in interaction and the advance in technology, a large number of global problems have come into existence.

The reason for this is apparent. In the eighteenth century the world still seemed almost infinite in size. Ships sailed until their crosstrees dropped below the horizon and, perhaps, were never heard from again. The outlines of continents were not yet clear and on maps vast areas were still marked *terra incognita*. Throughout most of the nineteenth century global population was growing only slowly, global resource use was modest, the impact of mankind on the environment seemed scarcely discernible, technological advances were still deemed to be synonymous with progress, and the level of global interaction was climbing but slowly. In a world that seemed infinitely large, who (save Thomas Malthus) could conceive of global crowding, resource exhaustion, environmental difficulties, "common pool" problems, and the "tragedy of the commons" writ large?

By the end of the nineteenth century, however, the locomotive, the steamship, and the wireless were beginning to shrink the world and by the last third of the twentieth century the infinite globe had come to seem very finite indeed. At one moment the polar regions were a setting for heroic exploits of explorers using dog sleds, the next moment they were crisscrossed by air routes, and governments were concerning themselves with their strategic significance or their untapped resources. For centuries the sea had been a metaphor for mystery, infinity, and nature's limitless power. Where else should Melville's Moby Dick roam but in the vastness of the seas? Yet, an instant later, mechanical devices began crawling over the ocean floor, giant drilling rigs began to suck oil from the depths, the globe-girdling seas began to be over-fished, and whales themselves were fighting extinction. Yesterday the earth was immense and replete with riches; today it is small, its resources dwindling, and men are troubled by the limits to growth. As technology and interaction stride ahead, humankind encounters, ever more frequently and sharply, the finite nature of the great planet itself.

Most individuals live in a microcosm—a village, a town, a neighborhood in a city. In the right kind of world, their lives would be smooth and undisturbed save for problems arising in that microcosm. Unfortunately, as the global system becomes more interactive and as technology moves forward, those little worlds become more vulnerable to happenings in the big world. With increasing frequency the big world fires thunderbolts at them—the consequences of inflation or recession, of trade and payments disturbances, of population and food problems, of resource problems, of new technologies, of disputes between developed and developing nations, and the consequences of assorted environmental problems. For a long time movement out along the interaction/technology continuum seemed to matter little. With the passage of time, however, it has come to matter a great deal, for global processes are thrusting themselves forward. Increasingly the dangers that must be dealt with are produced not by traditional power politics or conflictive actions but by the working of potent, impersonal processes vast in their scope.

As a social system becomes more interactive, the way it works becomes increasingly important to the individuals within it. Since that holds for the global system as well, it is not surprising that scholars have, in recent years, taken an increased interest in interaction. Interaction tends to be viewed as an unqualified good, however, and so, presumably, the more of it the better. It is normally taken for granted that interaction leads toward cultural enrichment, improved understanding between peoples, and, perhaps, toward peace as well. The dark side of interdependence—its "cost"—is being perceived only slowly. The benefits of interaction should be considered, however, only in conjunction with costs. As the amount of interaction in the global system climbs, may not costs climb as well? Furthermore, might not costs begin to climb more sharply after some critical point, significantly altering the ratio of costs to benefits? Later chapters will deal with these points.

2. Inadvertent Change

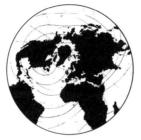

Given humankind's great capabilities, how is it that actors, both alone and working together, have so much trouble achieving those things they want and avoiding the things they do not want? Since activities in the global realm would not exist but for the actions of humans, why do so many things come to pass that no one wants? How explain the fact that human purposes so often produce unplanned historical outcomes? How has the global system developed its capacity to manufacture problems, seemingly on its own?

The Unintended

The generation of unintended consequences must surely be one of the most ancient of phenomena. Homer provides evidence of it in his account of the kidnapping of Helen, the Trojan War, and the destruction of Troy. Paris surely had no intention of destroying his own family and city. The *Iliad* and the *Odyssey* highlight another unintended consequence with their frequent references to wooded islands, wooded groves, and forest undergrowth. For centuries individuals cut wood for cooking and heat and the building of ships, and domesticated animals grazed on young shoots. By the time of the classical era, much of Greece, the area around the Mediterranean, and many of the islands, such as "woody Zacynthos" (*Odyssey*, 1:246), were becoming barren. There had been no plan to deforest these areas: it simply happened as the result of hundreds of thousands of individual decisions.

The horizons of most Athenians of the classical era were bounded by the city-states in which they lived, but the influence of Greek culture radiated outward for centuries in ways that could never have been imagined by its originators. In the first and second centuries A.D. enterprising sea captains, seeking only their own gain, were building a more or less continuous commercial network extending from Alexandria down through the Red Sea, the

Gulf of Aden, and thence east across the Arabian Sea to India and across the Bay of Bengal to Malaya and on to China. Their intent was not to link civilizations and to diffuse culture, but that is nevertheless what they were doing.

On 12 October 1492 the ships of Columbus reached the Bahamas, and the Old World forced the New to begin to interact with it. The initial contact was quickly followed by others, and many of the consequences were not at all intended. For example, the Europeans brought smallpox, measles, and typhus with them, and each of these diseases flourished. They also brought pigs, cattle, horses, sheep, and chickens, and these, too, flourished:

> One who watched the Caribbean islands from outer space during the years from 1492 to 1550 or so might have surmised that the object of the game going on there was to replace the people with pigs, dogs, and cattle. Disease and ruthless exploitation had, for all practical purposes, destroyed the aborigines of Española by the 1520s. Their Arawak brothers in Cuba, Puerto Rico, and Jamaica followed them into oblivion shortly after. The Bahamas and Lesser Antilles were not occupied by the Spanish, but as the Indians of the larger islands disappeared, slavers sailed out to the smaller islands, spread disease and seized multitudes of Arawaks and Caribs to feed into the death camps that Española, Cuba, Puerto Rico, and Jamaica had become. Thus, within a few score years of Columbus's first American landfall, the Antillean aborigines had been almost completely eliminated.
>
> As the number of humans plummeted, the population of imported domesticated animals shot upward. The first contingent of horses, dogs, pigs, cattle, chickens, sheep, and goats arrived with Columbus on the second voyage in 1493. The animals, preyed upon by few or no predators, troubled by few or no American diseases, and left to feed freely upon the rich grasses and roots and wild fruits, reproduced rapidly. Their numbers burgeoned so rapidly, in fact, that doubtlessly they had do with the extinction of certain plants, animals, and even the Indians themselves, whose gardens they encroached upon. [Crosby, 1972, p. 75]

All that the Indians could offer in return was syphilis but, since the Europeans were as little prepared for that as the Indians were for smallpox, it soon spread through the whole of Europe (Crosby, 1972, chap. 2). Though it would have offered little solace to the Indians who died in silver mines, the rich flow of that metal to Spain created an unplanned and disruptive inflation throughout the whole of Europe.

Eric Wolf has captured the unintended nature of the consequences that flowed from the Spanish experience in Middle America:

> It is one of the ironies of the Spanish Conquest that the enterprise and expansion of the colonists produced not utopia but collapse.
>
> All the claims to utopia—economic, religious, and political—rested ultimately upon the management and control of but one resource: the indigenous population of the colony. The conquerors wanted Indian labor, the crown Indian subjects, the friars Indian souls. The Conquest was to initiate utopia; instead, it produced a biological catastrophe. Between 1519 and 1650, six-sevenths of the Indian population of Middle America was wiped out; only a seventh remained to turn the wheels of paradise. [1959, p. 195]

It is perhaps only fair to note, however, that the Europeans also introduced into the New World draft animals, the drawn plough, the use of the wheel, ocean-going vessels, and a variety of foods including sugar cane, grapes, salad greens, radishes, onions, melons, and wheat.

The trading efforts of the Europeans contributed to the building of a world economy. To be sure, individual traders were not *trying* to build a world economy but only to achieve a series of immediate objectives. This result of their efforts, though important, was inadvertent. The division of labor that began to emerge in the global system, though unplanned, led to significant increases in production, also unplanned. When England, late in the nineteenth century, ceased to be self-sufficient in foodstuffs and became an importer of food, it led to a clearing of forests elsewhere in the world. Industrialization and the development of world commodity markets may, therefore, be said to have contributed, inadvertently, to global deforestation. Alfred North Whitehead suggests that historical processes often unfold without deliberate human control: "We have here history on its senseless side, with its transitions pushed forward either by rainfall and trees, or by brute barbarians, or by coal, steam, electricity, and oil. . . . Fragmentary intellectual agencies cooperated blindly to turn apes into men, to turn the classic civilization into medieval Europe, to overwhelm the Renaissance by the Industrial Revolution. Men knew not what they did" (1933, pp. 8–9). More generally, Karl Popper emphasizes that the growth of human knowledge, on which so much else depends, is not a guided process. The same holds for the growth of most human institutions. Popper maintains that "only a minority of social institutions are consciously designed, while the vast majority have just 'grown,' as the undesigned results of human actions" (1957, p. 65).

Although the phenomenon of unintended consequences is ancient, its frequency has increased sharply during this century. The unintended consequence is now part of everyday international life. In the early 1930s individual trading nations, to minimize the impact of the spreading depression, took defensive economic actions and ended up making the depression worse and increasing its impact upon each one of them. The improvement of medical and public health services in developing nations contributed to an increase in world population and may have increased the total amount of suffering in the world. Economic growth and development was long thought an unqualified good and was pressed in many lands, and now resource use has reached a level that cannot be sustained. Scientists knew enough to develop DDT, which ended the threat of malaria, but they did not anticipate the ecological consequences that would flow from its widespread use. American scientists were successful in releasing atomic energy for military purposes, for the generation of electricity, and for medical purposes, yet they also helped to create, by their success, a host of unanticipated problems having to do with politics, military affairs, survival, terrorism, waste disposal, nuclear accidents, health, and the environment.

An unintended outcome may or may not be desirable. When it is desirable, observers remark on the happy results of serendipity. More often, however, such outcomes are undesirable. In a highly interdependent global system, with numerous subsystems that must be kept in operation, there are many developments that would be undesirable and relatively few that would be neutral or beneficial.

The reason that unanticipated consequences have become so common has to do with the movement of the global system along the interaction/technology continuum. As the global system has become more interactive, it has necessarily become more complex. Each year more ships, planes, trains, and trucks set forth to carry larger quantities of a greater variety of materials and persons to an increasing number of destinations. Countless linked decisions and actions and reactions are required to maintain distribution networks and keep things moving through them. Patterns of dependence and influence become increasingly complicated (LaPorte, 1975). The emergence of each new actor or new type of interaction creates the possibility of hundreds of new actions and new dyadic relationships.

The global system is a man-made construction and new components are added each month. It is the most extensive social system that man has ever created and is probably the most complex as well. In fact, it has achieved such complexity that men do not fully comprehend it. We are like a breed of spiders that can spin vast webs in the night but have trouble finding our way through them by day.

It may seem strange that men can construct something more complex than they can understand, but such a thing is not uncommon when one is dealing with interactive social systems. Americans, for example, have fashioned both a national economy and an urban society so intricate that they can neither comprehend nor manage them adequately. This is the Labyrinth Effect. Daedalus, so mythology tells us, designed the Labyrinth in Crete, at the order of King Minos, to contain the minotaur. Later, when angry, the king imprisoned Daedalus and his son Icarus in the Labyrinth, but so well had the designer done his job that not even he could find his way out of it.

Men can fashion extreme complexity out of the relatively simple, and the secret of how they do it is to be found in the incremental character of such constructions. The human capacity to create intricate social systems deliberately and all at once is quite restricted, but the capacity to build by accretion is remarkable. Parts can be fitted together piece by piece by actors who do not understand the whole and do not need to. They need to understand only those components that are immediately adjacent. The growth of multinational corporations provides an example. A corporate manager needs to know how to expand his company's operations abroad, but he need not understand the general impact of multinational corporations on the international economy. It is by incremental means that the global system has been brought to its present level of complexity. New actors have appeared and have begun, step by step, to interact with others. New forms of action and interaction have gradually emerged. New technologies have been devised and have come into play, but often slowly and, initially, on a small scale, so that adjustments in the beginning are easily made.

To say that interaction and complexity have increased does not, on the face of it, explain why unanticipated consequences have become so important. The analysis must be carried a step further.

Immediate Consequences and Distant Consequences

An actor may take an action that has a set of immediate consequences. The matter does not end there, however, for a major event does not produce all of its consequences at once but may go on generating them for a long time. The consequences of an initial action will mix with the consequences of other actions and produce waves of more distant consequences. Several years ago Garrett Hardin noted: "We can never do merely one thing, because the world is a system of fantastic complexity. Nothing stands alone. No intervention in nature can be focused exclusively on but one element of the system" (1970, p. 18).

Distant consequences may differ from immediate consequences in three ways. First, they will occur later in time. Second, they may be spatially distant. Third, they may be functionally distant. An initial action may produce a set of consequences that may then generate further sets of consequences. As the number of such linkages increases, consequences may appear that are remarkably different from the initiating action. A given distant consequence may, but need not, involve all three dimensions, as when DDT used by farmers in the American Midwest appeared some years later (temporal distance) in the Antarctic (spatial distance) in the bodies of penguins (functional distance).

Since three dimensions are involved, and all are scalar, no sharp distinction can be made between "immediate" and "distant" consequences. Why, then, bother with the distinction at all? Because it is helpful in understanding the problem of unintended consequences. It underscores an important condition and illuminates a trend. Immediate consequences are often intended, whereas distant consequences are rarely intended; they simply happen. As the global system evolves along the interaction/technology continuum, becoming more tightly knit and more permeated by powerful technologies, the ramifications of a given kind of event become more numerous and spread more widely. Functional, temporal, and spatial distance are not as effective inhibitors as previously, and therefore the system produces a greater number of distant consequences. Since distant consequences are normally unintended, an increase in their production means that unintended consequences will play a progressively more important role in the operation of the global system.

The Bretton Woods system was designed to foster increased trade, the improvement of payments procedures, and economic development. It succeeded in accomplishing these objectives. It also "accomplished" the following things that were not intended:

— It furthered inequality between developed and less-developed nations.
— It contributed to the buildup of international debt.
— It provided the institutional framework within which an extraordinary growth of multinational enterprises took place.

— It tied global economic conditions to domestic and foreign policy
decisions of the United States.

— By contributing to the increase in trade it also contributed to the
growth of interdependence and to the vulnerability of the global
economic system to disruption.

In 1973 the OPEC nations raised the price of oil fourfold and achieved the
desired immediate consequence of increasing their income from the sale of oil
and applying political pressure on the developed nations in connection with
the Arab-Israeli dispute. The action had a variety of other consequences as
well: it worsened the economic position of fourth-world nations and increased
the amount of malnutrition and starvation in them; it increased the volume of
arms shipments to the Middle East; it exacerbated the Arab-Israeli conflict; it
changed the relations of OPEC members to one another; it further undermined
the economic situation in countries such as England, France, and Italy; it
speeded the process of nuclear proliferation, with whatever additional consequences that might have, contributing to a variety of important power shifts;
it magnified and transformed the Eurodollar problem; it altered the financing
of balance-of-payments deficits and diminished the position of the International Monetary Fund; it changed the role of international banks, enormously
increasing the indebtedness of developing nations; it encouraged demands for
the development of a New International Economic Order; and, by sharply increasing the cost of energy, it influenced the worldwide direction of economic
and technological development. The OPEC nations did not plan or anticipate
the distant consequences of their initiative any more than did the architects of
Bretton Woods.

In general, the more distant a consequence is from an initiating act, the
greater is the opportunity for intervening, undirected processes to have an
impact and the harder it becomes, therefore, to anticipate consequences.
Individuals are often not aware of their part in an undirected process. They
may not be aware, that is, that they are playing a part in something that historians will later speak of as a "demographic shift," a "population explosion," or a process of "modernization." When English businessmen began to
work with engineers in the nineteenth century they did not realize they were
ushering in something that would be called "the industrial revolution."

The mind usually becomes lost in the wilderness when it tries to calculate
consequences at three or four removes. Complexity easily defeats analysis.
Furthermore, because of progressive mutation at each stage, an initiating act

may produce consequences that seem shockingly disproportionate. How could the assassination of one young man at Sarajevo, albeit an archduke, plunge so many nations into the convulsion that was World War I? A mist often lies between actors and the distant consequences of actions they may take. Not in their wildest moments did those who designed the use of fluorocarbons in household and industrial spray cans dream that their act might have an adverse effect on a thing called the ozone layer![1]

Aggregation and Combination

Ecologists are fond of pointing out that it is not possible to throw anything away. No matter where we put old bottles and beer cans or nuclear wastes, they are still somewhere. The same thing holds for the global arena. Actors are inclined to think of it as a vast sink into which they can toss all kinds of behaviors and artifacts and then forget about them: an individual buys a foreign car; a corporation opens a new plant abroad; international air routes are shifted; a terrorist organization strikes. Yet these bits and pieces must all go somewhere, and when they do they are likely to aggregate with one another. Almost nothing disappears into the global arena without a trace.

Actions leave residues, and these residues impinge on one another even though the initial actions were taken without regard to the possibility of such an impact. Pollutants discharged into the atmosphere from countless points around the world aggregate and constitute the problem of global air pollution. Wastes discharged into rivers and those pumped into the oceans by ships, industrial concerns, and cities aggregate to constitute the problem of pollution of the seas. Thousands of boats and ships from scores of countries fish the oceans and create the problem of over-fishing. Births and deaths around the world aggregate into a global population problem, and empty stomachs aggregate to create a world food problem.

"Aggregation" is a characteristic of many global processes and is of fundamental, and increasing, importance. As the number of actors and forms of action climbs, the number and variety of inputs into the international arena skyrockets. There are more things and larger quantities to be aggregated—commercial transactions, industrial wastes, aggressive behaviors, cooperative actions, technological innovations, social innovations, and communications behavior—and therefore more aggregative processes must come into play.

The presumption must be that all actions taken in international affairs will have consequences. In a given instance those consequences may be great or miniscule, even below the level of visibility, but they will be there, for there are no throwaway actions.

Despite its historical importance, aggregation has been little analyzed as a general process. Friedrich Engels did understand such processes, however, and the way in which they could produce results quite different from what anyone had intended. In 1890 he wrote:

> . . . history makes itself in such a way that the final result always arises from conflicts between many individual wills, of which each again has been made what it is by a host of particular conditions of life. Thus there are innumerable intersecting forces, an infinite series of parallelograms of forces which give rise to one resultant—the historical event. This again may itself be viewed as the product of a power which, taken as a whole, works *unconsciously* and without volition. For what each individual wills is obstructed by everyone else, and what emerges is something that no one willed. Thus past history proceeds in the manner of a natural process and is also essentially subject to the same laws of movement. But from the fact that individual wills—of which each desires what he is impelled to by his physical constitution and external, in the last resort economic, circumstances (either his own personal circumstances or those of society in general)—do not attain what they want, but are merged into a collective mean, a common resultant, it must not be concluded that their value = 0. On the contrary, each contributes to the resultant and is to this degree involved in it.

A process may be referred to as "aggregative" when it has the following features:

— a substantial number of actors is involved;
— each actor pursues its own interests, taking such actions as those interests dictate;
— no single actor, or small group of actors, is in a position to shape process outcomes;
— actors do not plan or coordinate their behavior with an eye to the consequences their actions may bring about when they are all taken together, that is, when they are aggregated.

Economists will quickly recognize these as characteristics also associated with competitive markets. In such markets, a substantial number of buyers and sellers will be involved but no one controls supply, demand, or price. Each buyer or seller pursues its own interests and formal coordination of behavior is absent. There are multitudes of micropurposes but no macropurpose. Price moves about, not in response to collective purpose, for there is no such purpose, but in accordance with the dynamics of an interaction system expressed in terms of aggregate supply and aggregate demand. The operation of a competitive market always involves apurposive processes and the production of unintended consequences. There is collective agreement that there should be a price, but the location of that price is left to the market.

As international trade has grown year by year, markets have become bigger and more numerous. With the growth of the economic aspects of international interaction, apurposive processes, and therefore the production of unintended consequences, move steadily to the fore. The unintended, therefore, would have become increasingly important if for no other reason than the increase in economic exchange.

Aggregation is not the only process going on in the "sink" of the ecosphere and the global arena. Since behaviors and their consequences cannot be "thrown away," it is apparent that scores, or perhaps hundreds, of aggregative processes are going on at a given time and that these processes must necessarily interact with one another. This may be referred to by the term "combination."

Combination involves the linking of processes within functional categories as well as across functional boundaries. The resulting combinations, which may be quite elaborate, often offer impressive examples of interdependence. For example, industrial waste disposal practices may lead to increases in air pollution, which may change environmental conditions, which may, in turn, lead to changes in temperature and rainfall, which could precipitate a sharp drop in food production, which might lead to hunger and then to political instability and, perhaps, to war. As functional boundaries in the international system become more permeable, opportunities for combination increase sharply. Developments in the political realm may affect those in the communications field, which may affect economic processes, which may have an impact on the environment, and so on. By means of combination, entire trains of consequences can link up with one another and go on to produce other trains of consequences. The number of pathways along which processes can combine multiplies so rapidly as to border on the incomprehensible.

Undirected Processes and Unanticipated Consequences

If one considers interactive global processes, one can imagine them arrayed along a continuum with, at one end, those that are completely directed and, at the other end, those that are completely undirected. Any given process could be located somewhere along that continuum, although its position might change over time. For example, structural controls over trade and international payments are less effective at present than they were in the 1960s. The process could therefore be thought of as migrating from the more-directed to the less-directed end of the continuum. A process would be located toward the middle of the continuum when it was semi-directed.

Semi-directed processes produce consequences, some of which are intended and some of which are not. At the other end of the continuum would be located processes that are without any collective international direction, and they would, of course, produce a continuing flow of unintended outcomes. If a process is not directed by the actors involved, unplanned consequences are inevitable. If half a dozen chefs were using the same mixing bowl at the same time to prepare their favorite dishes, the expectations of each would be frustrated by the actions of the others and the outcome would be something that no one intended or desired—or could eat!

So it is with the global system. Thousands of actors are pouring actions into the global arena and into the ecosphere, and those inputs are variously aggregated and combined with one another and sometimes affected by the characteristics of the arena itself. Small wonder observers are frequently surprised by the results. Processes of aggregation and combination move by their own dynamics and what takes place is neither controlled nor directed by actors and may be neither observed nor comprehended by them. Whenever interactive social processes go forward without effective direction they must develop according to their own dynamics, for there is no alternative. Coordinated, deliberate social choice does not come into play. Uncoordinated energy use must, ultimately, produce an energy crisis. Lack of coordination among fishing nations will, eventually, lead to overexploitation of fishing grounds. Inadequate international economic coordination will allow economic processes to produce periodic global crises.

Because it is a playground for scores of processes of aggregation and combination, the globe is insistently dynamic. When a number of undirected change processes are simultaneously at work, impinging on one another, their interaction guarantees the production of novelties and discontinuities. The world system has become highly inventive; it produces surprises easily and as a normal thing, as the following examples indicate:

— The development of the nation-state system was an unplanned consequence of a great many disparate activities. Certainly the signers of the Treaty of Westphalia in 1648 did not intend to signal the birth of a new kind of organizational entity that would dominate history for centuries to come.

— The global depression of the 1930s resulted from a multitude of microdecisions, each of which was purposeful but, when aggregated, combined into a macrodisaster. As is so often the case, the gap between micropurposes and macrooutcomes was immense.

— Pollution of the air, lakes, rivers, and seas results from the aggregation of countless microactions, none of which are specifically aimed at environmental degradation. The same holds for inadvertent climatic change, the killing-off of species, and a variety of other environmental consequences.

— Emerging scarcities of selected natural resources result from the aggregation, over decades, of countless microdecisions involving the use of resources that were made without deliberate, collective concern for the overall impact of such decisions.

— Demographic changes are usually aggregative in nature. World population growth, for example, has resulted from a multitude of microdecisions by individuals, each representing a response to an immediate situation. These decisions have aggregated into a global population problem. More recently, fertility rates have started to decline. This does not reflect collective decision making, either, but rather decisions by hundreds of millions of individual women to marry later and to work during more of their child-bearing years.

— Technological innovation, globally considered, has been an aggregative process. Inventors and laboratories around the world have contributed to the development of technologies—steam, electricity, radio, aviation, rocketry, computers, lasers—and have introduced their innovations as quickly as was feasible. No collective international effort, based on an assessment of likely consequences, has guided this process. The diffusion of technologies, once developed, has also been undirected as a rule. Scores of transnational enterprises and national and international agencies are involved in technology transfer, but coordination and a shared philosophy seldom guide the process.

— For years the United States and the Soviet Union have sought to guide and regulate the spread of nuclear technologies. However, as the number of actors involved has increased, control of the overall process has weakened. An individual government or corporation can now shrug its collective shoulders and say, truthfully and accurately, that it can do little to change things. The process has become apurposive, and the inadvertent consequences that may flow from it could be serious indeed.

— The growth of multinational corporations is the result of an aggregative process. Individual companies sought to expand their international business and succeeded in doing so. The multitude of similar microactions, when aggregated, constituted a profound modification of the global economic system and its associated political relationships, but these developments were inadvertent and were driven by no collective international purpose.

— Global inflation, likewise, results from processes in which millions of microdecisions aggregate and combine in complex ways to produce a result that is both inadvertent and unwanted. Domestic sources of inflation combine with international monetary developments, resource scarcities, political factors, and the shifting winds of financial confidence. Many actors have some small degree of influence on one or another aspect of this global process, but the process as a whole proceeds without direction. All major governments deplore inflation, but it has little regard for their distaste.

— A free flow of investment funds across national borders is part of the familiar liberal economic dream, but what happens to that dream when the amounts involved become immense? Hundreds of billions of dollars worth of stateless credit and currency, beyond the control of any government or international governmental organization, now move through the global economy. Computers and advanced electronic communications techniques speed the transfer of these funds and contribute to their volatility. This astonishing growth of private international banking did not result from a calculated, coordinated plan. The Euromoney pool was brought into existence by the aggregation of thousands of microdecisions over a period of years, accelerated by the unplanned accession of hundreds of billions of petrodollars. Eurobanks did not intend to weaken the position of the International Monetary Fund, but the size of their deposits and the amount of their lending did it nevertheless. The stability of the global economy as well as its operation is now profoundly affected by system-wide developments of this nature, none of which was deliberately and collectively planned.

— The impressive growth of economic interdependence since the end of World War II is itself an inadvertent outcome of undirected processes of aggregation and combination. The change might be welcomed by many, but it did not result from a planned, coordinated campaign. It just happened.

— Since governments did not intend to create a more interdependent global economic system, it follows that they never planned that an increasingly large number of factors important to the functioning of a domestic economy would cease to be under the effective control of national governments. It was also an inadvertent consequence that the internationalization of the world economy reduced the capacity of governments to control developments in domestic economies.

— Finally, it should be noted, the emergence of a global system capable of producing a continuing flow of significant inadvertent outcomes was, itself, an inadvertent outcome.

3. Crises and System Vulnerability

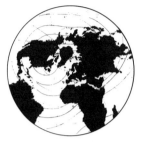

In recent decades one threat after another to the functioning of the global system has appeared: shortages of fossil fuels, environmental deterioration, trade and payments difficulties, inflation, threats of nuclear war, tension between rich nations and poor, and so on. Devising new scenarios for disasters that might befall mankind has become a popular pastime: mass famine resulting from overpopulation, perhaps combined with drought, an errant man-made disease; resource depletion; heating of the earth; cooling of the earth; oxygen exhaustion; a freshwater crisis; damage to the ozone layer; or a catastrophic increase in cancer because of the increased production of carcinogens.

Where do such threats spring from and why is their number increasing? Little attention has been devoted to the mechanics of threat-production, perhaps because of a natural tendency to assume that existing favorable conditions will last forever. It was a point emphasized by John Maynard Keynes when he wrote concerning the *Economic Consequence of the Peace*: "The power to become habituated to his surroundings is a marked characteristic of mankind. Very few of us realize with conviction the intensely unusual, unstable, complicated, unreliable, temporary nature of the economic organization by which Western Europe has lived for the last half century. We assume some of the most peculiar and temporary of our late advantages as natural, permanent, and to be depended on, and we lay our plans accordingly" (1920, p. 3). Without an improved understanding of threat-production it will not be possible to anticipate crises or to act collectively to head them off. Since the perception of threat at an early stage is largely a conceptual matter, it will not be enough simply to try to be more alert in general. The analyst needs a frame of reference that will help by indicating what kinds of things one should be alert for.

Major Sources of Change in the Global System

The origins of many threats of a nonpolitical/military kind are to be found in basic change processes in the global system.[1] Such threats, therefore, should not be explained primarily as products of oversight, carelessness, or hostility among actors but should be seen, rather, as natural consequences of the evolution of the global system.

Some of these sources of change are familiar and are associated with the movement of the global system on the interaction/technology continuum. A number of problems and crises derive, to a substantial degree, from technological advances. Nuclear technology, for example, brings with it problems relating to nuclear accidents, the disposal of nuclear wastes, nuclear proliferation, nuclear arms races, and the dangers of nuclear war. Economic growth is another change process that has been at work, and it, too, combining in some cases with technological advances, has fostered scores of problems. There are environmentally connected problems (air pollution, pollution of the seas, the CO_2 problem, the ozone layer problem, etc.) and resource-related problems (energy, minerals, fresh water). Increases in interaction are associated with problems relating to the instability of the world economy, trade and payments difficulties, and communications.

Change processes such as these will have many direct consequences. In addition, they will contribute to the formation of what might be termed second-level problems. For example, the rapidity of change these factors induce creates another problem, which is the continuing necessity for forced-draft adjustment. How are actors to adjust, month after month after month, to rapid and perpetual change? And, if they fail to adjust, what then? Looking at economic development, and given the fact that actors are starting from different points, an observer could be virtually certain that *uneven* economic development would result. That being the case, that observer could also anticipate that serious frictions and interest conflicts would emerge between rich nations and poor nations. Or, again, if there is to be pressure on a number of scarce resources, an observer should expect that that would contribute to global inflation, which would, in turn, have a set of important consequences.

Subsystems and Requisites

It is helpful to be aware of these basic sources of change in the global system, but it would be even more useful to be aware of the way in which those sources may affect existing structural arrangements. Each social system has requisites, that is, requirements without which it cannot be maintained as it is. If a requisite is not satisfied, a problem or a crisis must soon emerge.

The global system cannot function without flows of people, foodstuffs, energy, minerals, finished products, payments, credit, information, technology, and without the services of key kinds of personnel. It incorporates a number of subsystems that, with varying degrees of success, help to satisfy the requisites of the larger system. It can only function satisfactorily if they function satisfactorily; they are its life-support systems.

As the global system has evolved along the interaction/technology continuum the number of life-support systems on which it is dependent has necessarily increased. For instance, with the rapid growth of the potentially disastrous effects of technology, it is now a requisite of the global system that disruptive technologies not be introduced at too rapid a rate nor without careful consideration of potential consequences. That requisite is not yet recognized as such, however, and so new technologies are introduced, helter-skelter, as they are developed, with almost no collective consideration of their possible consequences. A global system that places no barriers in the way of actors fashioning and introducing powerful new technologies having to do with weaponry, space, communications, transportation, production, and consumption, is obviously creating serious problems for itself. Technology does not automatically represent "progress" and there is no "invisible hand" to arrange for the painless absorption of whatever the human mind can devise and let loose on the world.

Each subsystem, in turn, has its own requisites. Since each of these subsystems is open to modification as a consequence of the broad processes of change already mentioned, as well as the changes taking place in other subsystems, the situation is always highly dynamic. The number of subsystem requisites, therefore, is not fixed once and for all but changes over time. Older requisites may sometimes pass out of existence but the arrival of new ones will more than offset the loss. Tomorrow's requisites will be different from today's—and more numerous. The production and distribution of large quantities of petroleum has not always been vital, but it is at present. It has not always been essential that information move around the globe at the speed of light, but it has now become so.

Requisite Disruption: Discrete Events and Continuous Processes

Each day brings a rush of discrete events—births, deaths, business transactions, an election, a coup, an assassination, a flood, a drought. Sometimes such an event will be important in its own right, but often it will recur over a period of time and become part of what can be conceived of as a continuous process. Births and deaths aggregate over time and result in important demographic shifts. Riots recur, and we soon feel justified in speaking of a condition of political instability. Nuclear facilities are built, now here and now there, and we soon find it necessary to speak of a process of nuclear proliferation.

A continuous process may involve a change in nature, such as a shift in rainfall patterns, or it may result from human behavior, as with a population increase or the advance of industrialization. In addition, because of the impact of people on environment, continuous processes may be set in motion by the interaction of social and natural processes.

To say that a global process has a requisite is to say that its continued functioning depends on the performance of a particular variable. A threat to the process in question, and hence to the global system itself, normally comes into existence when that variable climbs too high or drops too low. The danger may be that there will be too little of the variable (rain, food, political stability, capital investment, energy, transportation) or too much of it (air pollution, pollution of the seas, radiation, economic instability, etc.).

Threats to a requisite, therefore, are likely to take one or the other of two forms. A gap is either opening up, or threatening to open up, between the variable and a minimum (Figure 2), or a gap is closing, or threatening to close, between the variable and a maximum (Figure 3). Some threats to requisites are more easily identified than others, and those deriving from continuous processes are easily overlooked because of the slow and undramatic character of movement of variables. When a situation worsens by small increments, the gap between the desired condition and the emerging condition

FIGURE I

	Natural	Social	Mixed
Discrete Events	a flood; an earthquake	an election; a riot; a strike; a change of government	rainfall from cloud seeding; radioactive fallout; death from acute pollution in a city
Continuous Processes	movement of glaciers; continental drift; circulation of ocean currents	increase in civil unrest; change in volume of trade; economic growth; shifts in power of nations	creation of the dust-bowl in the 1930s; damage to the ozone layers; shifts in temperature and rainfall because of cities, roads, pollution

FIGURE 2

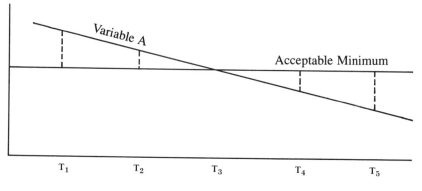

FIGURE 3

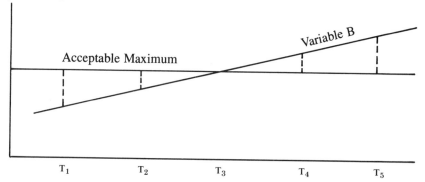

develops so slowly that a threat may not be perceived at all or, if perceived, may not be taken seriously. To be sure, as the gap opens up, the character of the threat will become increasingly clear.

System Vulnerability

It is important to develop ways of assessing the vulnerability of the global system to the total range of threats existing, but the task will not be easy.

The Interdependence of Support Systems

As long as everything goes smoothly, the operation of the global system is impressive. Systems and subsystems mesh with one another in complex ways that allow the work of the world to be accomplished. The complexity that allows the global system to perform so many tasks is also a source of vulnerability. As long as a social system is relatively simple, a step upward on the scale of complexity may provide it with increased stability because the redundancy of its safeguards will provide it with additional ways to meet its needs. After a certain point, however, the advantage of redundancy begins to be outweighed by the demand for unremitting efficiency in performing essential tasks. Beyond that point, an increase in system complexity means an increase in system frailty.[2]

To illustrate the point, the developing nations, the developed nations, and the international banks are all deeply involved in the Eurodollar/Eurobank system. Each cluster of actors has good reason for wanting to keep the system operating and each would be adversely affected by its collapse. Self-interest would seem to assure a measure of stability (Aronson, 1977). On the other hand, while each has an interest in the maintenance of the system, each also is aware that the other actors also want the system maintained. Each will, therefore, be aware of its strategic position relative to the others and may be tempted to hold the system hostage. Although none of the actors wants to end the system, each may be tempted, under certain circumstances, to overplay its hand in a bargaining process, and therein lies a source of instability. Continuation of the system depends on continuing cooperation and restraint on the part of all major participants.

At the global level, the larger the number of intricate interactive systems that must work right all the time, the greater is the likelihood that they will not work right all the time. Perhaps the point can be made in connection with the increasing incidence of accidents. The frequency of accidents—oil spills, chemical spills, explosions, nuclear mishaps—is increasing and so is their severity. As offshore drilling rigs become more numerous and bigger, accidents involving them will become more numerous and bigger. The same holds for aircraft, oil tankers, nuclear facilities, and weapons. As technology produces and uses new materials, the problem of carcinogens in the environment will become more serious. As the chemical industry has become larger and more advanced, problems with toxic wastes have mounted rapidly. A high-technology world is necessarily a high-risk world. As David Orr notes, "In an era when almost everything seems to be increasing exponentially, the growing number of potentially catastrophic occurrences appears to be no exception" (1979, pp. 41–42).

Things That Can Go Wrong

To say that the number of requisites of the global system is large and climbing means that the potential dangers facing that system are becoming more numerous. Not only has the number of system and subsystem requisites increased but so also has the number of things that can interfere with their satisfaction —sabotage, official miscalculation, congestion, the working of apurposive processes, the disruptive behavior of groups occupying strategic positions in relation to life-support systems, and so on.

The point can be illustrated, again, with reference to the Eurodollar market. That market is now part of the global economy and if it were to collapse the shock would be widely felt, yet threats to its stability are numerous. A sudden withdrawal of a substantial proportion of the liquid assets now in the hands of oil-producing nations might produce collapse. There is also potential for disruption in a continued increase in oil prices; a continued growth in the indebtedness of developing nations; the exposed position of the Eurobanks because of the amount of credit they have extended to developing nations; failure of the banking system to find a way to finance the rapidly rising balance-of-payments deficits of developing nations deriving from oil needs; the financial collapse of a major debtor nation such as Brazil; a liquidity crisis among Eurobanks deriving from the absence of effective regulation of banking practices; the weakening of the economy of a major industrial nation such as the United States; a sudden, contagious loss of confidence in the international economy; or a war involving one or more of the major powers.

Propagation and Containment of Shock

Increasing interaction in the global system causes processes to be more closely linked as well as more numerous. Simple and local problems tend to be replaced by those that are complex and broad in scope. It is a rarity to encounter a problem that can be dealt with in isolation from others. Energy, growth, resources, unemployment, trade, payments, and pollution are all entangled with one another.

That means that a shock in one part of the system can easily be transmitted to other parts, perhaps bringing them to a critical condition as well. In a highly interactive system, problems characteristically piggyback on one another. The onset of the world depression of the 1930s was an early example, and the elements of the global economic system are more tightly integrated today than they were in the 1930s. Once a serious crisis gets started, can it now reliably be prevented from spreading through a highly integrated economic system?

Because of the high degree of interdependence among component parts, crises are likely to be hard to contain and the rolling crisis may become more familiar. That is, an unsatisfied requisite may create a threat in one sector, which will trigger difficulties in another, and the two together may precipitate difficulties in still others. Such a crisis might acquire momentum as it proceeds, moving through the global system like a wave.

The Calculation of Vulnerability

For the global system to work tolerably well, a large number of subsystems must function effectively without letup. The failure, or imperfect functioning, of any of them will create problems. Peril is therefore built into the system and would exist even if all actors were to abandon hostility to one another in favor of unremitting cooperation. With the movement of the system on the interaction/technology continuum, the character of individual threats changes and the magnitude of the overall threat increases. Scholars trying to explain the decline of previous civilizations have sometimes centered their attention on the carrying capacity of the hinterland around major cities or ceremonial sites—Chichen Itza, Teotihuacan, Uxmal. Now, however, analysts must consider the carrying capacity of the globe itself.

It would be helpful for statesmen if scholars could devise ways of calculating aggregate risk but, thus far, there has been little interest in the matter. First, of course, one would need to calculate the probable magnitude and likelihood of occurrence of each individual threat (Orr, 1979, pp. 46–47). That would depend on the number of requisites affected, the importance of the processes associated with those requisites, and the extent of the disruption (i.e., the extent to which variables were passing minima). One would then need to move on to calculations about the likely contagion of a given crisis and the impact it might have on other dangerous situations. The theory of failure for complex social systems needs to be developed systematically, for intuition can be misleading. Complex systems have more ways of failing or of being subjected to stress than observers generally appreciate.

Several years ago E. F. Schumacher made an interesting observation:

> Our civilization is uniquely expert in problem-solving. There are more scientists and people applying the "scientific" method at work in the world today than there have been in all previous generations added together. . . . (I can imagine someone becoming slightly anxious at this point and inquiring: "If this is so, aren't we running out of problems?" It would be easy to reassure him: We have more and bigger problems now than any previous generation could boast, including problems of survival.) [1977, p. 121]

He does not go on to ask why it is that we have more problems despite unparalleled efforts at problem solving, but the answer is evident. Actors no longer need to take deliberate action in order for problems to occur; they have fashioned a system that takes care of problem-creation by itself. If nations and their leaders abandoned hostility and aggression in favor of relentless friendship and cooperation, massive problems would still remain. There was, of course, no deliberate plan to create a global system so dynamic and inventive that it would jeopardize its own survival; it just came to pass, one more inadvertent outcome resulting from the combination of scores of apurposive processes.

Conclusion

What are some of the characteristics of the present situation and of the crises that now abound?

— Many crises are connected with the evolution of the global system. The system, so to speak, has learned to create problems as it goes along.

— Problems are increasingly man-made. Humankind is now challenged far less by the problems of wild animals, the weather, or acts of nature such as earthquakes and volcanoes than it is by socially produced problems such as wars, recessions, depressions, inflation, resource shortages, and arms races.

— Setting aside for a moment the category of political-military problems, many of the matters that now have to be dealt with involve threats without enemies.

— Although problems are socially produced, they are, nevertheless, increasingly created inadvertently. Humans have not been trying to upset the ecological balance, to create an unstable world economy, to load the environment with ever-new carcinogens. These things are just happening.

— There are many points at which potential crises may arise in the global system, and their number may be expected to increase with time.

— Because there are multiple sources of change in the global system, crises cannot be counted on to come one at a time, nicely spaced out, but, instead, are apt to come in bunches from now on.

— A change process of any significance will be connected with other change processes. That means that a problem produced by a given process will be linked to those produced by other processes. A characteristic of contemporary problems and crises, therefore, will be their interdependence.

— Since these problems will be linked, their scope will often be extensive and sometimes global.

— Because of this linkage, a disruption in one problem area is likely to generate consequences in other areas as well. A disruption that may seem relatively minor may, as a result, have consequences that appear quite disproportionate. This is the "for want of a nail" phenomenon.

— The vulnerability of the global system at a given moment would be calculated, first, by examining the number of threats to system or subsystem requisites and assessing the aggregate impact of those threats, second, by estimating the resilience of the system, and, finally, by offsetting the one against the other. (Operationalization is, of course, another matter.)

— Since many of the serious problems of the times are associated with evolution of the global system, it is not likely that they, or their successors, can be entirely done away with, although they may be ameliorated.

As the global system moves along the interaction/technology continuum, its capacity to produce problems for itself will increase. In the absence of a distinct improvement in human problem-solving capabilities and the ability to work cooperatively on international problems, the global system is likely to become increasingly disaster-prone, vulnerable, and hard to manage. The penalties for management failure will also climb. If today's threats are survived, we may be sure there will be a fresh crop tomorrow. From the perspective of tomorrow, today, with its roster of problems, may be viewed with nostalgia as a time when life was charmingly trouble-free, a pleasant era before humankind settled into serious nonstop efforts to survive system-generated problems.

4. Purpose, Process, and Time

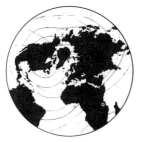

When historians analyze the errors of an age they often discover that its failures were associated with those beliefs about which it was most confident. Perhaps such beliefs, taken to be self-evident, help explain why several decades of analysis and empirical study have nevertheless left so many gaps in the understanding of global system dynamics.

The purpose of this chapter is to identify and examine three beliefs that appear to have hampered serious inquiry:

— a belief that one need not go beyond the purposes and behavior of national actors in order to explain developments in the global arena;

— a belief that, although change occurs in relations between nations, the global system itself is relatively stable and one need not, therefore, be overly concerned with long-term systemic change factors;

— a belief, based on the preceding one, that the time spans one should focus upon are days, months, and years rather than decades or generations.

Purpose and the Apurposive

Chapter 2 began by noting a paradox: how is it that activities that could not exist but for the actions of human beings are nevertheless not under effective human control? The paradox rests upon a tacit assumption, which is that human purpose customarily controls outcomes in the global arena.

Observers often assume that if something has happened, or is happening, there must be a controlling purpose behind the event. This conviction has so long been part of the accepted way of looking at things that its origins would be hard to locate, and it is seldom thought to require explicit statement. Actor purposes were the "causes" that produced the "effects" seen on every hand. There is an obvious corollary: every outcome represents someone's purpose.

The difficulty is that "common sense" points to a conclusion that is out of keeping with day-to-day observation; hence the paradox. The paradox disappears as soon as one dismisses the intentional fallacy, the assumption that developments in the global arena are controlled by the intentions of actors.

People prone to the intentional fallacy take for granted a world in which there is a low level of interaction and a slow rate of technological change, a world in which effects have clearly identifiable causes and causes do not have distant consequences. They presume a world in which aggregation, combination, and the production of inadvertent outcomes can safely be disregarded. They assume, that is, a pre-twentieth-century global system in which there are relatively few actors, few actions, and in which technology has not bound the parts closely together. In that earlier world the purposes of actors were indeed important. Apurposive processes did not then play the role they now do, and events could therefore be explained in terms of actor purposes without doing serious violence to reality. Unfortunately, that simpler world has become more distant with each decade of this century.

Ideas long held are not automatically set aside because, by some objective measure, their relevance has declined. On the contrary, as in this case, they may persist and inhibit the development of new ideas. Because observers "knew" that purpose ruled in global affairs and that the unintended could not come to pass, there was no incentive to examine other conceptions of global change, to explore the possibility of an apurposive process, or to be on the lookout for inadvertent outcomes of such processes. Those who fall victim to the intentional fallacy need not worry about the working of "forces," the presence of "trends," or whether the global system might develop dynamics of its own, for only those things happen that are intended by major actors. The assumed centrality of purpose has also helped to keep the study of international affairs firmly anchored in a state-centered outlook, focusing primarily on matters of national policy.

Although scholars have been slow to explore the apurposive, limited insights concerning the unanticipated consequences of human actions go back at least to Homer. The unintended has had a strange career in social thought, however: it was too important a phenomenon to be overlooked altogether but not so prominent as to demand systematic attention. Individual examples have been noted again and again, but each instance has been presumed to be unique. The circumstances in which the unintended might be expected to occur have not been probed.

Adam Smith's *The Wealth of Nations*, appearing in 1776, might have provided a starting point for the analysis of the apurposive, but, except in economics, it did not. Smith's analyses, after all, are sprinkled with discussions of aggregative processes and automatic regulatory mechanisms. His theory revolved around the way in which a multitude of individuals, pursuing limited ends, may nevertheless bring about a host of beneficent, but unintended, consequences. The individual, said Adam Smith, is "led by an invisible hand to promote an end which was no part of his intention." That hand was busily at work allocating resources, promoting efficient production by eliminating the inefficient, establishing competitive market prices, and evening out profits. Microdecisions, he was pointing out, when aggregated, can produce macro-outcomes bearing little resemblance to the purposes of the actors involved.

Charles Lindblom has emphasized the debt that analysts owe to Adam Smith:

> We also owe to him [Adam Smith] our still quite imperfect understanding of the degree to which man accomplishes many of his ends as an epiphenomenon, a by-product of activities pursued for other purposes. Income distribution, resource allocation, and economic growth are accomplished as by-products of petty self-serving individual decisions to buy and sell. Sociologists subsequently picked up the idea of epiphenomenal effects in their concept of latent functions of social institutions. But the inquiry into epiphenomena begun by Smith remains to be completed. [1977, p. 8]

It is worth noting, however, that Lindblom, along with Adam Smith, assumes that the by-products of these processes will be helpful to humankind. Yet, if a process is really undirected, there is no reason to assume that its outcomes will be beneficent. The metaphor of the "invisible hand" has always been misleading because it bootlegs in the assumption that a mind, perhaps that of the Almighty, but certainly beneficent, is guiding the hand. To be sure, an extensive literature has pointed out that the outcomes of apurposive economic processes need not always be beneficent (Schelling, 1978).

Apurposive forces and unintended consequences bulked large in Marx's thought. The bourgeoisie did not plan its rise as a class and certainly did not intend to take actions that would lead to its downfall. The proletariat emerged, not because individual proletarians planned it that way but, presumably, because of the aggregative consequences of millions of microdecisions and actions. Indeed, in Marx's analysis, human purpose and intent virtually disappear in favor of apurposive aggregative processes.

Why, then, did Marx not serve as a starting point for empirical investigation of the apurposive? It is hard to say, but perhaps it had something to do with his conception of the dialectical unfolding of history. Marx's descriptions of the working of capitalism were perceptive and were based on observation and careful analysis. His discussions of the future of the proletariat and of revolution, on the other hand, were largely anticipatory and so the likelihood of error was much greater. When he discussed the emergence of the proletariat and its future prospects, the volition of individuals disappears to be replaced by historical necessity. At that juncture he ceases to be concerned with genuine aggregative processes. His proletarians are rather like automatons possessed of a single will, and in aggregative processes there is, by definition, no single will or purpose. The development of Marx's ideas in this connection was also hindered by the way in which succeeding generations hardened his ideas into a formalized set of arguments and answers, with official interpreters of orthodoxy and punishment for the deviant.

Max Weber's treatment of the emergence of capitalism in *The Protestant Ethic and the Spirit of Capitalism*, first published in 1904–5, presupposes the existence of apurposive processes. Calvinist theology, he argued, came to justify and legitimate, and therefore, to encourage, the capitalist way of life. At the time (beginning with the religious revolution of the sixteenth century), however, this development was not planned, not controlled, not anticipated, and not understood. The ascetic values and a readiness for hard work that individuals exhibited in their behavior revealed an unexpected capacity to produce wealth. The existence of this wealth, in turn, led individuals to become more anxious to acquire material goods. In time, nevertheless, the pleasures of affluence tended to undermine the ascetic ideals that had brought the capitalist system into existence in the first instance. Both the rise of capitalism and its later modifications were inadvertent consequences of aggregative processes unfolding in accordance with their own dynamics.

Weber's entire system of thought is bathed in notions of evolution powered by apurposive processes (1968). For instance, he sums up some of his ideas on the development of bureaucracy in the following way:

> The bureaucratic structure is everywhere a late product of historical development. The further back we track our steps, the more typical is the absence of bureaucracy and of officialdom in general. Since bureaucracy has a "rational" character, with rules, means-ends calculus, and matter-of-factness predominating, its rise and expansion has everywhere had

"revolutionary" results, in a special sense still to be discussed, as had the advance of *rationalism* in general. The march of bureaucracy accordingly destroyed structures of domination which were not rational in this sense of the term. [1968, 3:1002–3]

What is interesting and surprising, however, is that Weber, as systematic as he was, nowhere examined the characteristics of the kind of process he so often took for granted. He discussed change in regard to status, groups, legitimacy, the sociology of religion, the market, bureaucracy, conflict, association, domination, rationality, the division of labor, and charisma and its routinization, but he did not examine apurposive processes as a general phenomenon.

R. H. Tawney, in *Religion and the Rise of Capitalism* (1926), writes in somewhat the same vein as does Weber. The change in religious ideas and practices scrutinized by Weber and Tawney was the aggregate result of many disparate actions. The Protestant Revolution, like most other important revolutionary changes, was unplanned. It grew by accretion and cannot be explained in terms of clear-cut human purpose. Tawney, like Weber before him, emphasized the powerful impact that changes in the religious sector had on the economic sector: "The revolutions, at once religious, political and social, which heralded the transition from the medieval to the modern world, were hardly less decisive for the economic character of the new civilization than for its ecclesiastical organization and religious doctrines" (p. ix). To put it in the terminology used here, aggregative processes in the religious sector combined in an unplanned way with those in the economic sector to produce a set of important but inadvertent consequences.

John Maynard Keynes, an economist with a strong historical sense, came to believe that the purposes of statesmen had only a limited capacity to shape the flow of events. His participation in the Paris Peace Conference contributed to that view. Although he did not use the term, he was acutely aware of the importance of apurposive processes, particularly those having to do with economics and population.

> The great events of history are often due to secular changes in the growth of population and other fundamental economic causes, which, escaping by their gradual character the notice of contemporary observers, are attributed to the follies of statesmen or the fanaticism of atheists. Thus the extraordinary occurrences of the past two years in Russia . . . may owe more to the deep influences of expanding numbers than to Lenin or to Nicholas; and the disruptive powers of excessive national

fecundity may have played a greater part in bursting the bonds of convention than either the power of ideas or the errors of autocracy. [1920, pp. 14, 15]

Fernand Braudel's monumental work on the Mediterranean world, first published in 1966, revolves around apurposive processes, for it is they that dominate the two slower moving rhythms of time, "geographical time" and "social time." They provide the "deep-seated forces" (1:21) at work, the "deeper realities of history . . . the running waters on which our frail barks are tossed like cockleshells" (1:21). Braudel looks at economic systems, civilizations, the impact of trade routes, the development of banking, the special role of towns, the significance of poverty and banditry, and the like. A historian who is interested in the relationship between history and geographical space and between economic and social history will be drawn inescapably into the study of aggregate behavior that dwarfs the purposes of any individual.

Not until Braudel moves to the third level, the level of individual time and individual lives, do the purposes of kings and princes come into play. At this juncture one may focus on "the actions of a few princes and rich men, the trivia of the past, bearing little relation to the slow and powerful march of history" (1:18).

European and British observers have recognized the importance of specific apurposive processes and have achieved insight into them, but they did not develop a general analysis of the apurposive. The same holds for American scholars.[1] Perhaps as long as Americans were confidently spreading across a continent, building cities, and fashioning a giant economy, it was to be expected that they would focus primarily on their own purposes and their capacity to shape their collective destiny.[2]

The reluctance of scholars to explore the apurposive remains something of a mystery. Firmly held convictions can, of course, be remarkably resistant to information that should change them. During the eighteenth and nineteenth centuries, for instance, evidence of the geological antiquity of the earth was abundant, but, because such evidence was not consistent with the biblical account of creation and seemed to diminish the position of humankind, scholars managed to disregard it (Eiseley, 1958, pp. 62–64). Similarly, there may be a distaste for the very idea of the apurposive. Humans have been the movers and shakers in history, and it might not be pleasing to discover that they are now creating a new world from day to day without knowing what they are doing. The human intellect, charmed by its prowess in the natural sciences and inclined to view its capacity for comprehension as all-encompassing, may not be flattered by the idea that an understanding of interactive human social systems may at present be beyond reach.

An illustration of this reluctance was apparent in the cool reception of much of the scholarly community in 1972 to the path-breaking work, *Limits to Growth* (Meadows et al.). Though the book focused on matters of major importance, its evolutionary assumptions and its interest in apurposive processes led scholars to concentrate on its shortcomings rather than its innovations.

Critics of the present international order do not automatically shed the beliefs noted here. For example, despite its innovations, the emerging ideology of the New International Economic Order does not yet incorporate an understanding of apurposive processes or the way they can produce unintended consequences. Since outcomes are assumed to be explainable in terms of purpose, it is thought to be legitimate to infer purpose on the basis of an observed outcome. That is, if a consequence can be traced backward through time to a given action, though at several removes, those responsible for the initial action can be presumed to have intended the distant consequence. Consequently, features of the international order that spokesmen for developing nations find unattractive are assumed to have been purposely created by the developed nations. If one believes that things do not happen unless powerful actors meant them to happen, the fact of occurrence, by itself, is conclusive evidence of intent. And, after all, if one does not recognize the role of apurposive processes, how is misfortune to be explained save on the basis of self-seeking by the great powers?

There is nothing difficult or counterintuitive in the idea that apurposive processes now play a major role on the world scene; it is simply an idea with which we have not yet become familiar. Vast tracts of contemporary experience are waiting to be explored with its assistance. Indeed, a number of important excursions have already been made by geopoliticians such as Mahan (1893) and Mackinder (1919) and also by Forrester (1971),[3] Meadows et al. (1972), Mesarovic and Pestel (1974), Choucri and North (1975), and others. Economists, in particular, have found it easy to deal with aggregative economic processes (for example, Cooper, 1968; Hirsch, Doyle, and Morse, 1977; Hirsch and Goldthorpe, 1978), perhaps because Adam Smith showed the way in the very beginning. As Rosenau puts it, "In studying politics one tends to posit actors as seeking to manipulate or control their environments, whereas the student of economics tends to treat environments as having their own dynamic with respect to which actors are essentially irrelevant and to which they must yield" (1979, p. 11). Despite this preliminary work, the vast realm of the apurposive is still to be mapped.

Process

For the most part, analysts of international affairs have given relatively little attention to long-term change. Grains of sand may cover mighty temples and drops of rain may wear down mountains and form mighty rivers, but in global affairs increments are seldom seen as constituting significant processes.

The discrete event—a diplomatic incident, a threat, a change in personnel or policy—is likely to be highly visible and to attract attention. Slow-motion change, on the other hand, the continuous process, despite the intrinsic importance it may have, tends toward invisibility. Braudel understood the problem: "Is it possible somehow to convey simultaneously both that conspicuous history which holds our attention by its continual and dramatic changes—and that other, submerged, history, almost silent and always discreet, virtually unsuspected either by its observers or its participants . . . ?" (1972, p. 16).

When Dr. Jekyll becomes Mr. Hyde in ten seconds, we register the metamorphosis with surprise and horror, but let the change take ten years and it goes unremarked. The global petroleum shortage approached year by year for several decades, but it did not become visible until OPEC took action in 1973. Environmental problems, increasing instability in the global economy, mineral shortages, increasingly severe refugee problems—all involve processes that worsen incrementally and that, therefore, have low levels of visibility. Before a process can attract much attention it must be dramatized by some discrete event, or its rate of change per unit of time must climb over a high threshold.

Why have observers of international affairs paid so little attention to long-term processes? Why is the "submerged" or unobserved realm so extensive? A large part of the explanation has to do with human perception, and something will be said about problem recognition in chapter 13. Here, it is enough to note that when a change is slow enough, it does not look like change at all. Part of the explanation may also be found in characteristics of the field that owe something to its origins. Hand in hand with a preference for stable-state explanations of change has been a lack of interest in evolutionary change processes that has amounted to an aversion, and both may have owed a good deal to Newtonian assumptions. If the universe was thought to consist of mechanisms created by God to work unchangingly according to universal principles, then evolutionary change is ruled out and one might focus, instead, on balance-of-power games that could be interpreted as international analogs of a celestial mechanism. If disequilibrating factors produced a power imbalance, counterforces were expected to materialize that would soon return the system to equilibrium. International politics, therefore, would be seen as involving little more than repeated plays, with variations, of a single game.

In addition, equilibrium ideas were, for generations, a reasonable response to conditions that existed. The realities of the global system wear a different aspect for observers at different times depending on the position of the system along the interaction/technology continuum. For centuries change occurred at a modest tempo as the system moved along the nearly flat portion of an exponential curve, and observers were understandably preoccupied with recurrent patterns and equilibria.

The problem with equilibrium formulations was that they directed attention away from long-term change. A balance-of-power enthusiast might fail to note that each game proceeds within a setting and that such settings may differ from one game to the next. Intent on similarities between individual games, one would find it easy to overlook a transformation of the global system from one game to another. There were always lessons to be learned, of course, because players would change and game-playing skills would vary, but those factors would introduce novelty of only a minor kind. Substantial or progressive system change could not be incorporated into equilibrium analyses.

With the passage of time, conditions changed, but ideas did not automatically adjust. The problem was not that analysts remained devoted to equilibrium ideas—they did not—but rather that they did not explicitly set them aside and, in so doing, clear the way for alternative ideas that would have an evolutionary basis. Unlearning is as important as learning and is often integral to it.

A "process" is said to exist when otherwise discrete events are perceived as linked together. Process thinking is learned. It involves the imposition of a mental construct upon events. It follows, then, that processes do not announce themselves but must be hunted out and that mental effort is required as well as a special cast of mind. At any given moment a number of trains of connected events are moving forward in nature and human affairs that have not yet been perceived as involving "process." An observer who is not open to the possibility that processes may exist is not going to see the connections.

Acceptance of the intentional fallacy has doubtless also impeded the recognition of evolutionary processes. After all, if actor purposes are thought to control all outcomes, then "process" is an unnecessary concept.

For these reasons, and probably others, a great deal remains to be learned about processes of global change. Observers should expect to find a world in which a variety of processes, directed and apurposive, unfold at different rates and, by their interworking, weave the rich tapestry of world affairs. The staccato events of the day should be seen as feeding into slower movements and both of them, in turn, mixing with movements so gradual as to be almost imperceptible. Braudel suggests the way in which processes unfolding at widely different rates may mesh with one another in complex ways:

> This book is divided into three parts, each of which is itself an essay in general explanation.
>
> The first part is devoted to a history whose passage is almost imperceptible, that of man in his relationship to the environment, a history in which all change is slow, a history of constant repetition, ever-recurring cycles. . . .
>
> On a different level from the first there can be distinguished another history, this time with slow but perceptible rhythms. If the expression had not been diverted from its full meaning, one could call it *social history*, the history of groups and groupings. . . .
>
> Lastly, the third part gives a hearing to traditional history—history, one might say, on the scale not of man, but of individual men . . . the history of events: surface disturbances, crests of foam that the tides of history carry on their strong backs. [1973, 1:20–21]

Time

During the nineteenth century the history of nature was rewritten along evolutionary lines. After Charles Lyell, Louis Agassiz, and Charles Darwin, most aspects of nature were seen as subject to change, and systems once viewed as static began to be seen as dynamic. Geology, zoology, and botany did not become sciences until they first became historical. In the field of international affairs, however, the nineteenth century might as well have never existed. Students of international politics have been notably un-time-conscious, for the most part. After all, if purpose controls, one does not need the factor of time to help explain observed change. Similarly, if the global system is presumed to be nonevolutionary, the possibility of gradual system transformation can be disregarded.

An individual who does not *expect* to encounter long-term system mutability will not find it. His time frame will be too short to allow him to pick up intermediate and slower rhythms. The individual who can devote only forty-five minutes to observing a glacier will find it changeless. Just so, observers can look at an evolutionary global system and have difficulty perceiving change except in power relationships among nations. Their circumstances do not encourage decision makers to think in terms of long time spans, and this trained incapacity could be costly. A foreign policy that is unaware of or insensitive to evolutionary elements in the global system could prove disastrous.

It is time to rediscover time (Toulmin and Goodfield, 1965). The present emerged from a different past and hurries toward a very different future. The global system, far from being in a timeless equilibrium, is undergoing rapid change and time is of the essence. As the rate of system change picks up, equilibrium theories will be less and less useful. The history of the global system must be reconceived, and the model must be Darwin not Newton.

The achievement of an evolutionary perspective would be likely to lead to a substantial reconceptualization of global affairs. The landscape that observers would look at would still be the same, but they would view it from a different vantage point. Familiar questions might be posed in a new way, and certainly new questions would be asked. Since social scientists have not devoted much attention to time, there is probably much to be learned. Speculation and playing with the concept might be useful.

Social Time and the Aging of Social Systems

The earth does not spin at an appreciably different rate today than when Phoenician traders first pushed the prows of their boats along strange shores, but how much now happens during a single rotation of the earth is a different matter. It is important to distinguish the passage of time—sidereal time, the time of the stars—from the question of what happens during a given unit of time. In dealing with social phenomena one wants to measure not just the passage of time itself but the rate of change in some variable per unit of time. That implies the use of a concept of "social time."[4]

Social time differs from biological or chronological time in an important respect. For organisms, time flows unidirectionally and unalterably. When life begins for an organism, its clock starts and it ticks on, without change, until its time is exhausted. The clock may stop part way through the cycle if the organism encounters disease or accident, but the organism can do nothing to significantly lengthen the time span available to it. For the mosquito, that may be a few days; for humans, a few decades; for the giant sea turtle, perhaps a few hundred years. Unthinkingly, we carry this biological conception of time into the realm of social systems and are immediately led astray by it, for social systems can alter their life spans.

Social time can stop and start repeatedly, stand still, or even change its direction of movement. It can slow down or accelerate. An increase in the amount of change per unit of time represents an acceleration of social time. When Henry Adams referred to the Law of Acceleration, he meant that the density of events per unit of time was increasing in a predictable way. When observers reflect that "time is speeding up," that is what they have in mind. References to "exponential growth," "doubling time," or to the "half-life" of radioactive elements call attention to the fact that the relationship between time and another variable is itself changing (but in a regular way).

Social systems do not have a life-expectancy that can be neatly measured in chronological time. For them, time must be measured in terms of some other, and more appropriate, variable. That variable, for highly complex social systems, should be the rate of movement along an interaction/technology continuum. Rate of movement along such a continuum provides the "clock" that measures the passage of social time. Time speeds up or slows down depending on change in that rate. This clock does not measure the ticking of seconds—they pass no faster than they did a thousand years ago—but the evolution of social systems. It measures their aging.

For organisms, aging and the passage of time are virtually equivalent notions; for highly complex social systems they are not. For instance, time can pass without a society becoming older. If, for some reason, it halts its movement along the continuum, it may stay forever young. By remaining fixed at a low level of interaction and technology it ceases to age. Neolithic tribes persisting in the Amazon basin are chronologically old but developmentally young. Traditional societies that see little change from one century to the next have ceased to age, for most practical purposes. Change processes—and therefore aging—have been placed on "hold." When "modernization" begins and advanced technologies are introduced, however, movement along the continuum resumes as does the aging process. When the Mayan civilization collapsed, the Indians remaining in the Yucatan were less advanced than their predecessors. In that instance, social time moved backward.

A society that is chronologically young may, nevertheless, be old according to its developmental clock. Those who do not see this may have fallen victim to the Ozymandian presumption:

OZYMANDIAS

I met a traveller from an antique land
Who said:"Two vast and trunkless legs of stone
Stand in the desert . . . Near them, on the sand,
Half sunk, a shattered visage lies, whose frown,
And wrinkled lip, and sneer of cold command,
Tell that its sculptor well those passions read
Which yet survive, stamped on these lifeless things,
The hand that mocked them, and the heart that fed;
And on the pedestal these words appear:
'My name is Ozymandias, king of kings:
Look on my works, ye Mighty, and despair!'
Nothing beside remains. Round the decay
Of that colossal wreck, boundless and bare,
The lone and level sands stretch far away."

Percy Bysshe Shelley, 1817

Ozymandias, we may speculate, had looked about his kingdom at the height of its activity and had concluded that it would last forever. Yet, even as he commanded that his words be carved in stone, the downward trajectory may have begun. Lacking the telephone and Xerox machine, the king of kings was unable to cope with a control crisis. He deserves sympathy from us moderns, and, who knows, he may have lived long enough to realize that, for complex social systems, a high level of interaction implies a short remaining life span rather than a long one.

In the disease of progeria, or premature aging, timing devices in an individual's body are set incorrectly, and the clock runs much faster than is normal. Individuals with this disease hurry through. After telescoping the entire drama of a life into a few years, they normally die of old age in their early teens. Fortunately the disease is rare.

The farther along the interaction/technology continuum a society is, the "older" it is and the less time it has remaining to it in terms of distance left to travel on the continuum. When a society develops rapidly, the "progress" it is so pleased with may constitute running through the cycle of maturation at an abnormal rate.

The United States is often spoken of as a "young" society by those who focus on its chronological age. However, the extraordinary vitality and inventiveness of Americans over several generations greatly accelerated the developmental process. Movement along the interaction/technology continuum was rapid, and the United States may have hastened into something approximating late middle age.

Since the visit of Commodore Perry in 1853, Japan has moved with remarkable swiftness through various stages of industrialization, urbanization, and development. It has, therefore, encountered, in an unusually short period of time, the full range of problems that accompany modernization—pollution, crowding, the reduction of privacy, social disruption, etc.—which other societies have spread out over a much longer period. A society "chooses" its rate of aging by the course it takes, and it could, therefore, conceivably decide to slow the process.

Since World War II the global system has been moving rapidly along the interaction/technology continuum. From one point of view, that is a splendid accomplishment; from another point of view, it means that the system is aging rapidly and that the time remaining to it (i.e., distance left to travel on the continuum) is fast dwindling. It is moving swiftly toward those increasingly difficult problems that lie farther out along the continuum. We should anticipate that crises will come at shorter and shorter intervals until they merge into a perpetual crisis.

The Two Clocks

Can we envision a "clock" that will monitor the condition of a society and note how rapidly it moves along the interaction/technology continuum? The setting of such a societal clock would indicate where, along the continuum, that society is at the moment of inspection, and the rate of change of the clock would correspond to the rate of development in that society. Each society, pursuing its own path of development, would move according to its own clock. The "time" in Kenya would not be the same as in India or Italy or Japan.

The idea of societal clocks, which measure the same variable but give different readings depending on local conditions, is perhaps unfamiliar, but it is implied by common-sense notions of development. When a judgment is made that one society is more or less "developed" than another, a yardstick is being taken for granted. Indeed a yardstick of some kind has been taken for granted ever since the idea of "progress" came into common use.

A second clock would measure the rate of development of the global system itself and would provide Global Time. Because it monitors movement along the interaction/technology continuum, its rate accelerates, like a Geiger counter brought into the presence of increased radiation.

No two societal clocks need have the same reading or move at the same tempo, and none of them need coincide with the Global Clock. Compared with the societal clocks in many developing countries, the Global Clock will read a later hour, but some of them are moving at a tempo that will reduce the gap. The societal clocks of some of the developed countries, on the other hand, may be later than the Global Clock and may be changing more rapidly. Since the end of World War II societal clocks in Japan and the United States have been running a good deal faster than the Global Clock.

Why bother with the two clocks? Because it is helpful in thinking about ways in which global and societal development relate to each other. As advanced societies feed technologies and techniques into the global system, its rate of development is accelerated, which is to say that the Global Clock speeds up. That is another way of saying that doubling time shortens because of exponential growth. It also means that the unit of time appropriate for the examination of global trends becomes smaller with passing decades.

A society that is completely isolated will live according to the time found on its societal clock. Global Time will be irrelevant. Diffusion processes, however, may draw such a society increasingly into the web of world affairs. A twentieth-century road system may be laid out, modern dams built, and an electrical grid constructed within its borders. Resources may be extracted by up-to-date technologies, and the lives of its people will be affected by television, communication satellites, transborder data flows, and the products, weapons, and ideas of the bigger world. As ties become more numerous and intimate, that society's development moves increasingly to the tempo of the Global Clock. When a developing society can seek to acquire nuclear power plants and nuclear weapons, it has begun to live much of its life according to the Global Clock.

Because of technology transfer and the contagion of social and economic developments, societal clocks in developing countries are being accelerated, as already noted. From one perspective, that means that world culture is being imposed upon individual societies; from another perspective, it means that those societies are reaching out for that culture and are eagerly embracing it.

However explained, domestic development increasingly keeps time to the tempo of the Global Clock.

Global Time could not exist as a useful concept until the global system had moved fairly far along the interaction/technology continuum. Before that, therefore, in phase 1, there existed only societal time. In phase 2 Global Time emerged and became increasingly important. Finally, in phase 3, which may be dated from World War II, Global Time can be thought of as providing the pulse of life in a growing number of societies. In phase 3, the Global Clock leads societal clocks to beat nearer in time with it and, simultaneously, continues to accelerate. With apologies to John Donne we might say "never send to know for whom the clock ticks; it ticks for thee."

Conclusion

Societal time is a human product, but societies rarely control its passage deliberately, and the movement of Global Time results from such massive apurposive processes that it might almost as well be built into the frame of nature itself. Is it conceivable that humans could bring the tempo of Global Time under control, or has it moved, by easy stages, beyond control? That question will be taken up in chapter 14.

Later chroniclers of the developments of these times will probably find much to be sympathetic with. They will understand the reluctance to allow "purpose" to be removed from its special position. It was bad enough to have had the earth removed from the center of the universe and to have evolutionists undercut the special position of mankind without also having to acknowledge that purpose does not always rule in human affairs. Nevertheless, there is also likely to be much that will surprise them. They will wonder that their predecessors, in trying to understand the pulsating times in which they lived, were so little interested in unearthing clusters of new questions and in focusing on the dynamics of the global system. They may decide that their predecessors lacked what Max Weber once termed a "relentlessness in viewing the realities of life" (Gerth and Mills, 1946, pp. 126–27). How else explain the popularity of the intentional fallacy as late as the final third of the twentieth century when it should have been evident by that time that a pitched battle was going on between purpose and apurposive processes? How else explain the persistence of static-state assumptions and the difficulty of perceiving and dealing with an array of long-term trends involving energy, resources, technology, environment, interaction, population, and the global economy? How else explain the slowness to realize that if major variables are moving directionally, then the global system itself is probably undergoing progressive change?

However they explain it to themselves, later observers will be aware that their predecessors operated under a grave handicap: they encountered a series of evolutionary systemic crises while they were preoccupied with issues of power politics and before they had learned to be at ease with the idea of evolutionary global change driven by apurposive processes.

5. The Dynamics of Global Processes

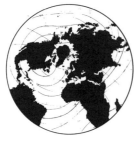

Why cannot humankind take events by the scruff of the neck and force them to shape up? How does the global system manage to fashion outcomes that humans never dreamed of? When and how did the global system learn to act as if it had a mind of its own?

Implications of the Continuum

The characteristics of the global system today are different in many respects from those of 1815, 1918, or even 1945. The single most important factor in explaining the difference is the position of the system on the interaction/technology continuum. If that was true in the past, may it not hold for the future as well? If movement along the continuum is going to be maintained, then it should be possible, based on extrapolation from past and present, to anticipate developments that have not yet emerged or are only beginning to emerge.

To be sure, in a time of rapid change, change processes themselves may undergo modification. Yet, if underlying dynamics are understood, those modifications can also be anticipated. Observation and extrapolation already suggest a number of emergent system characteristics. As movement along the continuum proceeds:

— the number and prominence of aggregative and combinatory processes will increase;

— unanticipated consequences will become more numerous and more significant;

— perturbations will be more effectively transmitted from one sector to others;

— problems will therefore tend to become increasingly broad in scope and more intertwined with one another (Young, 1969, p. 742); and
— the global system will become increasingly vulnerable to inadvertent or intentional disruption.

On the basis of these developments, a second layer of consequences can be inferred. Increases in interaction imply an increasingly prominent role for transnational institutions of various kinds. The position of the nation-state will undergo change as a result of the increase in interaction and will probably be weakened. Improvements in communications techniques will allow diffusion processes to become increasingly influential. In these changed circumstances, actors will need to redefine their interests and, among other things, give greater attention to collective goods. It also follows that familiar concepts, such as "power" and "influence," will have to be significantly revised. Later chapters will deal with each of these points.

Interaction and System Control

Another area in which movement along the continuum has important implications is that having to do with order and control in the global system. Order is not a natural, spontaneous product in complex social systems but must be imposed by deliberate effort. When individuals interact with one another in a large organization, a city, a nation, or the international system, their affairs go smoothly only if there is a framework of rules to channel and direct activities. Those rules are provided by constraint systems that may be products of law, formal agreement, informal agreement, or custom. Rules there must be, however, for uncoordinated action will produce disorder. There is no reason to think that a world will be orderly in which a multitude of nation-states jostle and mingle with thousands of transnational enterprises, international governmental organizations, and international nongovernmental organizations. The role of the invisible hand in human affairs has been much exaggerated. Even market activities, which may seem spontaneous and self-regulating, have to be organized in the first instance, must proceed in accordance with an agreed set of rules-of-the-game, and must be policed.

When there are many actors and a high density of interaction, a high level of social control is needed. A frontier community did not need the level of social organization that the same community would require, a century later, when it had become a thriving metropolis. In general, as a system becomes more interactive, the level of management that was adequate at an earlier stage will cease to be adequate. The problem is a familiar one. A man may begin by running his own family enterprise. As the enterprise prospers and expands, its management will also need to expand. Before long, teams of management specialists will be needed if the same degree of operational control is to be maintained. Harold and Margaret Sprout have noted that "the more complex a system becomes, the greater also becomes the cost of providing against breakdown for whatever cause" (1974, p. 26).

At first glance it may seem paradoxical that global problems should be piling up just as man is achieving the capacity to reach out to the stars. Individuals will sometimes say, in exasperation, "If we can put a man on the moon, why can't we solve such and such a problem?" There is nothing strange, however, in the fact that capabilities and problems appear to be increasing together; it is to be expected. The two are twin consequences of the same thing; global movement along the interaction/technology continuum. Our problems are increasing *because* our capabilities are increasing.

As the global system moves along the continuum, new technologies and conditions emerge in quick succession: a rapidly rising population; a tightening of the global economic web; increased global production; greater international exchange; the use of nuclear energy; the advent of rocketry, satellites, computers, and so on. Each of these developments brings special problems with it. In an earlier era resources were not consumed so rapidly and depletion problems were therefore fewer; energy consumption was much less than now and so there was no global energy crisis; the secrets of the atom had not yet been penetrated and so there was no fear about species-ending wars; nuclear and chemical industries were less advanced and so the problems of toxic waste had not become serious: the global economy was less interdependent and so threats to its economic stability were less worrisome.

We cannot take the good and leave the bad behind. As the system evolves along the continuum, actors may happily embrace the benefits that come with such movements; the associated problems will embrace us of their own accord. Major actors will therefore inherit progressively more difficult global management problems. That means that as the global system evolves there must be substantial, continuing increases in managerial effort if overall system control is not to suffer.

Given the circumstances of the time and the relatively low level of interaction that then existed, the international system was probably more effectively managed during the century following the Congress of Vienna than it has been since. Management needs were modest at the time, and informal collaboration between chiefs of state and ministers and an occasional conference went a long way toward satisfying those needs. That may seem a surprising judgment since the great growth in international governmental organizations has come in the period since World War I. But during that later period, the amount of interaction in the international system has doubled and redoubled and doubled again. Therefore, while existing control capabilities have increased since 1918, the *need* for control has increased still more. To move ahead only slowly in such circumstances is to move backward.

The worldwide economic depression of the 1930s signaled the fact that a global economic system had been brought into existence and that it lacked effective control. Since then, by accretion, actors have put together a vastly more complex and interactive system, but they have not been able to write an operating manual for it. It is only partly under control, and, because it is partly *not* under control, it generates a parade of problems—inflation, trade difficulties, economic instability, currency instability, maldistribution of wealth, uncontrolled action by multinational enterprises, and so on. Vastly more organization hours are being devoted to system management than ever before, but the drift is in the direction of less effective control over global processes rather than more.

Why is it that events outrun policy? Why has not the growth of effective management kept pace with the growth of interaction?

It is helpful to think of management as involving two closely related components: technology on the one hand and managerial skills on the other. The technological component is capable of rapid, indeed exponential, growth. For example, many technologies have been developed and put into service to meet skyrocketing information needs—the telephone, television, satellite communications, computers, and now telematics. The worldwide communication net is a wondrous thing, despite its strong skewing in favor of the developed countries, but there is no way that technology can solve the information problem once and for all. The increase in information needs continues without letup as the global system moves along the interaction/technology continuum, and the demand for better and more powerful communications capabilities never ceases. The facilities that seem splendid one moment will seem cramped a year later. The electronic computer represented a significant step forward in the capacity to handle vast amounts of data, but the pressure for improved information-handling facilities appears as great now as when the computer age dawned.

Nevertheless, the real difficulty lies with the managerial component. Constraint systems of the kind needed to manage global processes can be created only on the basis of agreement between nation-states. Since nations are deemed to be sovereign, suggestions for collective agreement and action necessarily touch a sensitive spot. Discussions are bound to be politicized and, if for no other reason than that, are certain to be slow moving. In addition, however, a problem must first be recognized and there must then be fact-finding, analysis, and an examination of possible solutions and the costs to be borne by each actor. In general, the more complex the issue, the longer is the time required to achieve agreement. Collective agreement remains hard to achieve and easy to block. Despite the onrush of problems and the pressure for speedy solutions, therefore, there has been no decrease in the time required to achieve international agreement.

Once agreement has been achieved, there remain the tasks of management, and managerial capacity does not improve very rapidly. Despite the use of techniques such as linear programming, operations research, and computer simulation, humans are not vastly better managers today than, say, the men who built the pyramids or who maintained the Roman Empire. Today's managers are often good at managing microsystems but less effective at running the macrosystems created by the accretion of large numbers of microsystems. An individual military base may be well run, for instance, but the Defense Department as a whole is less well run. An individual IGO may perform its job well, but its activities may not be effectively integrated into a higher level of management.

The management problem is created by the way in which the two components interrelate. The technological component of management could keep pace with the growth of system complexity, for its capacity for growth is exponential. The rate of growth of managerial skills, on the other hand, is linear. Since the two must work in harness, the rate of growth of the slower of the two establishes the maximum rate for the two. Overall, then, global management capacities grow only linearly.

Global problems of the kind discussed here are created by apurposive processes, some of which are fast-moving; the creation of constraint systems to deal with those problems involves slow-moving, purposeful processes. Disorder can arise out of interaction without anyone working at it, but order can be achieved and maintained only by strenuous effort. Actors get into trouble via processes of aggregation and combination that have an element of the automatic about them. Yet they must get *out* of trouble through reliance on analysis and purposeful collective action. To put it simply: problems tend to be generated effortlessly at the global level while solutions to them have to be produced laboriously at the constraint system level.

Since global problems are produced by semiautomatic mechanisms yet must be dealt with by slow-moving purposeful procedures, if they are to be dealt with at all, the two processes are out of phase. Problems are produced faster than solutions. The global system has therefore acquired a distinctly Sisyphusian character: no matter how long individuals and organizations work at dealing with global problems, there will not be a net reduction in the number of problems remaining to be dealt with.

The global system, if it is to function at all well, requires an ever-increasing amount of coordination, yet the actors in that system, for both political and managerial reasons, cannot provide coordination as rapidly as it is needed. Inadvertently, therefore, over a period of years, actors have created a system with a management requisite they cannot satisfy. The mismatch in rates calls to mind the Malthusian formulation. Population, Malthus argued, tends to grow geometrically and therefore outruns subsistence, which can only grow arithmetically. In the same way, apurposive processes create new global conditions that imply a need for a stream of managerial initiatives, yet the demand for such initiatives will tend to outrun supply.

The inability of actors to produce an adequate supply of new control mechanisms means that there has been a gradual attenuation of control. As the amount of effective control lessens relative to the amount of interaction in the global system and the state of technology, apurposive processes produce increasing amounts of disorder. That is why the global system is currently undergoing an entropic or disorder crisis. The global system, long markedly undergoverned in comparison with other complex social systems, is now dangerously so.

It is a requisite of any complex system that it solve enough of its problems so that the carry-over from one time period to the next is manageable. Otherwise, there begins to be an accumulation of problems and the possibility of breakdown arises. Because the global system is becoming relatively less directed with the passage of time, the capacity of actors to deal collectively with emergent global problems is weakening. Historically, manifestations of the movement along the interaction/technology continuum, such as increases in trade or the flow of messages, have been regarded as signs of progress. Although each such manifestation may represent a solution to a pressing technological problem of the moment, each is also apt to contribute to the broader problems of control. We may deal imaginatively with this or that microproblem by designing new control measures, but all the while the macroproblem worsens. The smaller problems are being dealt with, often by a "technological fix," but the larger problems are being merely survived, and their rate of accumulation is ominous. Actors have fashioned a game neatly rigged against themselves.

It might be useful to summarize the points made thus far about problems and system controls.

— Apurposive processes can be counted on to produce new problems. Since the number of apurposive processes in the global system is increasing rapidly, because of increases in levels of interaction and technology, the number of problems deriving from this source must be expected to increase rapidly.

— As problems persist and increase in numbers, they will combine with one another in unanticipated ways, creating new layers of problems.

— In addition, because of the complexity that now exists, purposeful collective attempts to cure one problem are likely to lead to the emergence of new, unanticipated problems.

— For these reasons, the total number of problems on the global agenda may be expected to increase rather than decline.

— This is likely to be the case regardless of the amount of effort devoted to problem solutions, for apurposive processes can often produce problems faster than purposeful collective efforts can produce solutions.

— This means that actors may get into more trouble than they can get out of, particularly since global problems will be piled on top of normal political/strategic problems.

— As problems pile up, their analysis becomes exceedingly taxing and their management difficult. The possibility of an unmanageable system overload begins to emerge.

— If the effort devoted to collective control of global system processes does not rise in keeping with movement along the continuum, effective control becomes attenuated.

— As effective control weakens in one process after another and as new processes emerge that have never been controlled, the global system drifts toward a condition of undirectedness.

— Its inertia increases, in the sense that the system is progressively more inclined to go "its" way and to resist efforts at guidance. As

inertia increases, an increasing amount of effort is required to provide a given degree of direction. When control is lost, it becomes progressively harder to regain with the passage of time. Because of its resistance to the imposition of control, the global system gives the appearance of "trying" to get out of control.
— Management and control problems become more pronounced as the system moves along the continuum. An increasing amount of time and effort must therefore be devoted to trying to patch things up and to survive the latest crisis. As a consequence, progressively less time and effort will be available for purposeful actions.

Hyperinteractivity

When a system evolves from a condition of moderate interaction and midrange technologies to high interaction and high technology, it transforms itself. Since the global system has only recently entered its highly interactive phase, a new world is even now being created before our eyes, a world full of subtleties and mysteries. For explorers, it is a golden age: opportunities for voyages to strange lands are on every hand. Voyagers may be surprised at the animals they encounter in those new regions, as Darwin was surprised when he first visited the Galapagos islands on the *Beagle* or as the first Europeans were when they encountered kangaroos in Australia. The animals that inhabit such regions are apt to have strange shapes, and people will give them unfamiliar names—perhaps like Aggregation, Combination, Inadvertent Change, Control Crisis, and Hyperinteractivity—and there is no assurance that they will be friendly. Such animals did not exist in the earlier, simpler world, and the fact that they can now be glimpsed is a measure of how far out along the interaction/technology continuum we have already traveled.

The global system has been in perpetual change since it first evolved in the sixteenth century, and it will continue to evolve. If that is the case, what lies down the road? In a later chapter aspects of a controlled future will be discussed. For the moment, therefore, let it be assumed that humankind has waited too long to bring the global system under effective control. What, then, would lie ahead in an uncontrolled future? What might happen if the global system continues to spin out along the continuum?

If present trends are extrapolated and, indeed, carried to their logical extremes, a zone of "hyperinteractivity" can be envisioned in which whole new sets of relationships would come into play. As interaction advances far beyond anything yet experienced, as technological advance moves decades beyond the present, and as technological innovation continues its progressive acceleration, the system might enter a no-man's-land between the unpredictable and the unimaginable, a wonderland in which not even Alice could be at home. For the social scientist, hyperinteractivity may be like the "black hole" for an astronomer, a condition in which normal expectations are set ajumble. In that connection we would do well not to mistake our own limited imaginative capabilities for limited inventiveness on the part of the global system. One recalls J. B. S. Haldane's remark: "The universe is not only queerer than we suppose but queerer than we can suppose."

Perhaps the following would be some of the features of a hyperinteractive world:

— The time interval between major scientific innovations (and technological innovations as well) declines toward zero. Innovations tend to become simultaneous with one another.

— The impact on society of scientific and technological innovations produces unceasing revolutionary change, something akin to a continuous explosion.

— Interaction within the global system becomes so great that the density of the system changes significantly. When new communications techniques are applied to that dense medium, it operates virtually as a superconductor. The diffusion of cultural items, for example, tends toward the instantaneous.

— In that dense medium, waves of diffusion crisscross one another and are slow to dampen. The virtual absence of friction allows items to move swiftly among societies, and ideological epidemics are therefore numerous, varied, virulent, and short-lived. Ideas move through the tightly knit network of communications as sheet lightning plays across a summer sky. National differences fade before the assault.

— As waves of diffusion follow one another in rapid succession, that which was new one moment is replaced as obsolete the next. The rate of obsolescence is extremely rapid and the costs of obsolescence are enormous.

— The rate of diffusion and of social and technological change generated by apurposive processes calls for a rate of adaptation on the part of societies, institutions, and individuals that cannot be satisfied. Institutional breakdown is seen on all sides.

— As the international system becomes hyperinteractive, the impact of any one government on the system as a whole declines sharply, which is to say that the efficacy of governments declines. Change in a single nation can only take place in conjunction with parallel change throughout the system as a whole. It also means little for a government to pursue an independent foreign policy.

— The number of nonstate actors is numbered in the tens of thousands and their existence contributes to the overwhelming inertia of the global system.

— The interests of national actors expand and overlap to the point at which one set is scarcely distinguishable from another.

— The number of metasystem requisites spirals upward toward infinity and so does the number of threats likely to be present at any given moment.

— Each problem is linked to every other problem. It is therefore no longer possible to decompose a broad problem into its constituent elements.

— Each problem that emerges, because of its linkages, is global in extent.

— Because of high rates of change and interaction, problems tend to be created in increasingly short periods of time.

— Problem solutions tend to be infinitely long in the achievement. Problems have therefore ceased to be disposed of by purposeful action. They disappear only when an apurposive process replaces one problem with another.

— Aggregation and combination are everywhere. Apurposive processes provide the basis for all significant change. The system is self-propelled but unguided. Surprise becomes the norm.

— Change, which is rapid and on an immense scale, is almost completely inadvertent.

— Constraint systems have ceased to be a significant factor in guiding change. Purposeful efforts to guide global affairs have been overwhelmed by apurposive processes.

— Crisis is total and perpetual. Actors are powerless to take hold of the situation.

If the global system continues to survive its control crises, it will encounter its final crisis as it approaches the zone of hyperinteractivity. Hyperinteractivity is a barrier in the social realm roughly equivalent to the speed of light in the natural realm: there is no going beyond it. Indeed, it is rather like the engineer's notion of a frictionless machine; it can be approached but can never be fully achieved. If the global system were to move into the zone of hyperinteractivity, limiting factors, alone or in combination, would come into play: resource exhaustion, communications overload, a breakdown of control measures, cumulative friction from big and small things going wrong, or the sudden appearance of overwhelming unintended consequences.

Conclusion

A veil obscures the dynamics of global change and ways must be found to penetrate it. A continent of new problems, just out of sight, may now be ready to be explored. The global system has long been moving out along the interaction/technology continuum, but, until the second half of this century, that did not constitute a problem. The movement was modest in pace and it appeared that such "progress" could continue indefinitely. As slow movement has given way to a headlong rush, the doubling time for important global processes has dropped steadily.

Is this formulation a revisiting of nineteenth-century theories of linear development, a kind of neo-Spenglerian determinism? To be sure, any discussion of social limits to growth must evoke echoes of Rome and other civilizations that collapsed because their size, complexity, and escalating needs outran their managerial capacities or the available resource base. Nonetheless, the analysis presented here is not deterministic and does not speak of irreversibility. It says only that as long as the global system continues to move out along the interaction/technology continuum the consequences described here must continue to unfold. World War III would derail the process but at enormous cost. Another serious worldwide depression would turn the clock back for a time. Furthermore, it would be possible, although not easy, for humankind to alter the scenario by deliberately slowing movement along the continuum. Man is not chained to a predetermined fate. As Lewis Mumford remarked, "A trend is not destiny."

This chapter has examined control problems associated with the global system. Are they peculiar to that system? The answer is not yet known. One may speculate—and it can be no more than that—that these problems, or others very like them, will be encountered by all large, highly interactive, high-technology social systems.

Part II. Constraint Systems

6. Constraint Systems and Rules of the Game

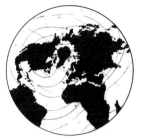

The global dynamics discussed in previous chapters are continuously altering the context in which the games of traditional power politics are played. Likewise, the preoccupation of actors with those games and, of course, the outcomes of the games themselves will often influence the development of those broader processes.

The phenomena of traditional politics are so varied, however, that it is difficult to treat them coherently unless they are organized in some way, a way that draws attention to essential features. At present, we have separate bodies of literature dealing with cartels, with special economic arrangements such as the common market, and with empires and imperialism, neoimperialism, satellite relationships, spheres of influence, colonialism, neocolonialism, center/periphery relationships, and dependency. Distinctive vocabularies and sets of concepts have been fashioned that seem to owe little to one another. An economist's discussion of OPEC or Bretton Woods would appear to have little in common with a historian's treatment of the Spanish Empire in the New World or a political scientist's analysis of relationships between the Soviet Union and eastern European nations.

Yet in the case of each of these arrangements there are noteworthy common denominators: (1) a set of power relationships between actors and (2) behavior that is constrained in a regularized way by the rules of the game. It should be possible, therefore, to bring these phenomena within the compass of a single analytic framework. Proposed here is a framework organized around a central concept, that of the "constraint system."[1]

Constraint Systems

A constraint system may be said to exist when behavior exchanges between actors on the world scene exhibit a pattern that persists over time and that serves to distribute scarce values or to regulate significant processes. The distribution of benefits and costs is one of the functions of politics, and, in the international realm, constraint systems are often the means of such distribution.

The actors in such systems may be nation-states, multinational corporations, alliances, international governmental organizations, international nongovernmental organizations, supranational entities, or, sometimes, subnational organizations such as foundations, terrorist groups, resistance organizations, and the like. The category of the constraint system is therefore broad. The free-trade system of the nineteenth century was a constraint system, for example, and so are NATO and the Warsaw Pact system. The scope of a constraint system may be extensive, as with the multiple arrangements set up at Bretton Woods, or more restricted, as with the International Air Transport Association, designed solely to foster international air travel and to influence its character.

The emergence of constraint systems is inevitable. When actors pull and haul, seeking to advance their particular interests, arrangements of some kind begin to emerge that serve to regularize their behavior. Constraint systems are natural products of interaction. Structure and some degree of ordering among relationships emerges on the global scene just as naturally as it does in family, tribe, or town—and may be just as imperfect and impermanent.

Each constraint system, by definition, provides some measure of order on the world scene. By so doing, it increases predictability and reduces randomness within the system. (That is not to say, of course, that each constraint system represents a net improvement in the global situation. A system might be organized, for instance, to coordinate terrorist groups or the aggressive actions of several actors against their neighbors.) Narrow-gauge constraint systems may also constitute the modules out of which more broad-gauge constraint systems can be fashioned.

The Rules of the Game

For most of the actors in a constraint system, behavior is governed by a set of rules. Such rules lay down the dos and the don'ts of the system, establish the terms of day-to-day interaction, and determine the distribution of the scarce values controlled by the system. As Christensen explains, "An historically important dimension of state action, especially for great powers with multiple resource bases and large repertoires of means, has been the attempt to structure or restructure the international environment. The idea is not just to control actors in specific situations, but to gain some control over the flow of events, over overall relationships, or over situations" (1977, pp. 127, 128).

The rules of the game can take a number of forms: legally binding agreements, nonbinding written understandings, a gentleman's agreement, or a tacit understanding (Cohen, 1980, pp. 129–50). Whether a given rule exists is an empirical question, and the test is behavior. A rule may be said to exist if it is observed with a high degree of regularity. If a rule ceases to be observed, for whatever reason, it has ceased to be a rule. An avowed principle, not operationally observed, is not a rule.

In the Western Hemisphere system, for example, a principle avowed by the United States has been that of nonintervention. The operational rule, however, is that the United States will intervene in the affairs of Latin American states if it concludes that interests of first importance are at stake. Similarly, in the Warsaw Pact system the avowed principles are those of national equality and socialist brotherhood. The operational rule, however, is that the USSR expects its wishes to prevail on all matters of central importance. A further tacit understanding is that if one of the socialist brothers were to seek a provocative degree of independence in its international behavior, it would risk Soviet military action.

System rules perform a variety of functions. They determine the payoffs actors receive and the costs they must bear. Rules help make clear to members of a constraint system which behaviors are required, permitted, or forbidden and what the costs of transgression would be. System rules may vary greatly, of course, in the amount of latitude they allow subordinate actors. The fit may be relatively tight, as in the case of the Warsaw Pact, or relatively loose, as in the case of NATO. Rules may also create opportunities of one kind and another. For example, the rules of the Bretton Woods system constrained actors but also provided a powerful stimulus to trade and investment for developed nations.

Furthermore, the rules of a constraint system may help provide continuity for the system as a whole despite regime changes in the government of a dominant actor. In a given system, leaders may come and go while basic system rules endure. The rules of the game also serve to regularize intrasystem relations so that behaviors and outcomes are consistent throughout the system.

The impact of an actor on system rules normally varies with actor capabilities. A dominant actor may be in a position to make its preferences the basis for the operation of the entire constraint system. For example, during the three centuries of Spanish rule in Mexico, precious metals were exported to Spain and the manufacture of anything that could be supplied from Spain was generally forbidden. "Nothing was permitted to Mexico which was faintly competitive to Spanish interests" (Wesson, 1967, p. 446). In addition there was a structure of privileges that helped to maintain the gulf between the Spanish-born and the Mexicans. The rules were made by Spaniards and were to be obeyed by Mexicans without discussion. In the words of one viceroy, "The colonists were born to be silent and obey, not to proffer advice on the higher affairs of government" (Wesson, 1967, p. 449). The pattern was similar with regard to Portuguese rule in Brazil: gold and diamonds were shipped to Portugal; trade was effectively confined to Portugal; and almost all kinds of colonial manufacturing were prohibited. In 1723, a memoir to the viceroy of Mexico stated, "The world's trade flourishes at the expense of the peoples of America and their immense labors, but the riches they draw from the bosom of the fertile earth are not retained" (Stein and Stein, 1970, p. 86). If a dominant actor succeeds in imposing its preferred set of rules on an entire system, the working of those rules will often, but not invariably, strengthen its position over time.

A dominant actor may be almost oblivious of the extent to which the rules it has established advance its own interests at the expense of the interests of others. During the nineteenth century, for instance, Britons did not as a rule perceive the imperial system as costly to subordinate members. More recently, Americans have been slow to appreciate the extent to which the rules of the game of the Bretton Woods system may have disproportionately advantaged the United States relative to the developing nations.

Symmetrical and Asymmetrical Constraint Systems

Constraint systems vary widely in the extent to which prevailing rules reflect the wishes of a single dominant actor, several powerful actors, or a more general consensus among system members. It is useful, therefore, to distinguish systems in terms of the degree of symmetry or asymmetry in the influence of actors on rule-making.

Highly asymmetrical rule-making is likely to be associated with empires, the control of the vanquished by victors in war, spheres-of-influence arrangements, economic relationships characterized by extreme inequality, and satellite relationships. From the point of view of a dominant actor, when rule-making works well it is an efficient form of behavior control because it allows for economy of effort. If dominant actor A can establish system rules, it can shape the behavior of B, C, D, and E without having to coerce each individually. For example, Soviet military action against Hungary in 1956 and against Czechoslovakia in 1968 made clear the overarching rule and made action against the other bloc nations unnecessary.

If a dominant actor wants to change the behavior of subordinate actors, it may be able to do so economically by changing the rules for all concerned. Furthermore, because rules represent the institutionalization of control behavior, they make action taken pursuant to those rules seem more predictable; a subordinate actor need not feel singularly oppressed, because it is only being asked to adhere to the same rules that govern the behavior of all subordinate actors in the system.

At the other end of the continuum are constraint systems in which rules are defined by members on a basis approximating that of one actor, one vote. No single actor or small number of actors dominates the system. The International Postal Union is an example.

Toward the middle of the continuum are "pluralistic" constraint systems consisting of actors, each of which has the capacity, formally or informally, to block the rule-making of the others. Only proposals satisfactory to all can be acted upon. OPEC and the European Economic Community are examples.

The form of a given constraint system may change over time. At the outset, rule-making in NATO was clearly asymmetrical because of American political, military, and economic predominance. With the passage of time, the capabilities of other NATO powers increased, and, beginning in the late 1950s, their fear of Soviet attack waned. The United States, in an effort to keep the alliance viable, emphasized the Soviet threat and offered a variety of benefits to other members such as support for "infrastructure" projects (roads, pipelines, port facilities, etc.), budgetary support, the transfer of technology, support in international organizations, and encouragement of private investment. When France, under the leadership of President de Gaulle, began to distance itself from NATO, however, there was little the United States could do to punish France, beyond denying her relatively unimportant benefits. Military action was out of the question. The weakening of U.S. dominance in NATO councils was also clear from its repeated failures to persuade European allies to maintain defense expenditures at levels desired by the U.S. government. By degrees, therefore, NATO moved down the continuum, becoming less asymmetrical and more pluralistic in its rule-making.

The way rules come into existence and are enforced will vary with the type of system. In pluralistic and symmetrical systems, rules are likely to emerge as workable principles agreed on by near-equals. A system member will normally obey them because it participated in their formation and therefore views them as legitimate and as reflecting its interests.

In the case of a highly asymmetric system, however, rules may be established unilaterally and with little regard for the interests of subordinate actors. As European nations extended colonial rule over the world during the eighteenth and nineteenth centuries, they did not think of applying to those areas the rules relating to sovereignty and nonintervention that prevailed in Europe. Operational rules applied to colonial areas allowed the Europeans great freedom of action, and even the avowed rules did not offer much constraint. *Kent's Commentary on International Law*, for instance, asserted that it had long been agreed that it was right for Europeans to war on and kill infidels (2d ed.; Cambridge, 1878, pp. 23–24).

Constraint System Profiles

Constraint systems can be usefully distinguished from one another in accordance with the following five variables:

1. the degree of symmetry or asymmetry in the distribution of capabilities among actors;
2. the degree of symmetry or asymmetry in the influence of various actors on the making of system rules;
3. the means used to enforce system rules;

4. the extent of the symmetry or asymmetry in payoffs (and costs) to system members;

5. the extent to which the system is or is not perceived by subordinate actors as being legitimate.

When these variables are considered, constraint systems emerge with distinctive profiles. Certain characteristics tend to be associated with one another. For example:

— Actors with substantial capabilities tend to have a pronounced impact on rule-making.

— Actors having substantial rule-making clout tend to receive a relatively high payoff from constraint systems in which they are involved.

— Systems that allow subordinate actors little input into rule-making are likely to be perceived by those actors as having a low level of legitimacy.

— Systems having low levels of legitimacy are likely to have to rely on elaborate systems of direct controls.

— Systems in which actor capabilities are relatively symmetrical are likely to have rule-making procedures and payoff schedules that are relatively symmetrical. Rules are likely to be enforced voluntarily rather than by severe sanctions.

System Legitimacy

Relations within a system will be greatly affected by the extent to which the position of the dominant actor is accepted as legitimate by subordinate ones. The concept of legitimacy will always be important in such relationships, but its precise definition will vary with the circumstances. It is a situational construct, and that is "legitimate" which is perceived as such by subordinate actors.

Several factors appear to affect perceptions of legitimacy: first, perceived substantive interests; and, second, a sense of what is equitable and appropriate. If, for example, decision-making arrangements are more asymmetrical than relative capabilities would suggest they should be, subordinate actors are likely to perceive them as inequitable. Furthermore, they are likely to perceive as illegitimate the substantive provisions resulting from such decision-making arrangements. Decision making does not need to be symmetrical to be perceived as legitimate, but the degree of asymmetry must be in accord with some accepted principle such as, perhaps, the extent of a subordinate actor's contribution to the system.

Constraint systems with a low level of perceived legitimacy are likely to be less stable than systems with a high perceived level, and a shift from high to low will tend to be destabilizing. The loyalty of Spanish colonies in the Americas was not seriously at issue until Napoleon invaded Spain and overthrew the Spanish monarchy. At that point the perceived legitimacy of Spanish rule, as well as its perceived inevitability, declined sharply and things were never the same again. For most of the colonial period England had little trouble maintaining rule over the American colonies. Once the issue of the legitimacy of English rule was raised, however, and nationalist sentiments joined with economic interest, things began to come apart at the seams and even the exercise of military power was not sufficient to maintain that rule.

When a constraint system has a low level of perceived legitimacy, the component units cannot be relied upon to administer themselves but must be closely supervised by the dominant actor. A fairly elaborate set of controls will be needed, including a readiness to use violence if need be. A system with a low level of legitimacy will be costly to maintain, whether it is a high-yield system or not. Maintenance of the French position in Algeria was costly to France because of low legitimacy, and benefits were slight. In an era of resurgent nationalism, such as the present, control of one nation by another will rarely seem legitimate to the controlled, and therefore domination will be costly, as the Soviet Union has learned in eastern Europe. In the view of the Soviet leadership, to be sure, benefits from the system still far outweigh its high costs.

7. Constraint System Dynamics

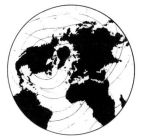

The central dynamic of an asymmetric constraint system is typically this: a dominant actor seeks to establish rules and arrangements that serve its interests while subordinate actors seek to modify them or escape the system altogether.

This pattern is historically familiar. One finds it in the Sumerian Empire, the Babylonian Empire, among the Hittites, the Assyrians, the Persians, the Macedonians, the Romans, the Napoleonic Empire, and the British Empire, to mention a few. Thucydides describes both aspects of the dynamic in his tale of the encounter between the Athenians and the ambassadors from the island of Melos:

> Of the Gods we believe, and of men we know, that by a law of their nature wherever they can rule they will. This law was not made by us, and we are not the first who have acted upon it; we did but inherit it, and shall bequeath it to all time, and we know that you and all mankind, if you were as strong as we are, would do as we do. [*Peloponnesian War*, bk. 5, sec. 105]

This chapter will examine the strategies used by dominant actors in trying to maintain constraint systems and the strategies that subordinate actors may use in trying to modify those systems or escape from them. Four patterns of domination should be distinguished: (1) reliance upon inducements and external pressure, (2) reliance upon a co-opted elite, (3) reliance upon political/administrative controls, and (4) direct military control.

Domination via Inducements and External Pressure

A dominant actor may be able to guide the behavior of a subordinate actor by modifying its external situation and by the use of inducements and threats. If the external situation has been successfully structured, the government of a subordinate society can exercise autonomous decision-making power and still come to the conclusions desired by the dominant power. The two governments remain at arms length, and the governing elite in the subordinate society is unambivalent in its national loyalty, yet it will usually choose to follow the line desired by the dominant country. Finland, for example, is independent, yet each major foreign-policy decision is conditioned by the fact that the Soviet Union is a neighbor and is extremely sensitive on certain matters.

Elite Co-optation

An actor need not go to the trouble of trying to structure the external situation of a subordinate country if it can, instead, co-opt its governing elite. The inducements that can be offered to members of the governing elite are many: appointment to office, maintenance in office, material rewards, status and prestige, protection, foreign travel, education abroad for children, and so on. In addition, members of the elite can be provided with other forms of support that may help keep them in power, such as military assistance, police training, military training missions, technical assistance, and economic aid.

A co-opted elite may be established in a variety of ways. A conqueror may install puppet rulers, as did Alexander the Great, Napoleon, the Japanese after their conquest of Manchuria, the Soviet Union in the case of the "Lublin Poles," and Hitler's government in Austria after the Anschluss.

Less dramatically, members of an elite may simply perceive it to be to their interest to work closely with a dominant actor. Students of Latin American history have pointed out the role of the so-called comprador class. The dominant actor and the local elite had a mutual interest in the exploitation of a subordinate country. It was not in the interest of the elite to press for any but minor changes since the existing rules of the game worked to their advantage.

Co-optation short-circuits the normal process of resistance to an exploitative foreign power. As a rule, the elite of a subordinate country would transmit to the foreign country the discontents and demands of the people. If the elite is co-opted, however, evidence of dissatisfaction may not be transmitted. If a subordinate actor does not make demands and try to further national interests, a dominant actor is under no pressure to make concessions. This is an advantageous arrangement because it costs less in the short run to prevent the articulation of demands than to satisfy them.

Only if co-optation ceases to be effective, or if the elite is ousted, can normal processes of resistance once again find expression. It should be noted, however, that in the case of co-optation, the elite in question still retains the integrity of its own decision processes. Decisions are influenced by the dominant actor but are not directly controlled by it.

At the height of the Vietnam War, for example, the United States had 500,000 troops and a great many military and civilian advisers in South Vietnam. From the outside it appeared that the governing elite must surely be co-opted and controlled. In fact, South Vietnamese officials retained a significant degree of decisional autonomy and often exercised it in ways American advisers thought unwise.

Domination via Political/Administrative Control

In this type of domination the governing elite is co-opted, as above, but, in addition, it is virtually incapable of genuine deliberation because its decision processes are infiltrated. Domination by this means can, therefore, be more thoroughgoing.

Imperial constraint systems have often relied upon this form of domination, although the extent of the penetration of subordinate societies has varied greatly. During its eras of empire, England established judicial, administrative, and military systems in its dependencies and permitted a fair amount of freedom. The Soviet Union, in its relations with the Warsaw Pact countries, has gone much further, establishing controls over press, radio, parties, labor, the police, the military, the arts, education, and the economy. Once again, pressure on the dominant actor to make concessions is held down, since demands for such concessions are not allowed articulation.

This is a high-risk arrangement, to be sure. When an elite filters out expressions of discontent, it is, in effect, tying down the safety valve. Denied a legitimate avenue for the expression of discontent, there may be a resort to illegitimate avenues. Denied evidence that would help them assess the degree of discontent, the local elite and the foreign masters may not realize the seriousness of a situation until it blows up. Apparently Soviet leaders did not realize they were confronting a revolutionary crisis in Hungary and Czechoslovakia until it was too late. They were left with a choice between losing control of those countries or using the Red army to reestablish that control.

This form of domination places the local elite between powerful pressures: actions taken to satisfy foreign clients are likely to worsen relations with domestic clients. The more reliable the elite is as an instrument of foreign domination, the less legitimacy it will have at home. Actions it might take to improve its image at home will be perceived by its foreign masters as evidence of a dangerous unreliability. Because of these conflicting pressures factionalism within the elite is almost inevitable, although it is likely to be expressed in a guarded way.

A controlled elite will normally insist that it is free and independent regardless of the transparent falsity of the claim, for such legitimacy as it has rests on that pretension. Behind that screen there will be contention between those who, above all else, want to demonstrate their reliability and those who, on the other hand, would prefer a greater degree of freedom of action, either for nationalist reasons or in the interest of increased administrative efficiency. The latter will believe that regulations made in a distant land often do not square with local realities and that they could do a better job of governing if they had greater freedom. In an era of nationalism, it is not surprising that nationalist aspirations within local Communist elites continue to be a problem for the Soviet Union.

Theoretically, there is no upper limit to the extent that a dominant actor can organize the life and resources of a subordinate country. As a practical matter, however, the more elaborate the political and administrative controls that are instituted, the more costly the control effort will be in terms of time and attention. Furthermore, establishment of an elaborate bureaucratic apparatus in a subordinate society will be likely to institutionalize conservatism, rigidity, and inefficiency. A further cost is that management of this apparatus may contribute to administrative overload in the dominant society.

Direct Military Control

In this category fall those constraint systems in which governance is based on an occupying military force. Examples would include joint occupation of Germany after World War II, U.S. military occupation of Japan, and the role of the French in Indochina after World War II.

This method utilizes a reliable instrument, the army of the dominant power, but it is almost guaranteed to be unpopular in the subordinate country. Furthermore, it will be costly and, because of that, may ultimately arouse discontent in the dominant country. The British discovered in India, in Malaya, and earlier in the American colonies the problems a military presence may create once nationalism is afoot. The French learned the same lesson in Indochina and Algeria. Generally speaking, the success of prolonged military occupation will turn on such factors as the role of the media in the two countries, the ruthlessness of the dominant actor, and the cumulative costs of military operations relative to the resources of the dominant country.

Constraint System Ideologies

Every substantial constraint system that persists will acquire an ideology. Its formation is unavoidable. If actors are to interact with one another in reliable ways, a set of shared values, perceptions, goals, and rules of the game will be needed.

A system ideology, then, is an instrument for guidance and coordination. Properly used, it is an efficient, low-cost instrument of control. It can legitimize the position of the dominant actor and the rules it favors, can transform a system based upon might into one that is perceived as based upon right, and can guide a great deal of behavior with a minimum of effort. The more a dominant actor can draw upon ideological support, the less it will have to rely upon political, administrative, and military controls. Conversely, the less it can count on ideological support, the greater the reliance it will have to place on other control measures. Because the Soviet Union cannot win genuine, broad ideological support in eastern Europe and has not succeeded in having its domination accepted as legitimate, it has no alternative but to rely heavily on other control measures.

The precise functions a system ideology performs will depend on the circumstances. Generally speaking, it will enunciate a set of system goals, will justify the means to those ends, and will go on to justify system rules, the way they are made, management strategies, the special position of the dominant actor, and payoff asymmetries in the system. It will try to convert the assumptions of the system into self-evident propositions and its operating rules into principles of abstract right. The ideology will emphasize the attractive aspects of the system and deny, de-emphasize, or explain away the less attractive aspects. The assumptions, values, and procedures of the system will be presented as more attractive than alternative arrangements. The special advantages that accrue to a dominant actor will be minimized or overlooked while the costs and cares of predominance will be stressed. A colonialist ideology, for instance, may dwell on the heavy burdens a dominant power must carry and may imply that it is quite decent of colonial powers to be willing to pick up the "white man's burden."

A dominant actor may or may not be aware of the extent to which the rules of a constraint system serve its needs, and there is room for wide variation, therefore, in the extent to which the manipulation of ideology by dominant actors is deliberate and calculated. In general, victims perceive the exploitative features of a system more easily than do beneficiaries. Ideological precepts that serve the interests of a people have a way of appearing persuasive to them. Dominant actors, in consequence, tend to become captives of ideologies developed for others. The concept of Manifest Destiny served American needs and was, accordingly, persuasive to many Americans. Only a later generation learned to treat that notion with scorn. The notion of a "free market system," with its assorted rules, served the interests of Western trading nations, and, not surprisingly, the ideas that it involved were persuasive to Western statesmen, businessmen, and analysts.

Ideas that once carried conviction may, in time, become objects of deliberate manipulation. Church history offers more than a few examples in which it appears that church fathers were deliberately manipulating symbols and doctrine. Lenin and Stalin were both adept at manufacturing "Marxist" or "Marxist-Leninist" theory to meet the needs of the moment (Scott, 1951).

Subordinate Actor Resistance

A subordinate actor may be content with its position in a constraint system in which case it will make no demands for change. If it is discontented, it may make minor demands that can be satisfied within the framework of the existing rules of the game. More severe discontents will encourage a subordinate actor to think in terms of rule change, for a significant redistribution of the values governed by the system will normally take place only after a successful challenge to the rules themselves. Prior to 1973 the oil-producing nations operated within the rules of the game established by the oil-consuming nations and the major oil companies. Bargaining revolved around changes of a few cents per barrel. OPEC then called for an oil embargo, which challenged the rules of the game successfully and allowed OPEC to dictate a 400 percent increase in the price of oil! At a stroke, the OPEC nations escaped from the old constraint system and established a new one, of which they were the masters.

It is common for subordinate actors to become increasingly discontented with the passage of time and, therefore, for their demands to escalate if their capabilities justify it. At the outset, for example, the American colonists had few complaints about English rule. The first demands, when they emerged, took for granted the context of English legality and were based on the provisions of colonial charters or on the rights that all Englishmen were thought to enjoy under law. Demands based on natural rights came later, as progressive radicalization continued. Demands for escape from the constraint system, that is, independence, appeared still later. India's demands against England also revealed a gradual ripening.

When a subordinate actor pressures a dominant actor to change the rules of the game, it is likely to be more concerned about the rules that are important to it than about those important to other members of the system. A subordinate actor may, that is, try to induce the dominant actor to make special concessions, whether or not those concessions are offered to others in the system. A constraint system might, therefore, be organized on the basis of several tiers of members, with more demanding rules applied to the weaker than to the stronger. NATO has long operated in this way. For instance, the heads of the British government and the government of the Federal Republic of Germany expect to be consulted before an American president has a summit meeting with Soviet leaders, and presidents have usually honored that expectation. The same thing does not apply to the governments of the Netherlands or Belgium. That does not mean, of course, that smaller allies are altogether without bargaining power. Denmark and Norway have made it clear that they do not want nuclear weapons stationed within their borders. The British Empire was also a tiered system, and subordinate actors were able to aspire to move from a less privileged to a more privileged category.

The strategy and tactics selected by a subordinate actor should reflect an estimate of the likely responses of the dominant actor to various courses of behavior. When demands are made, will it assess the costs and accede to them if it can? Or might it conclude that those demands represent only the first installment of a long series and that, therefore, no concessions should be made? A subordinate actor must be careful not to induce a more strenuous response than it can handle. More specifically, it should not shift the basis of the contest from bargaining to sheer military power until it is ready for such a shift. Hungarian dissidents were correct, in 1956, in perceiving that the Soviet Union would be reluctant to resort to the use of military power, but they overestimated that reluctance.

In general, as the capabilities of a subordinate actor improve relative to those of the dominant actor, its bargaining position will improve and it can escalate its demands. As the Athenians explained to the Melians, when the strong deal with the weak, it is not the justice of the claims of the latter so much as relative power positions that count, "for we both alike know that into the discussion of human affairs the question of justice only enters where the pressure of necessity is equal, and that the powerful exact what they can, and the weak grant what they must" (Thucydides, *Peloponnesian War*, bk. 5, sec. 89). Conversely, if the relative capabilities of a subordinate actor decline, its demands should be scaled down. Since it is relative capabilities that are in question, change can be brought about by an improvement or weakening in the position of either actor. If the capabilities of the dominant actor decline, in absolute terms, and those of the subordinate actor remain the same, the relative position of the latter will have improved.

The relative power positions of the two may also be affected by developments in the broader environment. For example, the powerful thrust toward decolonization that emerged after World War II changed the context in which colonial contests were fought. This wholesale ideological change placed traditional colonial nations on the defensive while dependencies aspiring for independence found it easy to attract support. This increased the maintenance costs of colonial systems at a time when colonial nations, following the devastation of World War II, could ill afford them.

An escalation of demands tends to be associated with increasing capabilities, but the relationship is not invariable. A subordinate actor might think itself well off and not escalate its demands despite an improvement in its relative capabilities. For the same reason, it might choose not to escape from the system even when it could. Canada, having achieved operational independence from the mother country, is nevertheless pleased to retain a formal connection and to profess loyalty to the British crown.

One of the quickest ways to increase the capabilities arrayed against a dominant actor is through the formation of a coalition. Individual oil-producing countries were ineffective in changing the rules of the game of the world oil system until they formed OPEC and began to coordinate their actions in order to take advantage of emerging market conditions. Developing nations have drawn more attention to their efforts to reform the international economic order since they began to pursue a coalition strategy via the so-called Group of 77. The formation of a coalition represents, of course, the creation of a new constraint system, a new set of power relationships, and new rules of the game.

Since a coalition strategy provides such an easy way to increase subordinate actor capabilities, why is it not resorted to as a matter of course? For one thing, a dominant actor may be in a position to prevent it. The governments of eastern Europe are so thoroughly penetrated by the Soviet Union that it would be extremely difficult for them to engage in the secret communication that would be required. Furthermore, potential members may be suspicious or envious of one another and find it hard to act on the basis of shared interests. OPEC was a long time in coming and even now has trouble achieving agreement. Actors have multiple interests, not just a single one, and although one interest may tend to unify a group of actors, another may divide it. Successful coalitions are usually based on the predominance of a single, salient, shared value. The absence of such a value, or the existence of a competing value, would militate against the formation of a coalition.

System Maintenance and Escape

In a highly asymmetric system a subordinate actor will normally seek (1) to modify system rules so as to increase benefits to itself; (2) to raise system maintenance costs that must be borne by the dominant actor; and (3) to find ways to lower escape costs. The dominant actor, on the other hand, will be trying (1) to improve the yield from the system by increasing the ratio of benefits to costs; (2) to lower maintenance costs; and (3) to keep escape costs at a high level.[1]

The interests of the two are in conflict but not in a zero-sum conflict; there are shared interests as well. For example, an inordinately high level of short-term exploitation would be destructive to a subordinate actor and might also be counterproductive for the dominant actor. In the years immediately after World War II a great deal of industrial equipment was removed from eastern Germany to the Soviet Union. After a time it became clear that this policy was contrary to the long-term interests of both parties and was abandoned.

There are common interests, again, in connection with escape and escape costs. If escape costs are very high, prohibitively so, this should be made clear, for avoidance of a bloody showdown is in the interest of both parties. The 1956 escape attempt was costly to the Hungarians, and the nonmilitary costs to the Soviet Union were also heavy. Indeed, those costs were so heavy that the Soviet Union, later, in the case of Rumania, allowed a subordinate actor partial escape rather than order military action. Indications that the USSR would be extremely reluctant to use military power against another Warsaw Pact member, because of political and other costs, provided Rumania with room for movement. In its turn, Rumania has, for the most part, avoided provocative behavior that would embarrass the USSR or threaten its overall position in eastern Europe. That is, it tried to hold down the cost to the Soviet Union of its freedom of action so as not to force a reassessment by the Soviet Union of its position.

If the use of military force is unavailable to a dominant actor, then there will be an upper limit to escape costs, as President de Gaulle realized in planning France's disengagement from NATO. In such a case the strategy of system maintenance relied upon by the dominant actor will have to emphasize benefits rather than the threat of punishment. One of the benefits enjoyed by members of the Warsaw Pact system is the confidence that they will not be objects of armed attack by fellow members. The rules of the game do not allow conflicts of interest to escalate into military conflict save in the event of an attempt at escape or an attempt to change the rules of the system radically. In eastern Europe, with its diverse nationalities and traditions of conflict, this benefit is a substantial one. Foregoing it, therefore, would be an important component in the cost of escape from the Warsaw Pact system.

Although a cost-benefit perspective is useful in thinking about the relations of actors in a constraint system, it is certainly not a precision tool. For one thing, estimates of costs and benefits are subjective. In addition, there is the difficulty of weighing "opportunity costs," or benefits foregone. Similarly, how is one to weigh the value of an evil forestalled? In assessing the value of the Warsaw Pact to the Soviet Union, one must ask how much is it worth to the USSR to minimize the risk of eastern Europe coming under the domination of a revitalized Germany? In assessing the value of the Western Hemisphere system to the United States, one must ask what has it been worth to have prevented any great power from gaining a significant foothold in this hemisphere?

Poland: 1980–1981

The events in Poland in 1980–81 illustrate a number of constraint system dynamics. When one country seeks to maintain forcible domination over another, instability is almost guaranteed. If the dominant actor tries to rule through consent, as a means of establishing putative legitimacy, consent may well be withheld to expose the emptiness of the claim. If it rules without consent, it surrenders any serious claim to legitimacy and lays bare the power relationship.

The techniques that Soviet authorities have developed for governing the nations of eastern Europe are sophisticated and, on the whole, have worked quite well. They offer not consent but a simulation of it by means of national leadership (co-opted) and doctrines that would seem to tie the Communist party to the masses.

Walking a Tightrope: The Polish Communist Party
The position of a co-opted national regime is a precarious one, as noted earlier. When strikes began to spread in Poland, Edward Gierek, head of the Polish Communist party, advised Soviet leaders that the way to defuse the situation was to make broad concessions to the workers, including agreement with the demand for independent unions.

Gierek was doubtless a disappointment to the Soviet leadership in a number of respects. For one thing, he did not seem to have a good understanding of the dynamics of the situation. After years of repression, small concessions will not satisfy the oppressed. Instead, they are likely to encourage hope and generate new rounds of demands. Concessions could never fully satisfy the Poles, for what they really wanted was freedom to choose their own government and to be free from Soviet domination.

Gierek should also have understood more clearly that, according to Marxist-Leninist control theory, the only legitimate organizations in a society are those controlled by the Communist party. An uncontrolled organization is a potential focal point for resistance to government and party. The demand for a "free" organization of any kind should, therefore, have been viewed as inherently "anti-socialist." The Catholic church has been tolerated in Poland not because it fitted in with Marxist-Leninist principles but because it was too strong to root out.

The demand for an independent trade union was radical, therefore, from the very outset. Gierek should have known that in Communist societies unions do not exist to represent their members and press their needs against other segments of society or against government but, rather, to provide the party with access to the workers so that the latter can be guided and directed. Unions are not supposed to project demands upward but instructions and official interpretations downward. From the Soviet perspective, therefore, Gierek was mistaken to have ever thought of temporizing with the demand for free unions.

If Gierek, a longtime Communist, did understand these things, then the only alternative explanation for his behavior was that he was insufficiently tough. Was he more responsive to the needs of his own people than to the needs of the Soviet leadership? That, too, would be a serious matter, for the Soviet Union had had enough experience with "national communism" —Yugoslavia, the People's Republic of China, Hungary, Czechoslovakia, Rumania—not to want to open the door to it in Poland.

Finally, and most importantly, Gierek's inability to control events in Poland revealed him as an ineffective leader. Party leaders in eastern Europe are worth nothing to the Soviet Union if they cannot rule effectively; that is their whole reason for being maintained in power. As soon as events in Poland were momentarily stabilized, the Soviet Union, therefore, forced Gierek out of office. He was succeeded by Stanislaw Kania, who was also later forced out of office for some of the same reasons.

The Dynamics of Resistance

The events in Poland illustrate a number of the problems facing dissidents in a subordinate country. At the outset, the leaders of the strike movement played their cards carefully. With normal channels of political and economic protest closed to them, they did not take to the streets with noisy demonstrations but, instead, began a quiet, unauthorized strike to shut down parts of the Polish economy. They sought to focus upon key demands and to assure the Polish government that the challenge was a limited one having to do only with collective bargaining and the welfare of workers. When the Gdansk strike drew forth sympathy strikes elsewhere, constituting virtually a general strike along the Baltic coast, Lech Walesa, leader of the strikers, asked a temporary halt in the spread of sympathy strikes. He also, initially, argued for a loose federation of unions rather than a strong central federation, presumably on the grounds that the latter would seem too direct a challenge to the Communist party. The strikers emphasized that they were not trying to escape from the constraint system but only to modify some of its rules. In their statements and negotiations they took pains to use the official euphemisms of Communist discourse in order not to give unnecessary affront. They took care to avoid a direct challenge either to the dominance of the Soviet Union or the "leading role" of the Polish Communist party. Their strike, with its associated demands, represented a probe, but a careful one. They were trying to find out how great a change in the rules of the game the party and the Soviet leadership would be willing to tolerate, and they were attempting to locate the threshold beyond which lay forcible repression.

The situation changed rapidly and soon developed a logic of its own. There had been nothing like these strikes since Soviet rule had been imposed, so the movement instantly became the focus of attention and discussion. Walesa became a national figure overnight. The movement helped to meet needs that extended far beyond the ranks of the workers. At that time there appeared to have been three major sources of discontent: (1) anti-Soviet sentiment, (2) antiparty and antigovernment feelings, and (3) economic dissatisfaction. The national union, Solidarity, and the broader reform movement that came into existence gave Poles a way to express all of these discontents.

The virus of reform spread from one part of the society to another: from labor to agriculture, the universities, the media, the arts, local government, and economic planning. Every demand for broadened consent increased the popularity and power of the movement and made it more certain that further demands would be forthcoming. Solidarity was engaged in a *pas de deux* with the population as a whole.

In a significant development, the contagion spread into the party itself. Dissidents in different factories and cities began to communicate with one another laterally and spontaneously instead of vertically through designated leaders. There soon emerged widespread demands within the party for the democratic election of members of the Central Committee. This demand represented a direct challenge to the Leninist conception of the party based on the principle of democratic centralism. Furthermore, and the point was probably not lost on Soviet leaders, democratization within the party would result in a national communist party that would almost certainly be anti-Soviet. Pro-Soviet hard-liners would not have won a popularity contest within the party.

Within Solidarity a familiar pattern emerged. Walesa tried to avoid a runaway escalation of demands and expectations that would end in precipitating forcible repression. As a result he was labeled a conservative by more radical emergent figures who argued that the movement had outgrown its early leadership. Walesa could only maintain his position by going along with the progressive radicalization of Solidarity's demands. In early December the government released tapes of a Solidarity meeting in Radom during which there was discussion of the need to gain control of the state Radio Committee, the need for a workers' militia, and the need for a coup. A few days later the leadership of Solidarity proposed to conduct a nationwide referendum on the desirability of setting up a noncommunist government.

In the space of sixteen months from its founding, Solidarity had evolved from a union with limited economic objectives into an organization with broad political objectives that was prepared to facilitate the overturn of the government and to then step forward and replace it. The proposal for a nationwide referendum was revolutionary in the full sense of the term, for if consent of the Polish people was to be the basis for deciding on a government in Poland, a Communist party controlled by the Soviet Union would be doomed.

Those must have been heady days for the leaders of Solidarity as the government made one concession after another. It seemed that the party might allow itself to be reformed right out of power without firing a shot. The limits of the possible seemed to advance steadily. In a repressive situation, such as the one that existed in Poland, any reform movement has the potential to become a revolutionary movement. If it is not prevented, it will happen, and, in this case, the party was no longer able to prevent it.

The Soviet Response

The Communist party was the Soviet Union's chosen instrument for rule in Poland, and, therefore, as the position of the party weakened, Soviet rule in Poland also weakened. There was never any real question about Soviet acceptance of the breakdown of Communist rule in Poland: too much was at stake. Poland is important in its own right, and what happened there could have repercussions in the other Warsaw Pact countries. Unless the Soviet Union was prepared to see its system in eastern Europe dismantled, which it was not, the only question was when and how it would act.

Presumably it would seek to bring the situation back under control while incurring the lowest possible costs. The strikes were damaging enough in themselves because, according to Marxist-Leninist theory, a communist government necessarily represents the workers and so strikes are never necessary. Therefore, if there were strikes and worker discontent, something must be wrong with the theory. In addition, the demand for free unions was a clear indication that the workers did not believe that their interests were really represented by government-controlled unions.

For a time, Soviet leaders apparently hoped that intimidation, combined with a strong stand by the Polish authorities, would repair the situation. Therefore, it organized extensive military maneuvers in and around Poland using Soviet forces and those of other Warsaw Pact countries, made military moves consistent with the preparations for an invasion, reminded Poland of the Brezhnev Doctrine, and arranged for conspicuous trips to Poland by senior officers in the Red army. These moves had a sobering effect, and, for a time, the situation was stabilized.

When reformist momentum picked up again it presumably became clear to the Soviet leaders that the Polish Communist party had no hope of reestablishing control on its own, that the threat of invasion was of limited utility, and that there was, therefore, no alternative to the use of military power. When Communist party control broke down at the time of the Hungarian and Czechoslovak uprisings in 1956 and 1968, the Soviet Union had moved directly to intervention by the Red army. In both cases the political costs had been substantial. The situation was also sensitive in 1981, for the Soviet invasion of Afghanistan was still fresh in many minds around the world and another military operation would spread alarm, strengthen a weakened NATO alliance, and prompt increases in alliance defense expenditures.

The Soviet Union, therefore, sought a Polish solution to the crisis. Arguing that there was a threat of a coup and that the nation was on "the brink of civil war," leaders of the Polish army declared a state of martial law on 13 December 1981. The scenario of the Soviet leaders probably called for the reestablishment of order by the Polish army and then the reinstitution of party rule. The Soviet Union clearly prefers to rule in eastern Europe by political rather than military means. The former generates less internal hostility and is more pliable. It is easier to force a party to change its policies or personnel than to force an army to do so.

If this scenario did not work out, and the Polish army proved unreliable or, for some other reason, inadequate to its task, the next step, almost certainly, would be the use of the Red army itself, despite the political costs involved.

Great Power Relations

The events in Poland also served to illustrate a general rule. When a superpower takes a military action within its own sphere of influence, other nations will not respond with military action. The Reagan administration, despite a strong anti-Communist bent, confined itself to warnings and to consultations with allies: it never threatened military action.

Constraint Systems and the Unintended

As already noted, global processes often produce unintended consequences; so, too, do constraint systems. It is useful to think of constraint-system change in terms of two principle variables: first, whether the source of the change is internal or external and, second, whether the change is purposeful or apurposive.

In Figure 4 cell 1 would include those examples in which the source of the change is internal to the constraint system and is purposeful. When a change is purposefully introduced, the initiator will have certain results in mind and the consequences may be as intended. Other consequences may also follow, however, that were not intended. For example, the dynamics of an asymmetrical control system may, over a period of time, generate forces that will tend to reduce that asymmetry. Exploitation is sometimes self-limiting.

A dominant actor, in the interest of system maintenance, may introduce measures pertaining to education, training, transportation, communications, administration, and the economy that can, in time, undermine its own position. British policy in India, for instance, encouraged the education in England of able young members of the administrative class such as Gandhi and Nehru. These individuals were instrumental in importing into India the ideas of political philosophers such as John Locke, which were then used against England in the struggle for independence. Or, again, it was the policy of England to encourage Britons to migrate to the young American colonies. In time, this migration made it possible for the colonies to challenge the mother country successfully. A short-term solution to a problem may generate a more serious long-term problem.

A nation that has utilized military power to maintain control over a subordinate society may discover that its own military activity has transferred knowledge to the subject people concerning weapons, logistics, military organization, and guerrilla tactics. Major international oil companies made a point of training capable young Arabs in the technology, management, and economics of the oil industry. In so doing they helped pave the way for the takeover of the global oil system by OPEC.

Robert Gilpin has argued that the investment practices of a core nation may, in time, induce a shift of power from the core to the periphery. He suggests that the Netherlands overinvested abroad in the seventeenth century to the detriment of the home economy and that England made the same mistake in the nineteenth century. Both became rentier economies, living off earnings from overseas investments. Gilpin concludes:

FIGURE 4. Constraint System Change

	Source Internal	Source External
Change Purposeful	(a) consequences intended	
	(b) consequences unintended I	2
Change Apurposive	3	4

> Foreign investment is both a cause and a response to the historic tendency of advanced economies to decline industrially relative to their foreign competitors. Through the spread of technology and know-how, the industrial leader, over a period of time, loses more and more of its initial comparative advantages relative to rising competitors. As a result, a gradual shift takes place in the locus of industrial and other economic activities from the core to the periphery of the international economy. . . . The consequence of this tendency is a gradual redistribution of wealth and power within the international system. [1975, p. 45]

> In a world of competing nation-states, wherein power rests ultimately on an industrial base, foreign investment contributes to an international redistribution of power to the disadvantage of the core. [1975, p. 77]

The other cells in the matrix of Figure 4 can be dealt with briefly. In cell 2 would be located instances in which a source external to a constraint system made a purposeful effort to induce change within the system. During the 1970s, for example, western European nations sought increased trade with eastern European nations, and their purposes were political as well as economic. They were trying to induce change in the Warsaw Pact system and were successful, at least to a degree.

In cell 3 would be located examples of change within a constraint system in which the source of the change was internal but the process was apurposive. If system rules do not control all significant forms of interaction within a system, the interaction that is uncontrolled may create problems for the rule-makers. For instance, the recent growth of multinational corporations was an unanticipated consequence. Economic conditions favored the development, and the rules of Bretton Woods allowed it but did not guide it. The problem had not really been imagined when those institutions were established.

Cell 4 would include examples in which change in a constraint system is external and apurposive. For example, the British Empire was weakened by the growth of the world economy and the relative decline of England's position in that economy. The working of the world petroleum system was affected by the increasing global demand for petroleum and by the approach of petroleum exhaustion.

What strategies might a dominant actor pursue in trying to control changes taking place in a constraint system and to minimize the impact of the unintended? Since uncontrolled behavior is disruptive to the system's normal functioning, one broad strategy would be to try to expand the scope of the system so as to incorporate the disruptive variables. The ideal of system managers, presumably, would be to have a system that changes only in accordance with the working of variables that are internal to the system and are controlled.

In pursuit of that objective, a dominant actor might try to reduce the amount of apurposive behavior in the system by making the rules of the game more inclusive. That is, it might try to bring under control all endogenous apurposive processes. The leading actors in the Bretton Woods system might, for example, have sought to establish controls over capital movement, the reserves that members must hold, and so on. The difficulty with this strategy is its doubtful feasibility.

A dominant actor might also try to expand the scope of its constraint system as a means for dealing with disruptive external factors. This would represent an effort to convert an uncontrolled exogenous factor into a controlled endogenous factor. For instance, the NATO powers have sought to use NATO as an organizational basis for attacking environmental problems, including air pollution.

For a dominant actor, trying to limit the impact of disruptive external factors, a possible alternative strategy would be that of insulation. The creation of a host of barriers between eastern European nations and the outside world represented an effort on the part of the Soviet Union to eliminate, or at least reduce, the disruptive impact of Western influences. During the life of Mao Tse-tung the People's Republic of China sought to insulate itself from the West. In a world that is becoming increasingly interactive, however, this is a difficult and expensive strategy to pursue. It is noteworthy that both the USSR and the People's Republic of China have found it necessary to relax barriers and to allow greater contact with the outside world.

Constraint System Decay

The number of constraint systems in existence has risen in step with the increase in the number of nation-states and nonstate actors and with the diversification of functional interests. One thinks of entities such as the Organization of Petroleum-Exporting Countries, the Organization of Central American States, the Organization of American States, the Organization of African Unity, the League of Arab States, the Nordic Council, the European Coal-Steel Community, the East African Community, the Danube Commission, the Cocoa Producers Association, the Central African Customs Union, the South Pacific Commission, and so on.

Most constraint systems are short-lived, although some have persisted for centuries. Each system will have a set of requisites, and the more numerous and demanding those requisites are, the more problematic is long survival of the system. Requisites of the Warsaw Pact system, for example, include an elaborate set of control measures, the proximity of the Red army, and the readiness of Soviet authorities to rely on military force if nonmilitary control measures break down. It is not easy to run an imperial system. Despite strenuous efforts on the part of the Soviet Union since the end of World War II, the USSR has not succeeded in persuading eastern European nations to be satisfied with Soviet rule. The Soviet leadership must know that the system would quickly disintegrate if, for example, a serious domestic crisis occurred in the Soviet Union or if the Soviet Union became involved in a demanding war elsewhere.

Requisites of the Bretton Woods system in 1970, say, would have included: the preponderant political, economic, and military position of the United States; the stability of the dollar; a strong global resource base including, specifically, plenty of petroleum at low prices; and acceptance on the part of developing nations of terms of trade that penalized primary goods and favored manufactured goods. Denial of any of these requisites would have constituted a threat to the system's continuation.

The military defeat of a dominant actor will normally lead to system collapse. The Austro-Hungarian Empire dissolved with the defeat of the Central Powers in World War I, and the Nazi and Japanese constraint systems collapsed with the defeat of Germany and Japan in World War II. Since constraint-system arrangements are commonly more to the advantage of some actors than others, disruption of a constraint system may be welcomed by the disadvantaged even though it is deplored by a dominant actor. Regime instability following Stalin's death in 1953 weakened the Soviet constraint system, and there were riots in eastern European countries and a restiveness until the Hungarian revolt was crushed in 1956.

The costs of system maintenance may become greater than the dominant actor can afford. Great Britain's weak financial and commercial base did not allow it to operate as a hegemonic economic and political power after 1929. Kindleberger suggests that "at the World Economic Conference in 1933, it was clear that Britain had turned away from a leading world role, cultivating the Commonwealth and freedom to manage sterling, and largely leaving it to the United States to devise a world programme" (1973, p. 297).

The relative power positions of dominant and subordinate actors may change, leaving the dominant actor unable any longer to discipline system members. The decline of imperial systems offers many examples.

Factors originating outside a system and beyond the control of the dominant actor may have an effect on system functioning. All colonial systems were affected by the ideological hostility toward colonialism that emerged after World War II. Similarly, the energy crunch of the late 1970s had an impact on many constraint systems.

8. Contemporary Constraint Systems

Constraint systems are subject to change and evolution and, like all man-made social structures, they come to an end. The Napoleonic system came and went, and so did the Concert of Europe, the British Empire, and scores of other empires, arrangements, and alliances known to history. This chapter will examine (1) the Bretton Woods system, now in a state of decline; (2) an emergent ideology, that pertaining to the New International Economic Order, which may, in time, provide the basis for a new constraint system; and (3) the Soviet-American constraint system.

The Bretton Woods System

The Ideology of Economic Liberalism

One function of an ideology is to justify the characteristics of the constraint system with which it is associated. For an economic system, the ideology may be counted on to explain how the international economic order works, why it works as it does, what features of the economy should be managed or not managed, by whom, and with what objectives in mind.

In the case of the liberal economic order dominant in the nineteenth century, elements in the associated ideology, explicit or tacit, included the following:

— The processes of the international economy reflect the play of market forces. The role of political factors is negligible.
— Market forces, such as competition and supply and demand, govern prices.
— A number of other equilibrating processes are at work including those relating to interest rates, capital flows, the costs of factors of production, and the distribution of profits.

— National governments should avoid interfering with these processes. Interference with automatic market mechanisms will cause the system as a whole to work less well than it otherwise would.

— Natural resources are allocated by market mechanisms. Those who possess resources, initially, or who can buy them, are at liberty to consume to any extent their financial means will allow.

— Resources are unlimited, for all practical purposes. If a particular resource should become scarce for a time, its price will rise and that will encourage substitution and decreased use. The price mechanism will therefore take care of any scarcity.

— Private capital flows in response to market opportunities. That assures the best possible global utilization of available capital.

— Increases in investment, production, and trade are of benefit to all nations and peoples.

— Buyers and sellers enter into exchange relationships voluntarily. Therefore, if an exchange were not mutually beneficial, it would not take place. If an exchange does take place, the presumption must be that the parties to it regard it as fair.

— Nations should engage in economic specialization when a pronounced comparative advantage exists. Such specialization is to the interest of all actors, for it involves an efficient use of resources and will therefore promote lower prices.

— The principle of comparative advantage implies that the more developed countries should concentrate on industrial production while the less developed, and least developed, should concentrate on the production of primary materials.

— If the principles of free trade and comparative advantage are observed, there will be a natural harmony of interests among trading nations regardless of size, wealth, and degree of economic development. Individual firms will have interest conflicts, for that is the nature of competition, but national economic interests will not conflict.

With the coming of the Great Depression of 1929–39 the free-trade system broke down. Governments took defensive action to protect employment and markets. Tariffs were raised, quotas were imposed, and preferential arrangements promoted trade discrimination. Governments also sought to aid industry in penetrating foreign markets. Export subsidies were established and currencies were depreciated competitively in pursuit of trading advantage (Kindleberger, 1973). The net result of all this was a sharp contraction of international trade, a condition that persisted until the advent of World War II.

Origins of Bretton Woods

As World War II began to draw toward a close, a few thoughtful Englishmen and Americans, in and out of government, began to turn to the question of the organization of the postwar international economic system.[1] Obviously international collaboration on matters of trade and payments was necessary, for otherwise there would be no way to escape the swamp of bilateralism and trade discrimination and no way to achieve currency convertibility. On the other hand, it was also clear that an exclusive reliance on automatic economic mechanisms would invite a replay of the earlier catastrophe. What was needed, they concluded, was a liberal economic system but one that would incorporate international institutional safeguards.

Three functions were deemed important:

1. nations would need to be assisted in negotiating joint, mutual reduction of tariffs so that trade could once again expand and the conditions of free trade could be achieved;
2. international investment should be encouraged and guided toward areas most in need of postwar reconstruction and development;
3. monetary and payments arrangements needed to be stabilized and facilitated so as to encourage the expansion of trade and forestall payments disturbances.

Each of these functions would, if given institutional form, modify an important aspect of the free-trade system. Taken together, they would amount to an effort to create, deliberately, a global economic system different from any that had existed before.

Once it was decided that the international system needed to be reconstituted, it was evident that the United States would have to play the leading role in the enterprise. The other great powers, in the wake of the war, were either defeated, disorganized, or impoverished, or some combination of the three. The United States alone had come through the war in good shape. It alone had the economic and political clout to press its ideas with any hope of achieving the broad collective agreement necessary if the new arrangements were to be vested with a sense of legitimacy.

The initiatives involved were bold and creative, and three institutions were ultimately established: the General Agreement on Tariffs and Trade; the International Bank for Reconstruction and Development (World Bank); and the International Monetary Fund.[2]

For each actor in a constraint system the problem is how to live within the rules of the game while still pursuing its interests as it sees them. For subordinate actors the problem is normally insoluble, in absolute terms, and so compromise and adjustment are necessary. For a dominant actor, however, the situation may be different. It is in a position to *make* the rules, and if the rules are fashioned so as to embody its interests, then it may be able to adhere to them while still pursuing its interests. It is predictable that the rules of the game in a constraint system will work to the advantage of a dominant actor, at least in the short run. Certainly, in the case of Bretton Woods, the United States was a major beneficiary of the rules. It was helpful to have the dollar as a reserve currency. This allowed the United States to run balance-of-payments deficits year after year without having to settle, for central banks in other countries were willing to hold dollar obligations as reserves for their own currencies. This made it easier for the United States to finance foreign aid, its military presence overseas, and the Vietnam War.

The Bretton Woods arrangements conferred significant decision-making power on the United States as well. It was in a position to have great influence on the decisions of GATT, the IMF, and the World Bank, and those institutions, in turn, together helped to shape the world economy. "In reality, however, and behind the facade of these institutions, the United States has run the international economy" (Gilpin, 1977, p. 56). The Bretton Woods system provides an interesting example of the leverage that a dominant actor can obtain by virtue of its role as rule-maker. For several decades institutions devised by the United States, and to which it continued to provide guidance, influenced the behavior of hundreds of actors, including scores of nation-states. It influenced decisions involving trillions of dollars, in aggregate, and all with relatively little effort.

In looking back to the origins of the Bretton Woods system, it is tempting to impute to American negotiators insights and perspectives that belong to a later period. At the time, they were concerned about American interests but were not thinking exclusively about them (Horsefield, 1969, vol. 1). American officials were not deeply troubled about the self-serving nature of their efforts because they were convinced that if the United States could help to organize a more stable world economy, trade and investment would increase and the benefit would be global. Those who operate within the framework of a liberal ideology find it easy to assume, if not a complete harmony of interests among nations, at least a high degree of interest overlap.

Nor were they wholly in error. It was helpful to other nations to have the United States take this initiative, and the system American negotiators designed did, in fact, promote extraordinary growth in international trade and investment. Although it was advantageous to the United States for the dollar to be a reserve currency, it was also useful to the economic system as a whole. The balance-of-payments deficits run by the United States increased reserves in the system and helped to finance the growth of trade.

The Decline of Bretton Woods

Despite the hopes of its designers, the Bretton Woods system began to encounter difficulties before long. First, there were problems that derived from the underlying liberal ideology. Each ideology incorporates a limited perspective and is certain to have blindspots. The liberal economic ideology assumed that the best route to economic development was free trade, but was that belief justified? The German economist Friedrich List noted in 1841, in his *National System of Political Economy*, that economic liberalism was a policy favoring the strong. Economically strong nations, because they are strong, need not fear competition. But what about the less efficient? In self-defense they may be pressed to use the mechanisms of the nation-state to shield their society and its economy from the impact of the international economy. This was a common thread running through mercantilist thought.

To Americans this idea should not be wholly novel. In December 1791 Secretary of the Treasury Alexander Hamilton, in response to a request from the House of Representatives, submitted his *Report on Manufactures*. He argued that manufacturing augmented the power of a nation and improved the well-being of its people. Free trade, with more fully developed nations, would inhibit the growth of industry and fix the United States in the position of a supplier of agricultural products. Hamilton wrote:

> In such a position of things, the United States cannot exchange
> with Europe on equal terms; and the want of reciprocity would render
> them the victim of a system which would induce them to confine their
> views to Agriculture, and refrain from Manufactures. A constant and
> increasing necessity, on their part, for the commodities of Europe,
> and only a partial and occasional demand for their own, in return,

could not but expose them to a state of impoverishment." [*Papers*, 1934, p. 210]

The proper policy for the young nation, he argued, was for it to foster economic development by deliberately encouraging the growth of manufacturing. It should do this by using governmental power to protect infant industries and shield them, for a time, against competition from more mature industries in other countries. One has to agree with Robert Gilpin, who claims that "the developing nations today, with their emphasis on protectionism, industrialization, and state intervention, owe more than they appreciate to Hamilton's conception of economic development" (Gilpin, 1977, p. 40).

A second source of difficulty for the Bretton Woods system lay in the domestic adjustments that a liberal, open, international economy calls for. It is essential to the liberal economic scheme that less efficient industries in one country give way to more efficient industries in another. That is all very well for the overall efficiency of the international economy, but it puts a heavy strain on the societies adversely affected. It means the closing of plants, the loss of jobs, and, perhaps, the onset of recession. Those groups in a population adversely affected by the adjustment are often not content to allow the forces of the international marketplace to work themselves out but seek, instead, to be shielded from them. The greater the extent to which a given national economy is tied in with the world economy, the more often it may be called on to make internal adjustments and, in consequence, the greater the political pressure for a defensive response is likely to be. Hand in hand, therefore, with the growth of economic interdependence, there may also be a growth in national demands for protection from the consequences of that interdependence.

A third source of problems lay in the specific arrangements of Bretton Woods. It was assumed that the dollar, a reserve currency, would be stable. But what if the United States did not act in such a way as to maintain the stability of its currency? What if, instead, it should choose to run heavy balance-of-payments deficits year after year? The IMF and, indeed, the entire system were so structured that they depended on the restraint and good judgment of the U.S. government. If that confidence proved unwarranted, the system could not survive. Events revealed that the United States was not prepared to act in a disciplined way. Because the dollar was a reserve currency, the United States came to act as if it had an unlimited credit line. It did not take action to end its balance-of-payments deficits, and so, slowly, as a result of an overabundance of dollars, the dollar weakened as a currency. On 15 August 1971, by action of President Nixon, the dollar ceased to be freely convertible into gold, and the system of fixed exchange rates had to be abandoned.

Without meaning to the United States contributed, one way and another, to the demise of an institution it wanted to maintain. Fred Block has depicted this remorseless logic as follows:

> Step by step, the United States either broke the rules of the old order or forced other countries to break them. The rule-breaking was deemed necessary at each step to save the international monetary system from an even greater crisis. The first major alteration of the rules was the creation of the gold pool in 1961, which relieved the U.S. of part of the responsibility of maintaining the gold price at $35 an ounce. The next step was the unilateral renunciation by the United States in 1968 of the obligation to provide gold to private purchasers at the $35-an-ounce price. This was followed three years later by the decision to close the gold window to official purchasers as well. The United States also renounced its informal obligations as a reserve currency country by blocking access to its capital markets, and the imposition of the 10 percent surcharge in August 1971 was a blatant violation of rules governing international trade. Finally, the United States was largely responsible for the final significant rule violation, the end of the regime of fixed exchange rates. The continuation of the U.S. deficit left foreign countries that did not want to accumulate additional dollars with only two options: instituting potentially dangerous controls over capital inflows or floating their currencies. Since the second alternative seemed less risky, it was the one for which Western Europe and Japan eventually opted. [1977, p. 203]

There were further difficulties. By the late 1960s the United States was deeply involved in the war in Vietnam, which contributed to its payments problem, and it neither felt like nor acted like the hegemonic power of the late 1940s. Exogenous factors came into play and added to the disarray. The sudden increase in oil prices placed strains on the system for which it had never been designed. The founding fathers of the Bretton Woods system had not anticipated the end of the era of cheap energy.

A final weakness in the ideology deserves mention, although it has been of little practical importance thus far. The ideology justifies managerial action to deal with some metasystem processes—trade, payments, investment—but not others. It does not provide for countercyclical action to head off a major metasystem disaster such as the depression of the 1930s.

The idea of countercyclical action for national economies was still being developed and elaborated in the 1940s, so it was hardly to be expected that the concept would be applied at the global level during the Bretton Woods discussions. John Maynard Keynes had developed proposals that would have allowed the IMF to adjust the price of gold to deal with global problems of recession and inflation and would therefore have given that organization a truly countercyclical capability (Horsefield, 1969, 1:17). The Articles of Agreement, however, gave the IMF a countercyclical capability only for dealing with the problems of an individual country (Horsefield, 1969, 3:192). Not until 1968 did the IMF acquire the ability to create new money in the form of a monetary unit of its own. In 1973–74 the IMF gave aid to Italy, Great Britain, and the Netherlands to ease payments difficulties brought on by the sharp increase in the price of oil. This aid doubtless had a countercyclical impact, but it was justified in terms of the balance-of-payments needs of those countries rather than in terms of the needs of the global economy.

The postwar era was one of rapid growth, and the actors administering the Bretton Woods system were never challenged by a massive downturn in economic activity. Had they been, this weakness in the underlying ideology would have stood out in sharp relief.

Demands for a New International Economic Order

Change in a major constraint system such as Bretton Woods is not an event but a process and may extend over decades or even generations (Gosovic, 1972; Singh, 1977). Change begins with the emergence of a system and continues until the system ceases to exist. The way a system works creates discontent, and the discontent gives rise to demands. A demand for minor changes in the application of system rules is likely to be replaced by demands for change in the substance of those rules.

Elements of an informed critique begin to develop and to be drawn together. Almost insensibly a counter ideology begins to emerge. Just as every constraint system will generate a supporting ideology given time, so, too, a challenge to a constraint system must be given an ideological form if it is to thrive. It is an axiom of American politics that "you can't beat somebody with nobody," and in the same way it could be said that it takes an ideology to beat an ideology.

By the early 1950s analysts in developing countries were beginning to have a perspective on the liberal economic/Bretton Woods system different from that of their counterparts in developed countries. This was reflected in terminology. One group of observers, in discussing the economic order, would use terms such as competition, economic laws, market processes, free trade, comparative advantage, and mutual advantage, while the other group would use terms such as exploitation, domination, oppression, asymmetry, and inequity. The terminological difference made it clear that appeal was being made to two different sets of values. The counterideology placed the principles of fairness, justice, and equality in opposition to those of efficiency and competition.

Economists in developing countries began to mistrust the principles of the liberal economic/Bretton Woods system. If free trade was supposed to promote economic growth for all, why were some nations not growing at all, or only very slowly, while the developed nations were enjoying rapid economic growth? If the parties to an economic exchange are equal, why was there so much evidence of gross inequality in bargaining power? Could it be that the principles on which the economic order was based actually served to impede the development of poorer nations? Were free trade principles fundamentally flawed in that respect?

The statement of the Afro-Asian Conference in Bandung in 1955 was significant in that it officially rejected the liberal economic proposition that all nations shared the same set of basic interests. It argued, on the contrary, that the interests of developed nations were distinct from those of developing nations and were often in conflict with them. It also maintained that the existing international economic system had been created by the developed nations to serve their interests and that it did so to the detriment of the interests of the developing nations. The Bandung views were reiterated at the Belgrade Conference of nonaligned nations in 1961 and again at the Cairo Conference in 1964.[3]

The growing numerical predominance of the developing nations in the United Nations General Assembly made it easier for them to establish agenda items favorable to their concerns. It also led to an increase in the number of UN organizations concerned with the problems of developing nations and thus to an increase in the number of forums in which new ideas could be articulated and refined. Economic commissions for the developing continents were established, the most important of which, for present purposes, was the Economic Commission for Latin America. In 1964 the United Nations Conference on Trade and Development was set up. At its first meeting a group of developing nations coalesced to form what came to be known as the Committee of 77. The committee retained that name even though its membership soon passed the hundred mark.

Subordinate actors were helping one another to realize that system rules were not part of the natural order of things but were man-made creations, reflecting a particular set of interests and assumptions. The Economic Commission for Latin America, under the direction of Raúl Prebisch, utilized its research capabilities in support of the interests of the developing countries and the same held for the UNCTAD Secretariat, also under the direction of Dr. Prebisch. Research was a form of political warfare, and reports were broadsides fired at a powerful enemy.

In December 1973 the General Assembly called for a special session to deal with international economic matters. Subsequent to that call the Sixth Special Session met in 1974 and resulted in a landmark document, the "General Assembly Declaration and Programme of Action for the Establishment of a New International Economic Order." The nineteen points in the declaration range from general principles to specific policy recommendations. The latter are aimed at increasing the flow of foreign aid, improving conditions of trade, stabilizing commodity prices, and improving the control by developing nations of foreign direct investment within their borders.

The most significant thing about the declaration, however, is its central focus, the demand for a New International Economic Order. This document takes it for granted that there is an international economic order, that it was set up by the developed nations to meet their needs, and that a new order is needed that will favor the developing nations. At one stroke, with the demand for a New International Economic Order, the debate was radicalized and moved far beyond the discussion of this or that limited demand. The declaration provided the nuclear ideas around which an ideology could be fashioned, and the demand for a New International Economic Order has been the principal item on the agenda of the developing nations since 1974.

Occasionally ideologies are the product of one mind, as in the case of Adolf Hitler and the Nazi ideology. Other times they may be the product of more than one mind, as in the case of Marx and Lenin and Marxism-Leninism. More often, however, ideologies are shaped by a collective process, as in the case of the democratic ideology or the liberal economic ideology. The emergent ideology centering on the demand for a New International Economic Order is of the latter kind. It has grown by accretion, albeit rapid accretion. Many strands of thought have contributed to what is an ongoing process, including the literature relating to dependency. This literature, in itself, contains various elements, including a theory of underdevelopment (Frank, 1969; Cardoso, 1974; Cardoso and Faletto, 1979) and an emphasis on the structural nature of imperialism (Galtung, 1971). To date there has been no master formulation of the emergent ideology, but the appearance of such a synthesis may be only a matter of time since the coherence of many of the components is already apparent.

The Emergent Ideology

The emergent counterideology challenges the liberal economic outlook and the assumptions of Bretton Woods at every significant point. It involves a mix of value statements, statements of presumed fact, and analytic ideas about the way things work. On the following pages the elements in that emergent ideology are enumerated and ordered in a preliminary way. Since the concern here is with ideology formation and rule change rather than economic analysis, no effort will be made to assess the merits of the various arguments.

I.

— The belief that the "economic laws" incorporated in the liberal economic outlook stand on their own as valid apart from any political system or set of value preferences is quite mistaken.

— Economic analysis reflects the preferences of the analyst, and it is part of the art of the economic analyst to build his preferences into his analysis in a persuasive way. Economic analysis must, therefore, be interpreted as "ideology."

— Economic arrangements, too, are rarely value neutral but reflect the preferences and interests of dominant actors. Although the rules of a system may be justified in terms of the working of impersonal historico-economic processes, they are better understood as products of powerful rule makers. Every economic order is undergirded by a political order and is brought into existence by the exercise of power. An economic system is always a *political* economy.

— Powerful nations are the rule makers for others. They are able to arrogate the role of rule maker to themselves because of power asymmetries.

— In an economic order rules help allocate scarce values. Therefore, those who fashion system rules are in a position to allocate scarce values and thus to advance their self-interest.

— Actors shaping an economic order can be counted on to devise rules that will further their interests. It must be expected that every significant arrangement in a constraint system will confer an advantage of one kind or another on the rule makers.

II.

— The free trade/Bretton Woods system was fashioned by the developed nations. The economic principles they propagated so confidently should be understood, for the most part, as expressions of their interests at a given time.

— The rules of the game of that system have created and perpetuated a worldwide division of labor advantageous to the developed nations and disadvantageous to the developing nations.

— The principle of "comparative advantage" instructs societies to concentrate on that which they produce to best advantage. In practice this principle has tended to lock developing nations into producing primary materials while manufacturing is left to the developed nations.

— Developed nations have encouraged developing nations to trade directly with them rather than with one another. This has promoted dependency on the part of developing nations and has tended to inhibit the emergence of interaction among them.

— Because the economic development of the poorer nations has been inhibited, they have not been in a position to generate their own capital but have had to rely upon capital from the developed nations. Since investment normally reflects the interests of the investor, this has allowed the developed nations to shape and constrain the development of the poorer nations.

— If nations were equal in circumstances and economic prowess, the same rules might then usefully be applied to all. Since they are not equal, however, equity requires that different rules should be applied to the economically strong and the weak. For example, the developed nations have favored the principle of nondiscrimination in tariff policy because, presumably, it is even-handed. However, once specialized roles have been allocated to societies, nondiscriminatory provisions only serve to perpetuate those roles. If developing nations are to break out of those roles and move rapidly in the direction of industrialization, their infant industries must be protected and favored rather than be subjected to even-handed nondiscriminatory treatment.

III.

— It is not correct to assume that parties to an international exchange come as free and equal actors, neither constrained by the other. In fact, the overall power and influence that each commands will have a bearing on any exchange and, in general, the weaker will lack the bargaining power of the stronger. Asymmetry in power and influence is therefore likely to be reflected in the terms of an exchange.

— A weaker actor may agree to a series of exchanges that are consistently more advantageous to the stronger. It does so because its options are limited and because the exchange is advantageous to it, even if it is *more* advantageous to the stronger. It is a characteristic of exchanges in the present economic order that they benefit one participant more than another and that the greater beneficiary is usually the stronger.

— According to the ideology of the free trade system, prices in international trade result from the play of supply and demand in the marketplace. In fact, stronger actors are in a position to exercise a disproportionate influence on prices. "Self-regulating" markets are not neutral and automatic but systematically favor the stronger economies. For instance, developed societies are often in a position to influence the price of the raw materials they wish to buy as well as to set the price of the manufactured goods they wish to sell. Since the rules of exchange reflect the interests of the stronger, they have no special claim to sanctity.

IV.

— As a consequence of asymmetric bargaining power, developed nations have been able to rig the terms of trade in their favor. This means that raw materials have been consistently underpriced relative to manufactured goods.

— This capacity to rig the terms of trade, maintained over a number of decades, has led to the accumulation of wealth in the developed countries and to persistent underdevelopment in the less-favored

nations. That is, the normal operation of the free-trade system has served to transfer resources from the less-favored to the more-favored nations. It has, therefore, both created and reinforced asymmetries in wealth, power, and status among nations.
— The free-trade system is not a self-correcting system. The rules of the game have provided for systematic, if unobtrusive, exploitation of one set of actors by another, and the longer the system persists the greater the disparities will be. Since that is the case, those rules should be changed to promote the needs of the many, not the few.

V.

— A New International Economic Order is needed, and it is in the interest of the developing nations to join with one another in trying to bring it into existence.
— The rules of that new order will unabashedly favor the interests of the poorer nations, just as the rules of the present order favor the interests of the richer, and will aim at the redistribution of global wealth.
— The major organizations supporting the existing international economic order—IMF, GATT, IBRD—normally reflect the assumptions and operating principles of that order. They are not "neutral" organizations, therefore, but are inherently political in their operation and in their impact. This means that the benefits from their working are likely to be distributed in an asymmetric way. Tariff negotiations under GATT, for example, have devoted noticeably less attention to products of concern to developing nations than to developed nations.
— These institutions, must, therefore, be replaced or, at the very least, be radically altered. Their decisions, for instance, should be based on majority rule rather than on weighted voting.
— There should be no presumption in favor of automaticity and market principles at the international level. The satisfactory functioning of global markets may require direct intervention in market processes by national governments or international organizations established to reflect the interests of developing nations.
— Since debt was imposed on developing nations by an exploitative system, demands that it be refinanced, scaled down, or repudiated altogether are legitimate.

— Since developing nations were forced to finance the prosperity of the developed nations over several generations, it would only be appropriate for developed nations to provide compensatory assistance now. Indeed, compensation for earlier exploitation is a moral imperative.

— Since the developed countries systematically inhibited the industrialization of the less-developed countries, it is now incumbent on them to make special efforts to speed the transfer of important technologies to those countries.

— The tariff system, which has given preferential treatment to the developed nations, should be altered so as to give preferential treatment to the developing nations.

— The terms of trade must be systematically set in favor of the developing nations.

— Multinational corporations have often been instruments for the exploitation of developing nations. The governments of developed nations, furthermore, have sometimes used their influence to smooth the way for favored multinational enterprises. It is both wise and proper, however, for a sovereign nation to wish to control foreign direct investment within its borders, and it should be free to take what measures it chooses without having to worry about the possibility of reprisals by powerful foreign governments.

The Future of an Ideology

The emergent ideology has come a long way, but it also has a long way to go. New kinds of questions continue to be asked, and new economic insights and interpretations continue to be incorporated. The policy and institutional implications of the ideology have only begun to be spelled out, and the hierarchy among value preferences encompassed in it has not yet been worked out. No economic system can maximize a plurality of values, so how are preferences to be ordered? If programs based on the separate values conflict with one another, as they are sure to do, which programs would take precedence? When attempts are made to determine priorities, interest conflicts are likely to emerge within the ranks of the developing nations.

The free-trade ideology systematically overlooked, or minimized, potential interest conflicts between rich and poor nations while the emergent ideology is grounded in the recognition of such conflicts. Although the dominant ideology was weakened by its failure to recognize the possibility of interest conflict, may not a weakness of the emergent ideology be the reverse—a systematic underestimation of the importance of *shared* economic interests? It would be unfortunate timing if the developing nations should acquire too firm an attachment to doctrines of interest conflict at a time when interdependence makes pressing the need for increased cooperation among nations.

The emergent ideology is ambiguous on the question of self-interest. On the one hand, it argues that the character of the present international economic order reflects the interest of the developed nations and that the latter can be counted on to pursue their interests. On the other hand, it assumes that the exploiters can perhaps be shamed into mending their ways and providing restitution. Yet if the developed nations are as single-minded in the pursuit of economic interests as the indictment suggests, considerations of guilt and justice would mean little to them. In practice, of course, the difficulty is not that intractable. Although the developed nations may have systematically exploited the poorer nations by means of the rules of the game they established, they did not do so with complete awareness of what was happening. They are not locked into patterns of heedless, self-interested behavior and may be open to pleas to change their ways.

Another shortcoming of the emergent ideology is that it takes it for granted that the global economy will be healthy and strong. It is a fair-weather ideology. That is understandable, for the ideology took shape after World War II in the decades that were characterized by unprecedented growth in world trade and the Gross World Product. Therefore, those who contributed to the formation of the ideology were not worrying about the overall economy but about matters of equity and the redistribution of wealth. Countercyclical elements in the ideology deal with commodities, alone or in groups, but only with an eye to stabilizing the position of third-world nations. There is no justification of countercyclical measures relating to the global economy as a whole.

This represents a notable gap in the emergent ideology, one it shares with the ideology it seeks to replace. It leaves it doctrinally disarmed and unable to cope with the possibility of a disaster such as the global depression of the 1930s. The emergent ideology offers no management philosophy and does not even consider the impact of such a depression on the needs of third-world nations. Hopes for large-scale income redistribution might be doomed by a depression, and a sharp move in the direction of bilateralism would also create serious problems for the poorer nations.

The ideology was developed within the framework of north-south differences and does not aspire to a global perspective at this juncture. When those shaping the emergent ideology begin to focus upon problems of the global economy, will they find it easy to embrace the principle of management as a means for satisfying those needs? A potential basis for conflict exists, therefore, between those, on the one hand, who would give first priority to the rights of nation-states to engage in restrictive practices in the interest of self-defense, and those, on the other hand, who would emphasize the need for global economic management, even if the rights of some nation-states would have to suffer. One suspects, however, that, if the issue arises, the emergent ideology will prove adaptable and will be made to accommodate the use of management for countercyclical adjustments in the global economy.

During the period when the ideology was taking shape, attention was focused on the way the global economic system operated to the advantage of the developed nations and to the disadvantage of the developing nations. The ideology, therefore, is attentive to the needs of national units rather than to those of individuals. There is a powerful concern about inequalities between nations but little explicit concern with inequalities between individuals. Its analysis is neo-Marxist in dealing with international conflict, but it has little to say about class conflict within nations. In addition, democratic values seem to play no important part in it. Therefore, at present, the ideology is consistent with the maintenance of regimes that are undemocratic, elitist, and devoted to the interests of privileged minorities.

As a result of more than two decades of thought and debate, the broad outlines of the counterideology are now identifiable and appear to be relatively stable even though change continues. One of the reasons for suspecting that they may be stable lies in the degree of convergence between the analysis associated with demands for a New International Economic Order and that elaborated by those concerned with the need to fashion a New International Information Order. Spokesmen for the latter, for example, argue that the developed nations control the production and distribution of information and that, as a result, serious and unfortunate asymmetries exist. These defects in the global information system exist, it is maintained, because the system was fashioned by the developed nations with only their own needs in mind. The developing nations have quite different needs, many of which are not being satisfied. The world information system should therefore be reorganized to do away with existing inequities and to meet those needs.[4]

The emergence of a counterideology has changed the context in which the debate between rich nations and poor nations proceeds and has noticeably affected the dynamics of social change. The ideology presents an alternative conception of the basis on which the international economy should be organized and envisions a new set of rules of the game. Developing nations have achieved a greater sense of solidarity because of the discovery of shared interests. Their spokesmen are impressed by the intellectual power of the critique they are using and are emboldened by the evident difficulty developed nations are having in responding to it. The emergent ideology strengthens their hand at the same time that it weakens the opposition. For the first time, developing nations are on the ideological offensive and have forced officialdom in the developed nations onto the defensive. A sea-change is taking place in underlying attitudes: support for the old rules and arrangements is less assured, and resistance to the demand for new rules and institutions is less confident and dogmatic. There is no way to tell, as yet, what the new economic constraint system will look like when it takes shape, but it will owe a good deal to the analysis and the demands incorporated in this counterideology.

The Soviet-American Constraint System

The Soviet Union and the United States are major actors on the world scene and each is the focal point of one or more control systems—NATO, Bretton Woods, the Western Hemisphere system, the Warsaw Pact, the Soviet sphere of influence. Since the planet is finite, these nations and their associated constraint systems necessarily impinge on one another. That being the case, it was in the interest of both major powers that rules be worked out to govern that interaction. Such rules reduce uncertainty and the possibility of serious misunderstandings. Informal rules governing competition have evolved, and the Soviet Union and the United States, in consequence, constitute a two-actor constraint system.

What are some of those rules? It is taken for granted that each side will gather intelligence about the other and that such activities will not be viewed as possible causes of war. Exposure of such activities may be used to embarrass the other, if it serves immediate tactical needs, but such incidents will not be allowed to get out of hand. Furthermore, whereas each may choose to imprison agents of the other, such agents will not be physically harmed. In fact, the common practice is that such agents will be either ignored, quietly expelled, or exchanged. It is also a tacit rule that, although covert actions may be engaged in, no attempt will be made to assassinate the leaders of the other country. Indeed, the assassination by either country of legitimate political leaders in third countries is deemed to be out-of-bounds. The interest of the United States for a time in trying to assassinate Fidel Castro was a clear aberration and is now a source of embarrassment.

As is widely recognized, a fairly elaborate set of rules of the game has been developed in connection with military deterrence. In the political and diplomatic realm, actors are also at some pains to avoid actions that might seem unduly threatening to the other. The United States has felt free to broadcast to the peoples of eastern Europe, but it has not sought to foment armed rebellion. It has worked with émigré organizations in the past but has always been careful not to set up governments in exile. It was also careful not to try to aid or arm insurgents in Hungary in 1956.

Spheres of Influence

Of special interest are spheres of influence (Kaufman, 1976; Steel, 1971–72; Hasner, 1972) and the evolution of rules pertaining to them. The term "sphere of influence" is misleading in some respects. To say that country X is in the sphere of influence of dominant actor Y does not necessarily mean that the latter has influence within X. For instance, public policy in Rumania is not as responsive to Soviet wishes as the Kremlin might desire, but Rumania, although effectively outside the Warsaw Pact system, remains securely inside the Soviet sphere of influence. The popularity of the dominant actor may be relevant in deciding whether a country is within a sphere of influence, but it is clearly not critical. The Soviet Union would win no popularity contests in eastern Europe, but the countries of eastern Europe are clearly in the Soviet sphere. The United States may not be very popular in Latin America, but that does not remove Latin American countries from the U.S. sphere. Economic and cultural ties may sometimes be relevant, but they, too, are not critical. Finland has close cultural and economic ties with western Europe but remains within the Soviet sphere. Conversely, although Cuba's political, economic, and military policies are coordinated with those of the Soviet Union in many respects, and although Fidel Castro's distaste for the United States is evident, Cuba remains within the U.S. sphere of influence, as Khrushchev discovered in 1962 at the time of the missile crisis.

The critical factor in determining whether a given country is within the sphere of influence of another is not the popularity of the latter, nor cultural ties between the two, nor the extent to which one controls the behavior of another. A sphere of influence is a constraint system, but effective control need not be a feature of that system. The critical factor is to be found in the way *other* great powers regard the assertion of special prerogatives in a given area. The identifying features of a sphere, then, are (1) the assertion of special prerogatives, and (2) de facto acceptance of that assertion by other actors.

The Monroe Doctrine involved an assertion by the United States of special prerogatives in the Western Hemisphere. In his Seventh Annual Message to Congress in 1832 President Monroe stated "that the American continents, by the free and independent condition which they have assumed and maintain, are henceforth not to be considered as subjects for future colonization by any European powers." Here is the United States arrogating to itself the right to determine what European powers can and cannot do in the Western Hemisphere. The so-called Roosevelt Corollary to the Monroe Doctrine adds the other prerogative usually associated with a sphere of influence, the right of an actor to intervene in its own sphere. In his Annual Message in 1904 Theodore Roosevelt stated:

> Chronic wrongdoing, or an impotence which results in a general loosening of the ties of civilized society, may in America, as elsewhere, ultimately require intervention by some civilized nation, and in the Western Hemisphere the adherence of the United States to the Monroe Doctrine may force the United States, however reluctantly, in flagrant cases of such wrongdoing or impotence, to the exercise of an international police power.

It is noteworthy that these American presidents were not addressing themselves primarily to those living in the Western Hemisphere but, rather, to European governments. It was the unwillingness of those governments to challenge the American position that gave the Monroe Doctrine practical effect.

The rules of the game for a sphere of influence are implied by what has already been said. The basic rule is that a major actor shall not intervene militarily in the sphere of another unless it is prepared for a frontal challenge to the actor asserting the existence of a sphere. This rule is based on the disparity in what would be at stake for each actor if the probe were to be successful. The challenged actor is likely to feel that a probe threatens vital national interests and would, therefore, be prepared to go to extremes to rebuff it. For the challenger, on the other hand, although the success of the probe might be advantageous, it would not be vital, and, therefore, the challenger would be prepared to take only moderate risks in connection with it.

The Soviet Union views eastern Europe as within its sphere of influence and would regard an American military probe as threatening to the entire, fragile Warsaw Pact system. The United States, aware of Soviet sensitivity on the matter, was careful neither to take, nor to threaten, military action at the time of the Soviet military interventions in Hungary and Czechoslovakia, or during the Polish crisis of 1980–81. When he enunciated the "Nixon Doctrine," Richard Nixon came close to a formal acceptance of the Soviet sphere. He noted that the time was past when any power would try to use eastern Europe to obtain a strategic advantage against the Soviet Union. The Helsinki accords went further in that direction. Similarly, when the United States intervened militarily in the Dominican Republic in 1965, the Soviet Union inveighed against the action and sought to score propaganda points but never threatened military action.

Since the rule concerning military intervention in the sphere of a major actor is widely understood, examples of nonobservance are uncommon. The Soviet effort to locate ballistic missiles in Cuba is such an example. Because the United States tolerated a pro-Soviet, anti-American government in Cuba, and did not follow through and overwhelm Cuba at the time of the Bay of Pigs incident, the Soviet leadership appears to have concluded that the United States was no longer prepared to maintain the integrity of its traditional sphere of influence. When Nikita Khrushchev chose not to adhere to the rules of the game but, instead, to probe the American sphere, he precipitated a direct and dangerous showdown between the two superpowers.

President Kennedy understood that a great power may choose not to intervene militarily against an actor in its own sphere of influence, even though it feels affronted, but that it could not fail to respond to military intervention by an outside power unless it was prepared to watch the dissolution of its sphere. In his speech of 22 October 1962 Kennedy noted that the Soviet Union was taking military action "in an area well known to have a special and historical relationship to the United States" and that the United States had no alternative but to respond to the challenge:

> . . . this secret, swift and extraordinary buildup of Communist missiles
> —in an area well known to have special and historical relationship to the
> United States and the nations of the Western Hemisphere, in violation
> of Soviet assurance, and in defiance of American and hemispheric policy
> —this sudden, clandestine decision to station strategic weapons for the
> first time outside of Soviet soil—is deliberately provocative and an

unjustified change in the status quo which cannot be accepted by this country, if our courage and our commitments are ever to be trusted again by either friend or foe.

The Soviet Union backed down, removed the missiles, made certain pledges, and the crisis passed.

A second rule, supported somewhat less passionately than the first, rejects intervention in a sphere in nonmilitary ways that the dominant actor is likely to regard as serious and unacceptable. As noted above, the United States did not, even at the height of the cold war, organize governments in exile for the eastern European countries. There was little chance that the United States would engage in "liberation" or "rollback" activities in eastern Europe despite the anti-communist rhetoric of Secretary of State John Foster Dulles.

Spheres and Probes

How and why do spheres of influence change? Since a sphere persists only as long as a dominant actor has the capacity and will to maintain it, anything that weakens the capability or determination of a dominant actor or that strengthens a challenging actor relative to it, will tend to undermine the stability of a sphere. Nevertheless, such changes have to be registered, so to speak, before changes in a sphere can take place. Defeat in a war registers weakness in an unmistakable way and so a sphere is unlikely to survive it.

A slow-motion decline presents more difficult problems for a would-be challenger. How is the extent of decline to be assessed and registered? Is one dealing with a tiger or only a paper tiger? Is the lion still the king of beasts or has it become a pussycat? At the end of World War II England was a victor and lost little time in reasserting its prerogatives as a sphere-of-influence power. Long-term economic decline and the strains of war, however, including the liquidation of British overseas assets, had left England seriously weakened. There was a lack of congruence, therefore, between its claims and its actual capabilities. How would the one be adjusted to the other?

The instrument used to assess and register underlying changes in capabilities and to determine the outlines of a sphere of influence is the probe. There are many kinds of probes—political, economic, cultural, paramilitary, military. A challenging power will use probes to test the geographical boundaries of a sphere, to determine what forms of intervention are currently acceptable or unacceptable, and to discover how determined a dominant power is to maintain its sphere. When a dominant actor rebuffs a probe, or deters a would-be challenger from probing, the outlines of the sphere are reaffirmed. Failure to rebuff a probe would encourage further challenges, which could be increasingly blatant and would invite the conclusion that a dominant actor no longer would, or could, defend its sphere of influence.

In the aftermath of World War II the Soviet Union initiated a number of probes in the eastern Mediterranean in areas that had traditionally been within the British sphere of influence. In 1941 Great Britain and the Soviet Union had invaded Iran to forestall increased German influence. Britain withdrew its troops after the war, but the Soviet Union did not. This was a clear-cut probe. If Soviet troops had been permitted to remain in Iran after British troops were withdrawn, the USSR would have been in a position to dominate the political life of Iran and move that country into the Soviet sphere. In early 1946 the United States joined Great Britain in delivering firm notes to the USSR implying that the two countries would, if necessary, use force to defend Iran. At that point the Soviet Union withdrew its troops.

In June 1945 the Soviet Union demanded that Turkey cede several districts to the USSR, that a joint Russo-Turkish administration of the Dardanelles be set up, and that Turkey sever its ties with Great Britain. In August 1946 it renewed its demands for a new administration of the straits. In these efforts the Soviet Union was again rebuffed, but the rebuff was administered not by England but by the United States. The latter sent a naval task force into the Mediterranean. The inability of England to respond to these probes on its own meant that England's sphere of influence no longer included this region. A sphere exists only as long as the nation asserting special prerogatives can sustain them.

When the USSR renewed its sponsored campaign of guerrilla warfare in northern Greece, and the fall of the Greek government seemed imminent, the British government faced a crisis. On 21 February 1947 the first secretary of the British Embassy in Washington officially informed the United States government that Great Britain could no longer discharge its traditional responsibilities in Greece and Turkey. This note was the British government's official recognition that its sphere of influence in the eastern Mediterranean was no more. In an address to a joint session of the Congress on 12 March 1947 the U.S. president enunciated the set of ideas that came to be known as the Truman Doctrine.

A successful probe may mean more than that dominant actor X can no longer include country Y in its sphere of influence: it may mean that Y has actually passed into the sphere of influence of Z. Traditionally Czechoslovakia had a close relationship with western Europe, and particularly with France. In elections in Czechoslovakia after World War II the Communist party received a larger percentage of the vote than any other party and came to hold key ministries in the government. The Communists were not long content to participate in a coalition government, however, and, with Soviet encouragement and advice, laid plans to consolidate their position. In February 1948 a successful coup took place and all important levers of power were seized. This coup was in the nature of a probe. Would the Western powers deliver an ultimatum and threaten action? If so, the Soviet Union was in a position to back down while denying it had had anything to do with the seizure of power. The Western nations, while shocked, did nothing. The probe was therefore successful and Western inaction registered the fact that Czechoslovakia had just passed into the sphere of influence of the Soviet Union.

As the great powers initiate probes and react to them over a period of time, the outlines of their spheres of influence are established, confirmed, or modified. The outlines of a sphere may be regarded as stable when a great power will respond reliably and vigorously to all probes that test it and when other actors, anticipating that it would do so, choose not to test it very often. For over a half century no major power chose to probe the American sphere of influence in the Western Hemisphere, but, when it was probed by the Soviet Union in 1962, it was found to be alive and well.

Since the central rule in the Soviet-American constraint system has been, until recently, that neither would intervene militarily in the sphere of the other, the freedom of action of each in its own sphere has been constrained only by intrasystem dynamics and a regard for political and economic costs. If the Soviet Union chose to invade Rumania, or even Finland, tomorrow, the U.S. government would grieve but would take no military action. By the same token, if the United States, in an aberrant mood, were to invade Canada or Mexico, the Soviet Union would not take military action against it.

A dominant actor will usually have little trouble devising an ideological justification for intervention in its own sphere. It was argued, for example, that the Monroe Doctrine was in everyone's interest. In his Annual Message in 1905 President Theodore Roosevelt declared of the doctrine: "It is of benefit to our people; it is of benefit to foreign peoples; and most of all it is really of benefit to the peoples of the country concerned." After its military intervention in Czechoslovakia in 1968, Soviet ideologues soon offered the "Brezhnev Doctrine":

The people of the socialist countries and Communist parties certainly do have and should have freedom for determining the ways of advance of their respective countries.

However, none of their decisions should damage either socialism in their country or the fundamental interests of other socialist countries, and the whole working-class movement, which is working for socialism.

This means that each Communist party is responsible not only to its own people, but also to all the socialist countries, to the entire Communist movement. . . .

The sovereignty of each socialist country cannot be opposed to the interests of the world of socialism, of the world revolutionary movement. . . .

Each Communist party is free to apply the basic principles of Marxism-Leninism and of socialism in its country, but it cannot depart from those principles. . . .

. . . The weakening of any of the links in the world system of socialism directly affects all the socialist countries, which cannot look indifferently upon this.

The antisocialist elements in Czechoslovakia actually covered up the demand for so-called neutrality and Czechoslovakia's withdrawal from the socialist community with talk about the right of nations to self-determination.

However, the implementation of such "self-determination," in other words Czechoslovakia's detachment from the socialist community, would have come into conflict with its own vital interests and would have been detrimental to the other socialist states. . . .

Discharging their internationalist duty toward the fraternal peoples of Czechoslovakia and defending their own socialist gains, the U.S.S.R. and the other socialist states had to act decisively and they did act against the antisocialist forces in Czechoslovakia. ["Sovereignty and International Duties of Socialist Countries," *Pravda*, 25 September 1968; reprinted in the *New York Times*, 27 September 1968]

The "Slow Probe"

A useful distinction is that between a normal probe and a "slow probe." A normal probe usually involves a single probing action that unfolds within a short space of time. The coup in Czechoslovakia in 1948 and the introduction of nuclear missiles into Cuba in 1962 would be examples of a normal probe.

A "slow probe," on the other hand, consists of a series of actions spread over a considerable period of time. The Soviet-sponsored guerrilla campaign in Greece after World War II was such a probe and so has been the Soviet military buildup in the Western Hemisphere. In the latter instance the Soviet Union has been testing to see if it can get away with nonobservance of the basic rules of the game for spheres of influence, provided it probes by modest increments and in slow motion.

Working with the Cubans, the Soviet Union increased its military presence in Cuba by stages as follows: it used Soviet troops for training purposes; it upgraded a brigade of Soviet troops to combat status; it improved the naval support facilities at Cienfuegos; it provided the Cuban government with a training submarine; it provided a nonnuclear operational submarine; it established electronic intelligence facilities in Cuba; it conducted with the Cubans air reconnaissance along the East Coast of the United States; it moved a nuclear-capable unit of Soviet fighter-bombers into Cuba; and it increased the flow of Soviet naval units through the Caribbean. The airlifting of twenty thousand Cuban troops to Angola, and their long-term logistical support there, demonstrate the existence of a technical capability that could just as well be used in Latin America if the United States were, for any reason, politically immobilized.

It was the U.S. discovery of the upgrading of the Soviet brigade to combat status that precipitated a brief confrontation in September 1979. That action had actually been taken some years earlier but had not been noted by American intelligence. It was, say, step four in the probing process and, by the time it was perceived, the Soviet Union had already moved on to steps six, seven, and eight. This may help explain initial Soviet puzzlement over the American response to the brigade. The Soviet leadership may have assumed, incorrectly, that the American government had long since perceived that step and had accepted it. They would probably have been less surprised if American officials had taken exception to more recent and more substantial incremental steps such as the establishment of the fighter-bomber unit or naval developments.

The slow probe takes longer than the normal probe, but it can be just as effective. Furthermore, its incremental nature makes it easy for the probing power to back off with a minimum loss of face if the reaction of the challenged power is stronger than expected. It can always maintain that the precipitating event—for example, the presence of a Soviet combat brigade—is trivial in significance and that the challenged power is responding in an unreasonable and hysterical way.

The major advantage of the slow probe is related to this point. Since incremental challenging actions are modest and separated from one another in time, it is difficult for the challenged power to take exception to any particular action. Individual increments may not seem significant enough to be used as grounds for a full-scale confrontation. In the United States, for example, in September 1979 opinion makers asked how a brigade of two thousand to three thousand men could possibly be a threat to the United States. What such persons failed to appreciate was that, in the case of a slow probe, its significance is not to be found in any *single* increment but in the *pattern* revealed by the series of increments. No one increment may be of great importance by itself, but, taken together, a series of increments may constitute a serious probe.[5]

The slow probe has a further advantage. It makes it possible for the challenged power to ignore or minimize a given provocation if it wishes to do so. After initially declaring the presence of the Soviet brigade to be "unacceptable," President Carter soon discovered that it was acceptable. He went on to pose the issue in the narrowest possible terms: Did a single Soviet brigade in Cuba constitute a direct, significant military threat to the United States? Since the answer to the question, as posed, was obviously no, the president felt justified in initiating only a minimal, and largely symbolic, response.

The president chose not to address the more significant question whether the pattern of Soviet military actions, in cooperation with the Cubans, constituted a challenge to the Monroe Doctrine and to the maintenance of the U.S. sphere of influence in the Western Hemisphere. The president made things easier for himself, in the short run, by posing the question so narrowly, but, in so doing, he left out of consideration an important aspect of the national interest. For the first time since the Monroe Doctrine was enunciated in 1823 a nonhemispheric great power, and one unfriendly to the United States, has been allowed to begin a systematic build up of versatile military capabilities in the Western Hemisphere.

The failure of the United States to respond vigorously to that probe doubtless sent a signal to the Soviet Union. The Soviet leadership may have concluded that if the United States was not ready to respond to a probe in its own backyard, it would probably not react strongly to Soviet action elsewhere. Four months later, in December 1979, Soviet forces invaded Afghanistan.

Difficulties between the Soviet Union and the United States have seldom derived from probes by one into the sphere of the other, for the rules of the game discourage that. Tension has more often been created by various kinds of Soviet ventures into gray areas outside the sphere of either actor. In this no-man's-land, spheres-of-influence rules do not apply. The most that can be said is that the closer an uncommitted area is to a superpower and the longer it has been viewed as important, the freer that power will feel to probe in that area and the more upset it will be about the probes of the other. In such circumstances opportunities for misperception and interest conflict abound and the consequences of probes, therefore, are hard to predict.

Sanctions

In a highly interactive world, major actors will be tied in with one another in scores of ways. How, then, is an offended actor to punish a transgressor without, at the same time, punishing itself and its friends? The answer is that it cannot.

The effort of the United States to organize sanctions against the Soviet Union following the invasion of Afghanistan illustrates the point. President Carter decided on a grain embargo against the USSR. The problem was, however, that such an action would also punish some American farmers severely. The sanction became politically feasible in an election year only when the federal government agreed to underwrite the cost to the farmers if necessary. The president also wanted to punish the Soviet Union by cutting back the flow of high technology to the Soviet Union from foreign suppliers. American suppliers were troubled by that effort and western European nations were not at all interested in the idea. They were sorry about the invasion and thought it improper but were not prepared to disrupt important trade arrangements simply to teach the Soviet Union a lesson. Besides, they could argue, over a period of years trade relations with the outside world would help domesticate the Soviet Union. The United States finally had to accept the political realities of the situation; it could neither force nor persuade its NATO allies to do as it wished them to do.

A given international exchange has value to the actors involved in it, or it would not take place. Exchanges of any significance will, therefore, quickly develop vested interests devoted to their continuance. The Olympics had a following, and, when President Carter called for U.S. abstention from the Moscow Olympics, he was bitterly opposed by many athletes, sports writers, and athletic organizations, including the United States Olympic Committee. In trying to punish the Soviet Union, it appeared that the United States was also punishing itself and its friends.

This is not to argue that sanctions were unwise; quite the contrary. If there is to be any international order, transgressors must be made to bear costs for their transgressions. The effort to punish, however, will lie heavily on the shoulders of those who undertake to police that order. Close involvement makes a unidirectional flow of punishment impossible, as affectionate parents have learned when they have had to spank their children.

The passions of power politics often interfere with attention to global issues. Again, the point can be illustrated with reference to the Soviet invasion of Afghanistan. To punish the Soviet Union, the U.S. Senate dropped consideration of SALT II. Yet if the treaty was of benefit to both nations, as its defenders had stoutly insisted, then the United States was punishing itself as much as the Soviet Union by dropping it. In the wake of the Soviet invasion, the U.S. government reduced cultural exchange with the Soviet Union. That was a natural response, but it should be noted that the long-term interests of the United States point toward increased cultural interchange with the Soviet Union, not less. The blow to Soviet interests was also, therefore, a setback to long-term U.S. interests. National interests relating to global processes cannot compete with national interests relating to the cold war. In the event of conflict between them, global interests come in a poor second.

There are costs involved in that allocation of attention and effort. Superpower rivalry is not the only game in town. Although the Soviet Union and the United States have been preoccupied with the great-power game, they have also been caught up in another game, the rules of which they have scarcely thought about. While they have been scoring points in the political-military game, global processes relating to resources, energy, population, the environment, and the global economy have been sliding slowly out of control. No matter which nation "wins" the cold war game, each nation is losing the global game and is losing control over its own national destiny in the process.

Part III.
Constraint Systems and
Global Processes

9. Interdependence and National Interests

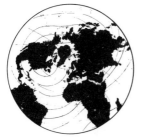

Since the global system is undergoing evolutionary change in key areas, as indicated in Part I, it seems probable that change in many other aspects of the global system will result. Virtually every aspect of the global system has already been bathed in change: the types of actor in the system, the role of nation-states, the nature of power and influence, the impact of communication and diffusion, and the character of the national interest in an interdependent world. The chapters in Part III will deal with some of these changes and the way in which they relate to the operation of contemporary constraint systems.

The Redefinition of Interests

The "national interest" is a familiar notion, one that underpins decisions on public policy and that has informed a great deal of scholarly analysis. What has not always been made clear, however, is that national interests should be perceived as relative to the circumstances of the nation involved. If the general principle is that interests must be situationally defined, then a change in the circumstances of a nation should lead to a reexamination, and possible redefinition, of its interests.

Its circumstances might change because of internal or external developments, and the latter, in turn, will be affected by factors both related to and unrelated to the global system. Whether a given line of activity would be in the interest of a nation might, therefore, depend on the state of the global system and the relationship of that nation to the system. If the global system has changed significantly from one era to another, the interest definitions of the earlier period will almost certainly be inappropriate for the later. With movement along the interaction/technology continuum, the global system has undergone remarkable change since the end of World War II, and it follows, therefore, that the national interests of major actors will have to be reexamined.

Many of the prevailing ideas about the interests of the United States, for example, emerged in an era in which nations were less interdependent than they now are, and those ideas are now suffering from obsolescence. They have not evolved as rapidly as have the conditions to which they are being applied. Since the United States has become closely linked to the operation of the global system, its interests cannot be defined save with constant reference to that linkage. If, as seems likely, it continues to become progressively more involved, its interests will have to be defined progressively more in terms of system concerns.

This chapter will examine some of the implications of this line of argument. For purposes of exposition, these implications will be presented in the form of a set of linked propositions. The points made will apply to other great powers as well, but illustrative material will be drawn largely from the experience of the United States.

Proposition 1:
The interests of a nation should be defined situationally.

Proposition 2:
When there is substantial change in the functioning of the global system, or in the relationship of a nation to that system, national interests will need to be reassessed.

Proposition 3:
As a nation becomes progressively more involved with the global system, it will normally define its geographic national interests in progressively broader terms.

If a nation were completely isolated and in no way dependent on the global system, it could define its national interests in purely domestic terms. As a practical matter, however, interdependence is now so pervasive that few nations can pursue the experiment of trying to operate as isolates or semiisolates.

When a major actor becomes involved in a geographical area new to it, it will begin to have preferences about what happens there. Before long, it will incorporate those preferences into a definition of its national interest as related to that area. "Interests" follow involvement. Therefore, as the geographic involvement of an actor expands, other things being equal, so will its definition of its national interest.

The point can be illustrated with reference to the experience of the United States. The expansion of its geographic interests began shortly after the colonies achieved independence in 1783 and has continued to the present. Even if one omits commercial treaties and the acquisition of military bases and small islands, the pattern is still impressive. In the two centuries since independence, the geographic interests of the United States have expanded so as to be virtually global in extent. A partial list of U.S. geographic interests follows:

1800 — Louisiana Purchase
1810–13 — West Florida occupied
1821 — East Florida purchased from Spain
1823 — Monroe Doctrine
1845 — Texas annexed
1848 — New Mexico, Utah, and Upper California annexed; Polk's corollary to the Monroe Doctrine; formation of Oregon Territory
1849 — Hawaii made a protectorate
1854 — Gadsden Purchase
1867 — Alaska annexed
1871 — United States secures perpetual free navigation of the St. Lawrence River
1898 — Puerto Rico, Philippine Islands, Guam ceded by Spain; Hawaii annexed
1901 — Platt Amendment concerning Cuba
1903 — Panama Canal Zone leased
1917 — World War I and the assertion of a vital U.S. interest in western Europe
1941 — World War II and the assertion of vital U.S. interests in the Far East

After World War II other geographical interests were quickly made evident with the Truman Doctrine, the Marshall Plan, NATO, the U.S. response in Korea in 1950, the U.S.–Japanese Mutual Defense Treaty, SEATO, and so on.

Proposition 4:
    As the global system evolves and becomes more interactive and as

technology develops, a national actor must define its interests more broadly and consider system-centered interests in addition to state-centered interests.

A preoccupation with state-centered interests is appropriate in a preinterdependent world. An increased concern with system-centered interests, however, is appropriate in an era of interdependence. State-centered interests, which may be political, economic, strategic, social, or cultural, are characteristically defined without reference to the impact their pursuit may have upon the global system and, because of feedback, upon the broader and more enduring interests of the nation. System-centered interests, on the other hand, will be defined with an eye to the way the parts of the system relate to the whole and are affected by the whole.

System-centered national interests may be related to global processes and may involve physical linkages, as with pollution processes or inadvertent man-made climatic changes, or may involve coordination and collaboration, as with efforts to maintain peace or achieve international economic stability. Finally, they may involve the positing of broad goals such as the achievement of universal human rights, an improved position for women, or rapid economic development.[1] The category of system-centered national interests includes regional phenomena, such as support of the EEC by its members. A regional arrangement fashioned and held together solely by a dominant actor would not, of course, qualify. That would remain an expression of state-centered national interest. The proposition might be restated, then, to take advantage of this distinction: As the global system evolves, national interest needs to be defined progressively less in state-centered terms and progressively more in system-centered terms. Such changes in definition can be seen even in connection with something as manifestly state-centered as the definition of "*national* security." Prior to World War II it was defined primarily in military terms. Now there is wide recognition that "national security" must be understood as involving far more.

Proposition 5:

System-centered interests are often pursued by means different from those used in the pursuit of state-centered interests.

State-centered interests may be advanced by the unaided efforts of an individual nation-state, but system-centered interests, if they are to be pursued effectively, must usually be pursued collectively. Global inflation, for example, cannot be dealt with effectively if it is defined as a purely domestic issue. The same holds for problems involving population, the environment, resources, or the global economy.

Proposition 6:
Because of the evolution of the global system, system-centered national interests have been increasing in number.

This point, too, can be illustrated from the experiences of the United States. In the wake of World War I the United States played an important part in bringing the League of Nations into existence, even though the Senate ultimately rejected American participation. After World War II the United States, by degrees, assumed a role of international leadership, which is to say that it perceived a national interest in connection with a number of system-related issues. It was instrumental in bringing the United Nations into existence, recognizing that its interests in a variety of important goals could best be advanced by collective means. The initiatives taken by the United States in connection with the Bretton Woods institutions reflected an awareness that the national interest lay in trying to regularize international trade and payments and in trying to foster international development. The United States has given expression to system-related interests in connection with arms control, nuclear nonproliferation, world population problems, human rights, the role of women, pollution of the atmosphere, pollution of the seas, the military uses of space, humankind's impact on climate, global telecommunications, the exploitation of ocean resources, nonrenewable resources, and the future of energy resources, to mention a few.

State-centered interests of the United States have grown over a period of two hundred years, but system-centered interests did not begin to expand in a significant way until the twentieth century. The explanation for that is, of course, that most system-centered interests are associated with the growth of interaction and/or the advance of technology. Since movement along the interaction/technology continuum did not become notable until World War I and did not achieve great momentum until World War II and after, the development of system-centered interests was correspondingly delayed. Pollution of the atmosphere and the seas, for example, did not emerge as a serious global problem until the growth of the global economy following World War II.

Proposition 7:

> For major nations new system-related national interests will be created with increasing rapidity in the future.

The emergence of national interests is a continuing process. If an effort had been made a few years ago to develop an exhaustive inventory of the system-centered interests of the United States, preservation of the ozone layer would not have been included, nor maintenance of the oxygen-producing capacity of the oceans, nor the holding of man-induced climatic change within narrow limits. A few years hence system-centered interests will doubtless have come into being that are not yet imagined. Since movement along the interaction/technology continuum is accelerating, the accumulation of such interests must also accelerate.

State-centered interests of the United States are close to their geographical limits (although not necessarily their numerical limits), which is to say the limits of the planet itself. New system-centered interests, on the other hand, will continue to multiply as long as the global system continues to evolve along the continuum and produce new conditions.

Proposition 8:

> As the system-centered interests of a nation increase, so does its dependence on the system. To the extent that a nation has such interests, it will be vulnerable.

Major nations, accustomed to a degree of freedom of action, have tended to view dependence on other nations as a threat to national security and have sought to find ways to reduce it and the vulnerability flowing from it. The United States, for example, formulated programs designed to reduce its dependence on the OPEC nations and their oil and, appropriately, dubbed the effort Project Independence. In an interdependent world, however, a developed nation will have so many dependencies and vulnerabilities that the numbers will pose an insoluble problem. It may be able to reduce a few dependencies, at great cost and effort, but many others will remain. Actors have inadvertently created a global system in which a great power can no longer hope to be sole master of its own affairs or its destiny. It is no longer feasible, therefore, for a major developed nation to attempt to define its national interest in terms of freedom from dependency and vulnerability. Instead, it must learn to live with its vulnerability, as smaller nations have long had to do.

Proposition 9:

As the system-centered interests of a nation are defined in broader terms, they will increasingly overlap the broadening interests of other nations.

Expansion of the realm of shared interests makes it harder to find clear-cut enemies. In a highly interactive world one's enemy is also apt to be one's partner. The government of the Soviet Union, for example, is ambivalent about treating the United States as an enemy, since it also wants to have the United States as a trading partner and a source of high technology.

If the area of overlapping national interests continues to increase, may not the interests of one nation, eventually, become virtually identical with those of another? No. Interests and interest conflicts do not disappear in a highly interactive world; they are only modified and transformed. A natural harmony of interests will not emerge out of interdependence and advanced technology. Utopia is not to be found farther along the interaction/technology continuum. The realm of shared interests may broaden, but significant situational differences, as well as differences in values and priorities, will guarantee the survival of interest conflicts.

Proposition 10:

As national interests increase in number, conflicts between various interests must also increase.

There will be conflicts between various state-centered interests, between various system-centered interests, and between state-centered and system-centered interests. In those circumstances it may be taken for granted that no combination of policies can simultaneously advance all interests. Decisions on trade-offs must be made continuously, and wisdom will lie in emphasizing the more important rather than the less important interests.

Proposition 11:

An increasingly common, and important, form of interest conflict will be that between state-centered and system-centered national interests.

Analysts have been intrigued by the way in which a hard-nosed pursuit of narrow self-interest can sometimes be self-defeating. They have looked closely at the "prisoner's dilemma." This involves a two-person non-zero-sum game that illustrates how "rational" considerations, combined with a lack of mutual trust, can lead to outcomes that are bad for both players.[2]

In one form or another, the prisoner's dilemma has long been with us. The account by Thucydides of the wars in the Peloponnesus can be interpreted in terms of the prisoner's dilemma. Individual city-states pursued a narrow definition of their interests and were unwilling to help one another. Because of their lack of confidence in one another, they could not achieve a collective solution to the problem and so suffered from a succession of wars destructive to all. They were dependent on one another but did not perceive the policy implications of their interdependence.

A contemporary variation of the problem, reminiscent of the story of the goose that laid golden eggs, appears in connection with "common pool" resources. When there exists a finite, common pool of resources, such as ocean fisheries, from which many actors may draw, the stage is set for another showing of the "tragedy of the commons." A narrow national-interest calculus dictates that an actor try to get as much of the common resource as possible in as short a time as possible, for what it does not get will be lost to it forever. When a multitude of actors all follow this policy, the resource will soon be exhausted and all will be losers in the long run, including those that got the largest share of the resource before it disappeared. Following this logic, eager national operators are busily over-fishing the oceans with the result that total yield is now dropping despite an increase in effort devoted to fishing.

The conflict between system-centered and state-centered interests will raise difficult ethical problems for American foreign policymakers. What should be the American stance on matters relating to resource use, the redistribution of global resources, the amount of foreign aid, the proper handling of U.S. food exports, and so on? To date, American policymakers are inclined to rely on a narrow national-interest calculus that undervalues concern for system-centered interests. This is understandable, for most individuals are more accustomed to thinking in terms of state-centered than system-centered interests. A systematic bias is, therefore, built into their calculations. State-centered considerations do not have to fight for recognition and are automatically assigned a high priority while system-centered interests, such as those having to do with the environment, are just as automatically assigned a lower priority.

The policy consequences of this bias were not extremely costly prior to World War II because important system-centered interests were far fewer in number. Now, because the proportion of system-centered interests in the mix of total national interests has increased, that bias leads to serious distortion of policy priorities. System-centered interests are habitually undervalued. As the web of interaction becomes more tightly woven and the dimensions of the globe shrink under the pressure of technology, interaction of every kind acquires an increasingly social aspect.

Perhaps in time, in response to events such as the energy shortage, this shift will be reflected more fully in the amount of attention devoted to system-centered interests by the foreign policy establishment of the United States. Reassessment of priorities is not something that comes easily to complex bureaucracies, however. Established conceptions of the national interest become embodied in entrenched bureaucratic structures while spokesmen for emergent interests, lacking effective organizational support, are at a disadvantage in the struggle for funding and attention. No invisible hand guarantees that the organizational potency of support for a given interest must tally closely with the intrinsic importance of that interest. Because of the lag involved in the recognition of new national interests and in finding ways to give them effective expression, national resources must always be misallocated to some extent and trade-offs among those interests will not reflect the policy priorities that should be in effect.

For a government faced with a concrete situation, the problem may not be so much that of understanding the situation and the need for a collective solution as it is the political problem of making and justifying a decision that will be unpopular. A government must sometimes choose between a tangible short-term interest defended by voluble, angry, and well-organized supporters, and a long-term interest not supported by delegations from the future, the costs and benefits of which are somewhat uncertain. It may have to choose between a limited national interest, which will do some damage to the global community, and the interests of the global community, which will do some damage to short-term national interests. In an era of interdependence questions such as the following must come up again and again:

— Should the United States protect domestic industries threatened by competition from abroad? On the one side, there are the imperatives of jobs and politics and, on the other, the U.S. commitment to liberal economic principles and global economic development and well-being.

— Should the United States discourage private investment abroad on the grounds that such investment represents the exportation of American jobs? If it does so, may it not slow the development of the poorer countries and work against its own long-term interests?

— Should the United States oppose demands for a New International
Economic Order on the grounds that they are designed to change the
rules of the game in favor of the developing nations and must,
therefore, adversely affect U.S. interests? Or might such opposition
reduce opportunities for change that could improve the long-term
stability of the international economic system and thus benefit the
United States?

— More concretely, should the United States oppose the efforts of
developing nations to get a larger share of world industrial production? Or should the United States support those efforts in the name
of justice, the development of the poorer nations, and the long-term
economic and political stability of the international system?

— Should the United States continue to seek high rates of economic
growth in the name of national interest and national security? Or
should the United States, considering the impact of high growth
rates on the consumption of scarce resources, start moving in the
direction of zero growth?

— Spokesmen of developing nations sometimes charge that the United
States, because of governmental policy and the activities of corporations based in the United States, has altogether too much
influence over global communications and is, as a consequence,
engaged in cultural imperialsim on a near-global scale. Should the
United States, acknowledging the communications asymmetry and
deferring to the increasing sensitivity of the developing nations on
communications issues, seek to be more restrained? Or should it, in
the name of national interest and freedom of communications,
continue to play as prominent a role in global communications as its
talents and energies will permit?

Other nations encounter the same kinds of interest conflict. Some OPEC
nations appear to be torn between the desire to maximize short-term benefits,
on the one hand, and a fear of bankrupting their customers and throwing the
world economy into a tailspin, on the other. Should the Japanese, in the name
of the national interest, continue to eat whale meat, or should the survival
of endangered species be an overriding concern? Should Japan continue to
maintain a very strong payments position, in the national interest? Or is it
in the interest of Japan to ease the payments pressure on other countries by
increasing its imports?

Proposition 12:

> The pursuit of the "national interest," even when it is enlightened and broadly defined, will not be an adequate guide to national policy; a sense of obligation must also come into play.

National interests must be defined more broadly: under what circumstances, if any, should a nation rein in its interests?

The basis on which the global system is organized—nation-states plus the principle of national sovereignty—does not obligate a nation to ever rein in its interests. Since it is a sovereign entity, it is not obligated, either legally or morally, to sacrifice its own state-centered interests in favor of the interests of the global system. In a highly interdependent, high-technology world, that approach is no longer viable, as can be illustrated with reference to resource policy and the position of the United States.

The ideas about resources that have long been controlling were developed during a period of plenty, a time in which global constraints did not seem to fit tightly around humankind. In recent decades those pre-scarcity assumptions and ideas have begun to encounter the reality of a planet that is finite and non-renewable resources that are limited. At present high rates of consumption, the global system can move quickly from a situation in which there is no apparent availability problem for a given resource to one in which a critical shortage is imminent.

As nations begin to realize that resources are indeed finite, the question of who gets how much of what will become more central. As long as the pie was thought to be unlimited in size, distributional issues did not seem vital. In conditions of scarcity, however, with a pie that is finite in size, the more that goes to Y the less there is for X. Before long, therefore, questions must arise concerning the basis on which global resources should be allocated under conditions of scarcity.

Any system of allocation will be based on a set of assumptions, principles, and ethical values, even though they may never have been explicitly stated. Certainly that holds for present arrangements, which are based on "supply and demand," the "market system," and the principle of "equal access" to resources for all nations. What could be more fair and natural, Americans might be inclined to ask, than that resources should go to those who can pay for them? Economic principles are seldom neutral, however. They represent choices of a kind, and they have serious political, moral, and distributional implications.

The doctrine of "equal access" favors the rich. Although all nations may have equal legal access to natural resources, the rich will be able to buy and consume them to a greater extent than will the poor. The "free play of market forces" has had potent distributional consequences. Economists from developing countries have pointed out that the free play of market forces contributed to the magnification of inequalities of wealth among nations. Continued adherence to that principle can be counted on to work strongly in the direction of perpetuating those inequalities.

The United States, with 6 percent of the world's population, accounts for 30 percent of the world's annual consumption of energy and selected minerals. That is quite in accord with the principle of equal access. Suppose, however, to explore the issue, U.S. consumption of key global resources rose to 50 percent or 70 percent. Is there still no problem? Does ability to pay confer a right to consume that is without limit? Is it altogether appropriate that scarce resources should flow to the low-priority, or even frivolous, needs of a highly affluent society rather than to the high-priority needs of a less wealthy society? Can one not sense a lack of congruence between the reality of global scarcities, on the one hand, and a principle of allocation, on the other, that allows unlimited consumption by the rich? Might it not be argued that the doctrine of "equal access" to natural resources should, in an era of scarcity, be viewed as a doctrine that legitimizes raids on the commons by wealthy nations? A principle that allocates resources to those who can pay simultaneously denies resources to those who cannot pay. Energy and mineral resources that now flow to the United States in such abundance will never be available to developing nations. May not the present use of scarce resources to maintain American affluence be effectively denying the possibility of economic growth to less wealthy nations?

More than any other nation the United States has benefited from the era of plenty. It cannot fail, therefore, to be heavily affected by the consequences of an era of scarcity. If demands should emerge that the United States restrict its resource use, should the United States refuse, on the grounds that to do so would be contrary to its national interest? Or, should it take the position that, in the event of conflict between the national interest and the human interest, a nation is under obligation to defer to the broader interest unless vital national interests are clearly at stake?

The issue has not yet been raised in a pointed way, but it may be before long. The principle of equity in the use of global resources has the potential for becoming the standard against which present resource use could be measured and found wanting. The matter of obligation will come up again in the concluding chapter (Johansen, 1980).

Proposition 13:

    When important actors do not defer to broader system needs but act
    in accord with narrow state-centered interests, the costs are likely to be
    heavy and to be borne by all.

The more important an actor is in the global system, the more important it will be to others that its actions be characeized by knowledge and responsibility. Because the global system is becoming increasingly vulnerable to disruption, its tolerance for irresponsible behavior is declining. A small nation may raid the commons, for example, and do relatively little damage, but when a superpower raids the commons—as the Soviet Union does with its giant fishing fleets—the impact will be felt by scores of others. By the same token, when the United States behaves irresponsibly by running successive massive-payments deficits or by failing to restrain energy use, the impact is felt globally.

The record of the United States in this respect leaves much to be desired. Since World War II, however, the United States has made significant progress in accepting the realities of interdependence. The Soviet leadership, on the other hand, has been slow to perceive that country's involvement in global interdependence, perhaps because that involvement has been less striking than in the case of the United States and perhaps, in part, because of ideological obstacles to perception. Classical Marxist-Leninist formulations say nothing about increasing interdependence, and, indeed, the implications of interdependence are at odds with Leninist notions about the imperialist thrust of capitalist nations and the necessity for hostility between imperialist and "socialist" nations.

How will the Soviet Union react when it begins to discover interdependence? Will it be made uncertain and truculent by the irrelevance of much of its ideology to emerging world conditions, or will it move slowly toward an appreciation that, although system membership dues are heavy for a superpower, they must nevertheless be paid?

Proposition 14:

    As awareness of system needs becomes more common, greater attention will probably be given to the question of who should make what decisions affecting the global system and on what basis.

Logic will suggest that decisions affecting the global community should not be viewed as legitimate unless there is broad participation in their making. If, for example, certain resources are finite and all of humankind must draw on that limited common pool, does not equity suggest that principles governing their use should reflect global needs? And if the allocation of global resources is everyone's business, might not entitlement to those resources be based more reasonably on need and the ability to put them to good use rather than on the ability of one nation to outbid others in paying for them? If the direction of global development is a matter of common interest, why should investment decisions totaling hundreds of billions annually remain in the hands of private banks and multinational corporations? Is corporate well-being the proper basis on which global investment decisions should be made, or should basic investment decisions increasingly reflect collective judgments about needs?

Proposition 15:

Formulation of an adequate, informed definition of the national interest will become increasingly difficult.

For one thing, a major nation will have multitudinous interests and they will criss cross and conflict in complex and baffling ways. For another, the content of the definition of national interest must evolve with the changing involvement of a nation in the global system and with the evolution of the global system itself. The content now given to the "national interest" would have seemed absurd twenty-five years ago.

An analyst must also weigh long-term interests against immediate interests and that, in turn, is complicated by the difficulty of discerning the distant consequences of present options. One would need to be able to perceive tensions between state-centered interests and system-centered interests and weigh one against the other judiciously. That, too, would be complicated by the problem of distant consequences. If an actor cannot know the more distant results of a set of actions, it might unknowingly, and with the best intentions in the world, endanger the common good. However, even if one *had* complete knowledge, one might still have to weigh a narrow national interest against the obligation of a nation to defer to the broader good.

10. Power and Impact in
an Interactive World

What will be the effect of the vast increase in interaction in the global system on the exercise of power and influence? That is the question which this chapter will address. First, however, something must be said concerning the exercise of power within a constraint system.

Types of Power in a Constraint System

Power has traditionally been analyzed by scholars and foreign affairs officials in terms of dyadic relations and relations of command and compliance. The focus has been on the capacity of actor X to use direct measures to force actor Y to follow instructions. Following the lead of Cheryl Christensen, we may refer to this as "behavior power" (1977, p. 127).

In addition, however, X may have the capacity to structure the environment and circumstances of Y in such a way as to shape the options available to Y and the payoffs associated with them. Actor X does not control Y directly but, instead, modifies the situation in which Y operates in such a way that Y, in calculating options, costs, and benefits will do as X wishes. Using the Christensen terminology, this might be referred to as "structural power," since X structures Y's situation. Christensen argues that "an historically important dimension of state action, especially for great powers with multiple resource bases and large repertoires of means, has been the attempt to structure or restructure the international environment. The idea is not just to control actors in specific situations, but to gain some control over the flow of events, over overall relationships, or over situations" (1977, pp. 127–28).

There is a third form of power that needs to be distinguished and that is the power accruing to an actor by virtue of its capacity to make rules of the game that other actors will follow. This might be termed "rule-making power."

Actor X shapes the behavior of Y by means of its capacity to fashion and enforce rules that Y must obey.

A subordinate actor may first obey constraint-system rules because obedience is enforced and, later, come to comply because obedience seems proper and the rules "legitimate." In the latter case, domination involves the exercise of "authority." A dominant actor will normally find it more efficient, as well as morally less burdensome, to rule by means of authority when it can. If rule-making in a constraint system is symmetrical and rules are fashioned by joint agreement, then rules are legitimate by definition.

Greater attention to structural power and rule-making power would encourage richer and more varied analyses of relationships in international politics. It would encourage observers to ask a broader range of questions:

— Does a given actor make the rules, or is it constrained by the rules of others?
— If it makes the rules, does it do so by itself or in concert with other actors?
— Are the rules reliably obeyed? Are they willingly obeyed?
— Can an actor block rules it thinks disadvantageous to itself?
— Can it modify existing rules in its own favor?
— If it wished to escape from the system, could it do so?

Answers to these questions will make it clear that some actors have but little effect on the operation of a constraint system and must take the rules as they find them, while others have a capacity to shape and modify them.

These three forms of power are, of course, closely related, and each contributes to the effectiveness of the others. An actor wielding substantial behavioral power will often be in the position to structure the external situation of other actors as well. Furthermore, if it can exercise both of these forms of power, it will almost certainly be able to shape the rules of a constraint system, and that last capacity, in turn, will tend to promote further increases in behavioral power and structural power.

The Strength of the Weak

In recent decades strong actors appear to have had increasing difficulty working their will on the weak. The United States, for all its vaunted military and economic power, could not find a way to deal with the seizure in

1979 of its embassy in Iran and the taking of its staff as hostages. The Soviet Union, for all its military might, found the path of military conquest difficult in Afghanistan following its December 1979 invasion. How can that be? When the capabilities of X are much greater than those of Y, how is it that X has trouble gaining compliance from Y? Why does not victory always go to the stronger? What allows weak actors to have such a powerful impact on the policies of the stronger? (Mack, 1975)

David Baldwin has dubbed this the "paradox of unrealized power":

> The frequent failure of power predictions has been noted so often by scholars, journalists, statesmen, and the "man in the street" that it deserves a label—something like "the paradox of unrealized power." How is it that "weak powers" influence the "strong"? How is it that the "greatest power in the world" could suffer defeat at the hands of a "band of night-riders in black pajamas"? How do we explain the "cruel and ridiculous paradox" of the "big influence of small allies"? How can the Arabs get away with defying the United States? How can tiny Israel exercise so much influence on U.S. foreign policy? [1979, p. 163]

He offers two explanations for the phenomenon. The first is the failure to use power resources effectively. "He had the cards but played them poorly" (p. 164). The second refers to the contextual nature of power, the "relative infungibility" of power resources. "He had a great bridge hand but happened to be playing poker" (p. 164).

Two other components of an explanation should also be mentioned, however. One is the bargaining power the weaker actor may achieve. If a subordinate actor in a constraint system can position itself so as to threaten a value important to a dominant actor, then its bargaining power will be substantial despite an asymmetry in overall capabilities. For a number of years Turkey had an importance for the United States beyond that based on its obvious contribution to NATO, because important missile tracking and other intelligence facilities were located there. Israel's bargaining power with the U.S. government was immense for many years because of the capacity of the American Jewish community to punish an administration that angered it.

Many options may be open to a subordinate actor interested in raising the maintenance costs of a constraint system. A partial list would include harder bargaining over trade or investment arrangements, demands for loan renegotiation, threats to nationalize commercial facilities, the development of a coalition strategy, strikes, slowdowns, civil disobedience, terrorism, or guerrilla warfare. A subordinate actor may also be in a position to deny a strategic resource, deny access to a strategic location, threaten withdrawal from an alliance or organization, or practice nuclear blackmail. As the global system becomes more interactive and its actors become more interdependent, the vulnerability of dominant actors to that kind of thing will increase.

The second component has to do with the way in which relative capabilities are customarily analyzed. Estimates of outcomes based on relative capabilities are much more likely to be accurate if they focus not on absolute differences but on differences in the capability *ratios* of the actors involved. The ease with which a stronger actor can constrain or punish a weaker is not a function of absolute differences in their capabilities but, rather, a function of the ratio of those capabilities. If the capability ratio of X to Y is high, then X can punish Y simply as a form of police action. If the capability ratio is less high, X may have to engage in a small war—or, perhaps, a not-so-small war—in order to punish Y. The point is implicit in the military injunction to concentrate maximum force at the point of contact with an enemy. A favorable outcome in a battle is far more likely, and losses will be fewer, if the ratio of forces is, say, 4 to 1 rather than 3 to 2. It follows that if a dominant actor can punish a subordinate actor more easily as the ratio in its favor increases, a subordinate actor is in a position to inflict greater costs on a dominant actor as the ratio declines. The costs involved may be military, political, social, psychological, economic, or all of those combined.[1]

As a capability ratio declines, the capacity of a subordinate actor to inflict costs on a dominant actor improves rapidly. The subordinate actor will not have to achieve anything approaching parity of capabilities in order to be able to have a powerful impact on system maintenance costs. For example, because of the characteristics of guerrilla warfare, a dominant actor may have to make ten to fifteen times as great an effort to suppress a guerrilla movement as the insurgents do to maintain it. Therefore, an incremental increase in insurgent capabilities will force the dominant actor to undertake a much greater effort if relative positions are to be maintained. If the ratio of cost burdens is sufficiently disparate, it may become easier at some point for the insurgent to escalate its efforts than for the dominant actor to escalate its counterinsurgent effort in step (Scott et al., 1970, chaps. 6 and 7). That will be the case even if the resources of the latter are far greater in absolute terms. (Appendix 5 in this volume explores the implications of the point.)

Power and Purpose

When the environment in which power is exercised undergoes change, the phenomenon of power itself must change. Evidences of change are readily apparent. As noted, major nations appear to be having increased difficulty, in certain respects, in working their will on smaller nations. The recent appearance on the global scene of thousands of transnational actors—multinational corporations, international banks, international governmental organizations, international nongovernmental organizations—further alters the exercise of power by nation-states. Because of the existence of transnational organizations and the increasing importance of transnational influences, national governments are less free than they once were to shape domestic policy solely to satisfy internal needs. Further, as remarked earlier, in a highly interactive system it is difficult to punish major transgressors because that will usually involve punishing oneself and one's friends as well. However, none of these changes takes us to the heart of the matter.

"Power" has been a key concept in the study of world affairs for several millennia and has been given close attention. Analysts have tended to focus on the way in which actor A has sought to get B to act so as to advance the interests of A. Does A coerce, does it persuade, does it induce, or what? The analysis in this volume suggests it would also be useful to give attention to another element in the concept of "power," and that is purpose.

A common denominator of analyses of power has been the assumption of purpose. It is taken for granted that actor A has purposes, and the question is whether, how, and under what circumstances actor A can or cannot lead B to do as it wishes. As Bertrand Russell put it, "Power may be defined as the production of intended effects" (1938, p. 35).[2] Powerful nations are those deemed to be in a position to give effect to a wide range of intentions.

Most analysts would quickly agree: "Of course 'power' assumes the existence of purpose. That is the reason for trying to exercise it." The point may seem obvious but it needs to be stressed, for the assumption of purpose points to a key limitation of the concept: it is relevant only in the realm of purposeful behavior.

Earlier chapters have emphasized the growth of apurposive processes and the key role such processes have come to play in global affairs. A common characteristic of these processes is the *absence* of a single, controlling purpose. Yet the concept of "power" *requires* the existence of purpose. Clearly, then, the concept of "power" cannot be used when one is examining apurposive processes.

Because of the emergence of apurposive processes the nature of discourse on international politics must change. "Power" is an appropriate concept for dealing with normal constraint-system issues because of the predominance of actor purposes in most such matters. The analyst is looking at things from the perspective of the actors involved and is considering their purposes, their behaviors, and the relationship between purposes and outcomes. The more ambitious the purposes and the more congruent the outcomes are with them, the more powerful an actor may be said to be. "Power" is not an appropriate tool, however, for dealing with apurposive processes, for then individual purposes have been aggregated into something else, and it is the something else that is being examined. That is why "power" has never seemed to be of much use in connection with global issues involving resources, the environment, population, or economic processes. (To be sure, actors caught up in an apurposive process may still be playing a power game, which could be examined in its own terms, but when an analyst examines an apurposive process, he will not, as a rule, be focusing on specific actors and their purposes.)

Impact

The significance of power (the reality, not the concept) will remain great, yet it is nevertheless clear that the emergence of apurposive processes makes power relatively less important than it once was in the totality of activities in the global system. Since the world of apurposive processes is off limits to the concept of "power," the domain of that concept has also undergone shrinkage. Significant areas of activity will have to be understood without reference to it. If "power" is falling from its traditional, exclusive place at the center of things, however, what conceptual tools might we use to complement it? What concept would stand in relation to apurposive processes as "power" stands to purposeful activities?

An apurposive process, by definition, is not under effective control. It might be largely undirected, as with world population, or it might be semi-directed, as is the case with the global economy. Nevertheless, despite the fact that it is not under effective control, the impact that different actors may have on it will vary greatly. Pollution of the seas, for example, is an apurposive process, but it is clear that landlocked nations do not contribute as much to it as do major trading nations with extensive shorelines.

To note that an actor has an impact on an apurposive process does not imply that it sought it or is even aware that it has it. For example, during the late

1960s and early 1970s, as a consequence, in part, of its involvement in the Vietnam War, the United States contributed significantly to the process of global inflation. At the time it did not mean to do so and was not even certain that it was doing so. In the same way, the United States has had an important impact on the process of global air pollution and has contributed to the worsening energy and resource picture. It had an impact on those processes long before their significance was officially recognized.

Generally speaking, the more interaction an actor contributes to a given apurposive process, the greater will be its impact on that process and on its outcomes. Impact, that is, is related to the percentage of the total activity in a process that a given actor contributes. If an actor is tied in with a large number of interaction networks and contributes a good deal to them, and if they are important, then the actor has a substantial impact on global affairs. The United States has a substantial impact because of the vast number of interaction processes it contributes to. Americans buy a lot abroad, sell a lot abroad, invest abroad, travel a lot, communicate a lot, provide economic and military assistance, and their cultural artifacts (television programs, music, films, dress, foods, technology, etc.) diffuse widely. Inescapably, then, the American impact on cultural change, the global economy, resources, the environment, and so on, is great.

Dependency

To be a great power in an interdependent world is to be tied in with other actors in scores of ways. With that involvement comes dependency. If there is to be a seller, there must be a buyer, and each will be dependent on the other. Richard Cooper puts it this way:

> Like other forms of international contact, international economic intercourse both enlarges and confines the freedom of countries to act according to their own lights. It enlarges their freedom by permitting a more economical use of limited resources; it confines their freedom by embedding each country in a matrix of constraints which it can influence only slightly, often only indirectly, and without certainty of effect. [Cooper, 1968, p. 4]

An actor's dependency is related to the extent of its involvement in the global system. The more it is caught up in the system, the more constrained its behavior will tend to be (Keohane and Nye, 1977).

To the extent that an actor is involved in interaction processes, it will have an impact on those processes; to the extent that it is involved, it will also be dependent. The flip side of impact is dependency. It has been a recurrent element in the American dream that the United States could be both a mover and shaker in world affairs and yet somehow dwell apart from the hurly-burly of world affairs. The above relationships suggest that there is no way that can happen. The only way the United States could escape dependency would be to forego all involvement.

Power and Impact

Since "power" and "impact" are analytically distinct, it follows that the realities to which they refer need not always go hand in hand. The concept of "power" has traditionally included two component elements: (1) the capacity of actors to shape the behavior of others in accordance with their purposes and (2) the capacity of actors to shape events in accordance with their purposes. The latter has usually been a silent partner, with attention focused on the first, because the capacity to shape the behavior of others has traditionally amounted to the capacity to shape events.

As the global system has moved along the interaction/technology continuum, however, it has developed the feature emphasized in this volume, the growing prominence of apurposive processes. As apurposive processes have become more significant, the ability of an actor to coerce others and shape their behavior no longer automatically confers the capacity to shape events. The two component elements have, therefore, become distinct and must be analyzed separately if confusion is to be avoided.

Foreign Policy

Changes in the character of the global system have created problems for those charged with the conduct of foreign policy. How does one design policies for a highly complex, interactive, high-technology world? And, just as important, how does one put them into effect?

Those who make and analyze foreign policy normally think in terms of power and purpose, and that mode of thinking builds a bias into their assessments. It is easy for them to assume that if a nation's power relationships (i.e., the capacity to shape the behavior of others) are in good shape, all is well. They have yet to grasp fully the fact that the power to shape the behavior of others, even when it exists, may not confer the capacity to shape events in accordance with one's purposes. A "powerful" nation may still be mouse-trapped by problems it did not anticipate generated by apurposive processes it cannot control. A nation's "power" position may, indeed, improve steadily at the same time that undirected apurposive processes are creating a world in which having power will not be worth much.

The foreign-policy calculus needed for a highly interactive world is different from that needed for a world in which the amount of interaction is far less. Because of its escalating complexity, that world is increasingly difficult to know and to understand. Since change is extremely rapid, by the time a set of conditions are recognized and understood, they may already have been altered. Because of interconnectedness, actions taken in one realm may produce consequences in areas that seem distant and independent. Power and influence are different in such a world, as we have seen, and success, because of that difference, becomes more problematic.

As the total number of inputs into the global arena during a given period vaults upward, the percentage of inputs that any one actor contributes to that total will almost certainly decline. Other things being equal, therefore, that actor's influence on the global system will also decline. Its policy aims, as before, may continue to be frustrated by the intentional efforts of other actors, but, in addition, its purposes will now be more frequently defeated because of the increased role of apurposive processes. Its "power," that is to say, will also be undermined. In absolute terms, that actor may be no weaker than it was before, but changes in the character of the system in which it operates have reduced both its influence and its power and, therefore, the effectiveness of its foreign policies.

This means that, in an interdependent world, actors, even major ones, will become progressively less masters of their own fates. It means, also, that the overall amount of foreign-policy disappointment felt by actors in the global system will increase, and one can wonder what the consequences of such continued, widespread frustration might be.

11. Transnational Actors and
the Global System

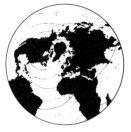

The growth in numbers of transnational actors since the end of World War II has been impressive. The total number of international governmental organizations is now in the neighborhood of 300 and the number of international nongovernmental organizations is over 4,600 (*Yearbook of International Organizations* [Brussels, 1977]). The number of IGOs has come close to doubling each decade since the turn of the century (Feld, 1972, p. 177). The number of transnational enterprises has also increased sharply in recent decades, and the percentage of international economic activity they account for is substantial and still climbing. Although the TNEs are associated mainly with the non-Communist world, a substantial number of major transnational socialist enterprises engaged in production, distribution, and finance do operate in eastern Europe and the Soviet Union.

This chapter will examine some of the effects of transnational actors and transnationalism on the operation of the global system.

Why Their Emergence?

What explains this lush growth? It is clearly associated with the movement of the global system along the interaction/technology continuum. It appears a threshold must have been passed in the late 1940s, for since then the growth in the number of transnational entities has been remarkable.

With the growth of industrialization, transportation, communication, population, and commerce, there has been an increasing differentiation of function both within societies and among them. As the number of activities, wants, needs, problems, and issues has increased, organizations have been brought into existence to deal with them. The increasing complexity of the global system makes it more difficult for organized interests to achieve what they want by acting through national governments, and, therefore, they may seek to get what they want via the formation of a transnational organization. To be unorganized in a world of organizations is to be disarmed and vulnerable.

The same differentiation can be seen in science and technology. The *Yearbook of International Organizations* lists approximately 250 organizations under the heading of "Sciences." These include institutions such as the North Sea Hydrographic Commission, the World Federation of Parasitologists, the Society for General Systems Research, the International Society on Soil Science, and the International Society for the Study of the Origins of Life. Under the heading of "Health, Hygiene, Medicine," approximately 370 organizations are listed.

Almost any new technology will have a spin-off of one or several organizations. With the coming of air travel a cluster of organizations, such as the European Organization of Civil Aviation Electronics, came into existence. Satellite communications produced a new set of organizations, including the International Telecommunications Satellite Organization. Cybernetics produced organizations such as the International Society of Cybernetic Medicine, and the use of liquified petroleum gas soon produced the European Liquified Petroleum Gas Association. The *Yearbook* lists 240 organizations under the heading of "Technology."

New organizations are created to articulate emergent interests, and, since those interests often cross national borders, the activities of the organizations must therefore be transnational. Simultaneously, then, as part of the evolution of the system, there is a proliferation of interests and an international institutionalization of those interests. The principal categories used by the *Yearbook of International Organizations*, in addition to those already mentioned, are the following:

Bibliography, Documentation	Economy, Finance,
Religion, Ethics, Morals	Economic Aid
Social Sciences, Humanistic	Commerce, Industry
Sciences	(approximately 350
International Relations	organizations)
(230 organizations listed)	Agriculture
Law, Administration	Communications, Tourism
Social Welfare	Education, Youth
Professions, Employers	Arts, Literature, Radio,
Trade Unions	Cinema, Television

Sports, Leisure	Development
Environment	Women

Another factor that helps explain the growth of nonstate actors is a change in the character of nation-states. NGOs and transnational enterprises could not operate in a world composed of relatively impermeable national units; it is in their nature to operate across national boundaries. Therefore, the existence of a substantial degree of border porosity was a precondition for the growth in the number and size of NGOs and transnational enterprises. At the same time, when that growth does occur, of course, it further increases the permeability of national borders.

The emergence of a lively world economy was also a precondition for the rapid growth of transnational enterprises. Large numbers of economic organizations, able to operate across national lines, could not come into existence until there were opportunities—in production, marketing, research, etc.—for them to seize upon. In addition, the advance of certain technologies facilitated their growth. The operation of these organizations presupposes high-speed global communications, the rapid movement of persons, and sophisticated information-handling capabilities. Their full development could not have come before the era of radio communication, air transport, and electronic computers. The same is true, to a somewhat lesser degree, of IGOs and NGOs. They feed on communication and the movement of persons.

The Impact of Transnational Actors

It is difficult to assess the significance for the global system of the growth in the number of transnational actors. For one thing, of course, that significance will doubtless continue to change as the number continues to increase. Furthermore, since the rapid growth of transnationalism is a recent phenomenon, learning on the part of such actors is likely to be rapid. Transnational actors will probably become increasingly skilled in pursuing their objectives and, to an increasing extent, will become forces for change in their own right.

Traditional international relations theory is not much help in understanding transnational actors, for it revolves around nation-states. Only now is a body of theory beginning to be fashioned that can accommodate transnational institutions (Keohane and Nye, 1972, 1974, 1977). A conceptual tool, such as "power," for example, does not seem well-adapted for use with transnationals. To be sure, transnational actors are sometimes involved in constraint systems and may exercise power. For example, before OPEC emerged into prominence in 1973 the informal constraint system operated by the major international oil companies provided them with effective control over the production, refining, distribution, and pricing of the world's oil. It is possible, therefore, to examine the "power" of individual transnationals and the constraint systems in which they operate, but the fit, nevertheless, does not seem very good. For one thing, purposes can be measured against outcomes only when outcomes are completed, and if a transnational organization is engaged in a long-term effort—to encourage family planning, to alert publics to an environmental problem, etc.—there may be no outcome that is readily measurable.

More generally, concepts are needed that fit the things transnationals do. Having an input into a network of organizations may not be "power" in the normal sense of that term, but it may nevertheless help to identify an emergent problem, build a consensus, or promote the coordination of international activities. When the analyst deals with a transnational organization, he may have to strip his mind of its normal concern with command, coercion, armies, treaties, and the like and, instead, ask how much activity a given organization is injecting into an important interaction process. The focus of attention must be on interaction, communication, and networking, for that is what many transnationals do.

An analyst who wants to assess the impact of transnationals must look beyond their purposes—and their success in achieving those purposes—to note the consequences that transnationals are helping to bring about without meaning to. The growth in the number of transnational actors resulted from an apurposive process; it was neither planned nor intended but was the result of countless microdecisions, each one of which was made in an effort to deal with an immediate practical problem embedded in a set of changing circumstances.

That inadvertent outcome, in turn, has served to generate a set of additional inadvertencies. The most important influence of transnational actors on the global system is probably the contribution they make to scores of apurposive processes. Each of the following, for instance, is an unplanned outcome of the transnational revolution, and the list could certainly be extended:

— The growth in the number of transnational actors is a result of the movement of the global system along the interaction/technology continuum and yet, also, helps to speed that movement.

— With the increase in the number of IGOs and NGOs, the system may be said to be becoming progressively more representative.
— The increase in numbers adds to the complexity of the global system and, in so doing, increases the need for coordination among actors.
— The increase in numbers means that transnational actors now comprise a significant part of the global environment that both transnationals and nation-states have to deal with.
— The increase in numbers may have led to a decline in the marginal effectiveness of the average organization. When thousands of organizations are at work trying to influence opinion and decisions, the contribution of most organizations is bound to be slight.
— The increase in numbers may have led to an increase in coalition activity among them.

Transnational Enterprises

The exuberant post-World War II growth of transnational enterprises was unplanned and inadvertent. Many of the enterprises are giants in their fields—CITIBANK, Exxon, IBM—and, in aggregate, TNEs now account for a substantial proportion of global economic activity.

Not surprisingly, therefore, TNEs have become a focus of research attention, much of it centered on the relationship between TNEs and host countries. For instance, although the investment, pricing, and employment practices of a TNE may have a pronounced impact on a given developing nation, the TNE will typically concern itself only with those consequences that translate themselves into balance-sheet items. In the same way, a TNE will not regard the balanced economic development of a country as its responsibility any more than it will the fact that a small economic elite may benefit disproportionately from its activities.

It became apparent to developing countries some time ago that the interests of TNEs do not automatically coincide with the interests of the countries in which they are operating, and it may now be becoming clear to developed countries as well (Vernon, 1971; Behrman, 1970, 1974; Barnet and Muller, 1974; Gilpin, 1975). For example, to at least some extent, the U.S. oil "crisis" of 1979 was the result of oil company decisions that the price of oil was likely to continue to rise and that it would, therefore, be prudent for the companies to build up reserves. In addition, oil that normally came from the

Caribbean to the United States was diverted to the spot market where it would fetch a price substantially higher than the regulated U.S. price. Behavior that appeared to the oil companies to be prudent management nevertheless had an adverse effect on the U.S. economy.

Although the TNEs have been the focus of abundant research, it is interesting to note the questions that have *not* received much attention. There has been relatively little concern with the aggregate impact of transnational enterprises on the global system despite the fact that they are large-scale buyers, sellers, investors, researchers, transferrers of funds and technology, etc. TNEs satisfy the conditions for aggregative processes (multiple actors; each actor pursuing limited objectives; the absence of coordination), and, since they are engaged in so many activities, they necessarily contribute to a variety of apurposive processes and, therefore, to the production of a raft of inadvertent outcomes. For example, each of the following developments is significant, yet none of them was deliberately sought by TNEs as they engaged in the pursuit of opportunity and profit:

— decisions of TNEs determine the amount, location, and nature of global investment;

— for the developing nations, TNEs have become the principal instrument of economic development;

— they are the principal means for the diffusion of technology and know-how;

— TNEs help to create new Westernized elites in the developing countries;

— they are major factors in cultural diffusion;

— their activities have a powerful impact on the rate and character of resource consumption;

— they have a profound impact on trade and payments;

— TNEs, including international banks, have contributed to the development of the Eurodollar market, making Eurodollars a major component of the world's money supply;

— TNEs are key instruments for achieving global economic growth;

— they are a means for tying nations into the global economy and, in that sense, have done a good deal to create the kind of world economy that now exists;

— they have been key factors in increasing the amount of interaction and interdependence in the global system and have, therefore,

helped speed the evolution of that system along the interaction/
technology continuum.

The cumulative impact of TNEs is great, yet they operate in a no-man's-
land as far as constraints are concerned. The following are the principal
nonmarket constraints at work: (1) rules and procedures of the international
economic system; (2) peer-group pressure originating in the international
commercial community; (3) requirements of host governments and governments in parent countries; (4) international law and codes of behavior. Observers appear agreed that these constraints have not amounted to much in the
past, however significant they may come to be in the future. For all practical
purposes, the individual TNE has been free to consult no interest but its own.

The funds of oil-exporting nations have been deposited in private international banks, swelling the "Eurodollar" market. Therefore, those banks,
and they alone, have had the resources to finance the balance-of-payments
deficits of oil-importing nations. As the foreign-exchange operations of these
banks expanded in the 1970s, the role of the IMF progressively declined.
It lacked resources on the scale that were needed and so ceased to be the
dominant monetary institution in the global system. This provides one more
example of the privatization of economic decisions having broad global consequences. Vital international monetary decisions are no longer centered in
the IMF, an international organization representing the collective judgment of
nations, but, instead, are "made" in an aggregative way by private banking
institutions having interests by no means as broad as the needs of the global
system itself.

Self-regulation is not an adequate substitute for international regulation.
Banks are in business to make profits, and it proves to be hard for them to pass
up immediate profitable investment opportunities in the interest of avoiding
possible system-wide problems at a later date. Bankers, understandably, tend
to think that banking, rather than the informal regulation of the global monetary system, is their main job. The result is that the Eurodollar market is not
sufficiently disciplined regarding reserve requirements or loan provisions, and
the absence of backing by an international agency adds a further element of
instability. Finally, the banks may already be so caught up in the existing
situation as to be in no position to assume the role of dispassionate regulator.[1]

The net result of the decline of the IMF and the failure of private banks to
take over the regulatory function is that international monetary processes that
were under effective collective control in the 1950s and early 1960s are no

longer so controlled. This attenuation of control is an example of the drift toward undirectedness referred to in an earlier chapter.

Transnational enterprises have not, as a rule, thought it part of their responsibility to be concerned about air pollution, pollution of the seas, an arms race, global inflation, payments crises, or international economic instability, save as such matters may bear on the corporate balance sheet. A transnational enterprise in the arms business will seek contracts and will not feel it is part of its responsibility to worry about the possible destabilizing effects of its sales on, say, the Mideast. It is engaged in commerce, and the responsibility for diplomacy and peacemaking belongs to someone else. In a given year the treasurers of TNEs may move hundreds of billions of dollars in liquid assets from one currency to another, but they are not likely to regard it as part of their job to plan their actions with an eye to maintaining the stability of a particular currency or to avoiding strain on global payments mechanisms. TNE plans have a powerful impact on global resource consumption, but, for the officers of individual concerns, that is neither here nor there. In the same way TNEs feel obligated to consider only the balance-sheet implications of technology transfers.

Multinational enterprises are major economic actors operating in a sensitive, interdependent global system, yet they proceed as if their activities affected none but customers, stockholders, and corporate managers. The consequences that flow from the aggregate behavior of TNEs are often important, but managers of individual TNEs feel under no obligation to coordinate the actions of these enterprises so as to avoid unfortunate macroconsequences. Since the purposes of TNEs are one thing, and the consequences that flow from their actions are another, and since there is no invisible hand to harmonize the two, rational behavior for individual enterprises, when aggregated, can sometimes have an adverse effect on the collective good (Schelling, 1978). In time, perhaps, officers of the larger TNEs may become increasingly aware of the impact of company policy on the global system, and a sense of corporate responsibility may begin to take hold. Under the best of circumstances, however, such a development would be slow and unreliable.

Transnationalism and the Nation-State

Nation-states are the key actors on the global stage and will retain that position for some time to come. Nevertheless, transnational actors, both individually and in aggregate, are already having a profound effect on the way in which the global system works. It was no part of a plan by nation-states (because they had no plan at all) to create conditions in which new kinds of organizations might thrive and multiply and, in time, compete with nation-states themselves in certain respects. National governments share scholarly puzzlement concerning transnational actors.[2] They are certainly not at war with them, for they have yet to fully appreciate the fact that they exist and might come to represent a threat. They have not yet begun to wonder whether the development should be encouraged, discouraged, or ignored.

An observer, however, can readily discern latent conflicts of interest. Until recently nation-states had the globe virtually to themselves; now they must share their turf with increasing numbers of transnational organizations. On the face of it, then, their position must be somewhat weakened. The proportion of the total inputs into the global arena deriving from transnational actors has also increased substantially, which means that the proportion of inputs driven by nation-state motivations and concerns has decreased.

There is also tension between nation-states and transnational actors because they tend in opposite directions. These tensions are expressed in the following ways:

— The world of nation-states is based on concerns that are national. The world of nonstate actors is based on concerns that are trans-national.

— Territoriality is the basis on which nation-states are organized; but territoriality gets in the way of transnational activity.

— The world of nation-states is constructed of box-like entities with clearly delineated borders. To transnational organizations, on the other hand, national boundaries are impediments to be overcome, barriers to their effective functioning.

— The logic of nation-states would create a world in which the permeability of borders was closely controlled; the logic of trans-nationalism would create a world in which borders were so permeable as to be of negligible significance.

— Governments want to be in charge of events within their borders; transnational organizations come into existence to emphasize, promote, and respond to the *internationalization* of activities, issues, and problems.

— National governments seek decision-making autonomy; nonstate actors are perpetual reminders that transnational exchanges and obligations create constraints on that autonomy.

— The nation-state, traditionally, has been the almost automatic focus of the political loyalty of its citizens; transnationalism offers alternative foci for loyalty, ones that cut across national lines— Marxism-Leninism, Zionism, Islam, Europeanism, and so on.

— The cultural primacy of a national society for its own people has long been taken for granted; transnational organizations undermine that primacy when they diffuse across national boundaries, music, dress, literature, popular culture, the performing arts, science, technology, films, television, sports, and life-styles.

In some respects, transnationalism is an alternative to nationalism and a solvent for it.

The declining efficacy of individual nation-states, and nation-states as a group, and the growing prominence of transnational organizations are responses to the same thing: changes in the nature of the global system as it evolves along the interaction/technology continuum. Nation-states were well adapted to the world that existed before World War I, but they are less at ease in the highly interactive, high-technology world that has since come into existence. Transnational entities, on the other hand, are quite comfortable in that environment, and why not? As species, transnational entities—IGOs, NGOs, transnational enterprises—emerged only yesterday and precisely in response to new global conditions.

Transnationals will probably go on increasing in number, for the factors that explain that growth in the past are still at work. Market forces will not soon, by themselves, limit the growth of transnational enterprises. To be sure, governments may become more interested in regulating the activities of transnational enterprises, in limiting their number, or in taking over activities that they have handled. For example, many governments now regard energy matters as too important to be left in nonstate hands, as they were when the Seven Sisters dominated the global oil scene. The instability of private international banking, and the threat it represents to national governments, may induce the latter to try to regulate the banking system. Effective action on this or other matters would require a degree of agreement among sovereign governments, however, and so the tide will not soon be reversed. Governments may become increasingly ambivalent about creating additional new international governmental organizations, recognizing that when IGOs are created, they sometimes take on a life of their own, even if, in theory, they are no more than agents of their creators. Unfortunately, however, from the point of view of nation-states, their freedom of action is limited: if the transnational problems besetting nation-states are to be dealt with, it can only be through increased reliance on a form of transnational actor, the IGO. Increased numbers of functions are being lodged with IGOs by national governments for the same reasons that functions flow from small geographical units to larger units within national societies. Only there can they be handled well or, perhaps, be handled at all.

An increase in the number of transnationals means that their aggregate impact on nation-states and the global system will probably increase. They will rub up against nation-states more often, and the tension between the two seems certain to increase. The nation-state will be fighting a war on two fronts. From one direction will come the challenge of transnationalism. Simultaneously, from the other, will come the challenge of separatism and micronationalism. Problems that cross national boundaries are too big for individual nation-states to handle very well, and that points in the direction of transnational solutions. Other problems are too small for nation-states to handle well, and that points toward decentralization or even fragmentation.

12. Communication and Diffusion

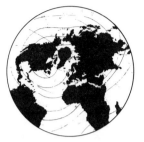

       The study of international communication has not traditionally been regarded as a part of the field of international relations. In recent decades, however, as the global system has hurried out along the interaction/technology continuum, communication has become a major engine of change. The international exchange process that was formerly devoted mainly to moving goods is becoming increasingly concerned with moving information. Communication is bringing about transformations at every level, from the life of the individual to the assorted subsystems of the world. Waves of communication-propelled change keep coming and are not easy to adjust to. Because of its importance, therefore, communication should be moved close to the center of this evolving field.

Communications technology has been undergoing extremely rapid change since the development of the telephone, the telegraph, and the vacuum tube. There are few fields in which technological innovations come with such pace and overtake human plans as swiftly and as reliably as in communications. Each new element can combine with already existing elements (microelectronics, satellite communications, fiber optics, computers, television, telephone networks, and so on) to produce still further waves of technological possibilities. In addition, vast and immensely complex man/machine networks are being fashioned by the linking of entire systems. The tempo of these developments continues to accelerate; the web of global communications draws more tightly around each nation-state and other actors and around the lives of individuals.

A phenomenon that goes hand in hand with communications is cultural diffusion. If we have an increase in the one, we must have an increase in the other. A prominent characteristic of an interactive world, therefore, will be the presence of a high level of intersocietal diffusion.

The subject of diffusion has a recognized place in fields such as sociology, psychology, geography, journalism, demography, biology, and epidemiology. The historian Fernand Braudel quite properly gives diffusion a role of importance in his masterful work, *The Mediterranean* (1973). Political science in general, however, and international politics in particular, have not been very interested in diffusion. Books on international affairs rarely touch on it explicitly, and it certainly has not been integrated into the body of theory in the field. The only phenomenon in international politics that has received substantial analysis in terms of diffusion is the occurrence of coups d'etat. Since diffusion phenomena are both common and important in world affairs, it may seem strange that they have not received more attention, but the world is full of things that should have been studied and have not been and so this oversight is not remarkable.

What Items Diffuse?

To say that diffusion is a prominent characteristic of an interactive global system is not to say that it is a new phenomenon, of course. Diffusion processes were important in fashioning human culture in an earlier world of limited interaction. One thinks of fire, the domestication of animals, agricultural techniques, hunting techniques, weapons development, the use of the compass, and so on. What is new is the amount of diffusion now taking place, the variety of items being diffused, and the speed of the process.[1]

One way to underline the importance of these processes today is to note some of the categories of items that move across national borders. Automobiles, television sets, wines, and soft drinks are only a few of the consumables that, in almost endless variety, are objects of diffusion. Styles in dress, from high fashion to jeans and army surplus clothing, move easily across national boundaries. The return to long hair and beards was a diffusion phenomenon. The hamburger and take-out fried chicken, for better or worse, are spreading around the globe. Advertising is an object of diffusion and it is also a formidable engine of diffusion. It teaches people to want the kinds of goods and services available in other societies—French wines, Japanese color television, Gucci shoes.

Entertainment forms diffuse easily. Classical music has long been international and so, too, some forms of popular music such as, for example, jazz, blues, big band, rock, calypso, and country. Television programs often find it easy to cross cultural lines. Some television series, such as "I Love Lucy,"

"Perry Mason," and "The Muppet Show," have appeared in more than one hundred countries. Even sports figures occasionally become international heroes despite the nationalist bias of most sports activity.

Scientific knowledge diffuses easily and so do some technologies. Examples are almost endless—agricultural techniques, road-building know-how, dam construction techniques, medical know-how, computer technology, administrative techniques, and so on. Language is changed by diffusion as words and phrases spread. The society that develops a new technology is likely to provide the terminology that goes along with it.

The international economy is, of course, one vast network of linked diffusion processes. The international prices of commodities and currencies—oil, wheat, soy beans, dollars, yen—are set largely by diffusion mechanisms. It is the diffusion of knowledge about supply-and-demand factors that allows the establishment of a market price. National governments are extremely sensitive about the economic behavior of other governments because the consequences of such actions diffuse so widely through the global economy. The failure of the United States to curb its oil imports during the period 1976–78 had a worldwide impact in a number of ways including its effect upon inflation. Inflation also diffuses easily among nations that trade with one another.

Attitudes and ideas are subject to diffusion. A complex of ideas may travel in the form of an ideology—communism, socialism, capitalism, the free-trade ideology, interest in a New International Economic Order, conceptions about racism and injustice, conceptions about the cold war, bipolarity, north-south conflicts, an increased emphasis on youth values, and so on. The rapid collapse of colonialism and the increase in the number of new nations in the decades following World War II cannot be understood save in terms of the development and diffusion of an ideology of decolonization. Religious beliefs and practices have often exhibited the capacity to migrate as, for example, Christianity, Islam, and, in recent years, a number of Eastern religions and cults. Anything that individuals can think or feel has a potential for dissemination across national boundaries.

Not surprisingly, styles in political action can be diffused. After all, if emulative behavior can be found in so many other realms of social life, why should it not appear in the political as well? For example, there is growing evidence that coups d'etat exhibit some of the characteristics of diffusion phenomena. There are fads in styles of terrorism. Political kidnapping, once almost unknown, became internationally popular in the 1970s. Airplane hijacking was epidemic in nature. The practice of seizing hostages as the basis for making a series of political demands also developed in epidemic fashion. Self-immolation, art thefts, and the defacement of valuable art works were all diffusion phenomena, although not all were political.

Attitudes associated with life-styles may also diffuse. When long hair first diffused, ideas about a life-style were also involved. It is not just jeans that diffuse but a way of thinking that can see jeans as an acceptable way of dressing. It is not only the use of drugs that diffuses but the appeal of a drug-related way of life. It is not only household items that diffuse—dishwasher, washing machine, vacuum cleaner, blender—but consumerism, a view that defines the good life as being intimately linked to consumables. It is not only jogging that diffuses but a way of thinking about the body and the importance of physical fitness.

Increasingly, in an electronic age, cultural items are converted into communicable elements—sounds, pictures, print—and transmission is therefore eased. The Philadelphia Symphony cannot travel easily, but recordings of its performances can. It may be cumbersome to ship heavy machinery from country A to country B but blueprints for making the machines are easily transmitted. When airplane hijacking spreads, what is it that travels? It is not the aircraft or the hijackers but the idea of hijacking. When diffusion takes place, what travels is often an idea, a concept, a set of plans, an attitude, an insight, a value. As these elements travel, they have consequences. Since ideas, attitudes, skills, preferences, behaviors, and material goods may all diffuse, diffusion analysis has wide potential application. It can be applied to any phenomena that move, or can be thought of as moving, within an environment through time.

Distributional Networks

Diffusion does not just happen. An item moves from one society to another only if there is a channel that allows such movement. Were it not for transnational distribution networks, Coca Cola would not be an international pause that refreshes. "I Love Lucy" and other television series would not be familiar around the world, and Hondas, Toyotas, and Datsuns would be driven only by the Japanese.

Transnational distribution networks are structures that persist for a time and serve to move cultural items across national borders. Such networks may, at one extreme, be custom-made and may involve only a few actors. At the other extreme, they may involve universal flows, such as short-wave broadcasting, into which actors can plug as they choose. Such networks, which may be organized for any of a number of purposes, are essential to the understanding of many diffusion processes.

The variety of such distributional systems is great. Multinational corporations are in the business of distributing something—services, goods, technologies, skills—whether we are talking about General Motors, Boeing Aircraft, IBM, or Holiday Inns, Inc. There are distributors of films, distributors of television series, and international banks are in the business of distributing capital. There are news agencies, television networks, airlines, international professional associations, travel bureaus, book publishers, music publishers, recording companies, publishers of technical journals, magazine distribution networks, transnationally linked computer and data bank systems, networks for the distribution of arms, underground drug distribution systems, and underground presses. There are even networks for the coordination and distribution of revolutionary activity. In the early 1970s, for example, there existed a Junta for Revolutionary Coordination that had offices in Rome and Paris as well as in Latin America and that sought to promote revolutionary activity in Chile, Argentina, Bolivia, Brazil, and Uruguay.

Many NGOs are distribution networks of a kind, and many IGOs are engaged in diffusing knowledge about public health, agricultural techniques, birth control, and so on. National governments have organized hundreds of agencies to distribute such things as information and propaganda, arms, foreign aid, intelligence activities, and covert operations.

The number of transnational distribution networks has been increasing rapidly since the end of World War II. This is explained, in part, by the increase in the number of actors and, in part, by increasing differentiation among those actors. The United States, for instance, is the starting point for many thousands of such networks. The emergence of a new technology is also likely to give rise to new distribution networks. Elaborate distributional systems are, therefore, associated with air travel, air freight, films, television, radio, and satellite relaying of signals. The increase in the number of networks is important because, other things being equal, the amount of diffusion will be closely related to the amount of effort devoted to it.

Subcultures

It is customary, as a kind of shorthand, to speak of items as diffusing from one society to another. As a practical matter, however, an item is not made available by an entire society nor is it received by an entire society. Rather it will be made available by part of one society and received by part of another. The item may move from one group to another, and it just may happen that the two groups are in different countries. Diffusion processes can be understood only if the role of these subcultures is taken into account.[2]

A "subculture" is a mini-culture existing within a broader national culture and having the characteristics that cultures have. One might also use the term "identity group" or "elite," but the term "subculture" has fewer pejorative overtones than does the term "elite," and is more suggestive than is the term "identity group." There are a great many subcultures in a country such as the United States, including the youth subculture, the business community, the scientific community, a criminal subculture, the academic subculture, the subcultures involving arts, sports, and so on.

Parallel subcultures in two societies are likely to be linked by a number of distributional networks. Cultural items move through these networks from a subculture in one society to a subculture in another. For example, life-styles, as well as styles in dress, music, and dance, may move easily from the youth subculture in one country to the equivalent in another. Cultural items may diffuse more readily from young people in New York to their counterparts in London, Paris, and Tokyo than to adults not many miles away in Maine. In such a case, diffusion across a national border is easy because the item moves through an established distributional network from one subculture to a parallel subculture. Diffusion between New York youths and Maine adults may not take place, however, because the two groups are unlike in important respects, and no distributional network can bridge the gap. In this instance, the barrier between nations is of less importance to diffusion patterns than the barrier between cultures.

Why do cultural items move so easily between parallel subcultures? There may be shared values, perspectives, and purposes, and this may facilitate the passing of certain kinds of information, gossip, and bits of conventional wisdom. A subculture, whether consisting of scientists, businessmen, or jet setters, is likely to have certain distribution networks that its members are attuned to. Items that come via these means are likely to seem prestigious and authoritative. Donald Schon describes the network that facilitated communication between black and student subcultures during the militant years of the late 1960s in this way:

> An underground press, with readership in the millions, services blacks, students and radicals of all shades and persuasions. Telephones permit connection and coordination of events across the nation. Records, tapes, and transistor radios spread words and music through which all shades of opinion and feeling find expression. Informal networks of students, blacks and radicals employ these technologies to establish a remarkable level of connectedness among individuals, organizations and communities throughout the world. The connectedness permitted by highly developed infrastructure technology allows the movement to retain cohesiveness in the face of shifts in the centers of leadership and the central doctrine. Because of the ease with which innovation can diffuse itself throughout the system as a whole, the movement can adopt an ethos in which transformation around the new is a value in itself.
> [1971, pp. 112–13]

Emulation is often important in the functioning of subcultures as well. Members of a subculture are likely to be quite interested in developments in a corresponding subculture in another society and may be prepared to take cues from it. Intersocietal emulation is largely a subcultural phenomenon. During the late 1960s members of the youth subcultures in a number of Western societies felt a noticeable affinity for one another and were attuned to many of the same things—the lyrics of popular songs, slogans, films that became cult objects, and so on.

There has apparently been a close affinity between the drug-connected subcultures in England and the United States and a good deal of emulation. Songs were written about drug experiences and a drug-related vocabulary was fashioned. The music/drug subculture had its own ethos, its own heroes and heroines—Janis Joplin, Jimi Hendrix, Bob Marley—and its own heroic exploits. Peer-group reinforcement across national boundaries was one of the factors that contributed to making drugs an international problem.

Diffusion of an item across a national border into another culture will often depend on the readiness of a subculture to accept it and that, in turn, may require some modification of the item. The study of the martial arts in an American setting is less disciplined than in Japan or Korea, for example, and "German" beer sold on the American market is said to be prepared by a different, and lighter, recipe.

Since items often move from one subculture to another, it would be quite possible for an item to enter a society via a subculture even though that item may be out of tune with the general thrust of the receiving society. Some years ago, for example, journalists expressed surprise that a society having as much respect for age as did the Japanese should nevertheless have so much campus activity aimed at humiliating elderly faculty members and administrators. The explanation lay in the fact that it was not Japanese society as a whole that was engaging in that activity but a particular subculture, which was alienated from traditional Japanese values. The point of entry for new values, which will serve to challenge the dominant values in a society, is often an alienated subculture.

Diffusion of an item from one society to another is commonly a two-stage process. Typically, the item (1) moves from a subculture in one society along established distributional networks to a corresponding subculture in the second society and, from there (2) it diffuses into other subcultures and perhaps, more slowly, into the society as a whole. Subcultures in the receiving society serve as brokers for the new. They receive the new item—a new style, a new idea, a new kind of music, new research findings—and launch it on its career in the receiving society.

Since individual subcultures differ widely in their concerns and perspectives, an item that may move quite easily from subculture X into subculture Y may have little chance of moving into subculture Z. Of the multitude of items available for diffusion from one society to another, some diffuse and some do not. It is as important to understand the constraints on diffusion as it is the conditions that promote it (see Appendix 6).

Asymmetry and Diffusion

The flow of cultural items often has a pronounced directional aspect. At present, an important flow runs from the more developed societies to the less developed. Since interaction processes involve influence, a society that interacts a great deal with others and is the source of many cultural exports will be influential in diffusion processes.

The United States is a source of massive inputs into global diffusion processes, and these inputs have taken a variety of forms. Herbert Schiller has noted that the volume of American cultural exports has been closely associated with the growth of its international economic activities. According to Schiller,

"The global invasion of American capital that occurred after World War II was accompanied by communications/cultural penetration and media saturation as well. The relationship between economics and cultural communications today is organic and inseparable" (1979, p. 1). The role of American firms in international advertising provides a striking example of predominance in a diffusion activity.[3]

Asymmetrical diffusion often produces feelings of ambivalence in those on the receiving end. There is obviously a demand for the cultural items in question, or they would not be imported. On the other hand, no society likes to be always on the receiving end of distribution networks. Asymmetrical diffusion easily generates resentment and can be perceived as a form of cultural imperialism. Not surprisingly, then, the development of cultural anti-Americanism has gone hand in hand with the growth of American cultural exports.

American "cultural imperialism" is largely apurposive in nature, however. It does not reflect settled national policy but is, rather, the net result of scores of organizations taking advantage of commercial and other opportunities. Furthermore, there can be no exporter without an importer. Despite the prominent role of American foreign advertising, it cannot, in fairness, be argued that American cultural items are being forced on unwilling victims. The results may, indeed, be unfortunate in some cases, but the responsibility for those results must be shared by both sellers and buyers, producers and consumers.

It should also be noted that not every activity or cultural item originating in a society need be ineradicably linked with that society. Rhine wines must always, presumably, be linked with the Rhine valley, but when IBM diffuses advanced computer technology around the world, is that the spread of an aspect of "American culture" or simply the spread of a new technology? Are not items such as jeans, rock music, hamburgers, and Coca Cola capable of becoming denationalized?

Much of what has been said above about the role of distribution networks and subcultures presumes the existence of open societies and a relatively free flow of cultural items in response to "market conditions," broadly defined. (See Appendix 7 for a discussion of a "market" analysis of diffusion processes.) In practice, of course, communication and diffusion may create problems for some societies. Governments may wish to preselect what their people shall hear and to prevent the outward flow of information about internal conditions. Such governments may seek to regulate communication, diffusion, and transborder data flows. The Soviet government, for example, seeks to shape the domestic interpretation of events, such as the invasion of Afghanistan, by preventing the dissemination of alternatives to the official explanation. Such efforts, though burdensome and costly, have nevertheless proved to be fairly effective. Those in the Soviet Union who read foreign materials, listen to foreign broadcasts, or travel abroad are relatively few. A certain amount of contagion is unavoidable, however.

Developing nations often betray an ambivalence about international communications. On the one hand, they are aware that they can be enriching, can speed development, are a basic resource, and that without them full participation in the modern world is impossible. They sense that "communication is power" and feel that, if they lack the communications capabilities that other nations possess, they are being somehow short-changed. On the other hand, communication with developed nations may also be perceived as an alien influence and one that is socially, politically, economically, and culturally destabilizing. Communications dependency has become one of the most sensitive of existing dependencies. Developing nations want to participate in global communications, but they do not want to be dependent on developed nations for information about and analysis of the world, their neighbors, and themselves. That explains the attraction of the idea of communications self-sufficiency and the interest in the formation of a New International Information Order.

This ambivalence is easy to understand, for the new communications revolutions are genuinely hard to live with, just as they are hard to live without. The growth of global communications does, indeed, pose a threat to cultural identity. Societies that import their films and television programming from abroad are subjected to a kind of cultural assault. The logic of international communication may run counter to the desire of governments to maintain a closed regime. Such governments, given their values, may be well advised to take steps to combat inadvertent electronic subversion. If communication pouring in from abroad fosters social change, a developing society might wish to ration communication as a means of slowing change and keeping it within manageable limits.

Consequences

There are communications processes with a degree of collective international direction, such as the allocation of frequencies within the framework of the International Telecommunications Union, but, overall, the development is apurposive. Despite their importance, communications/diffusion processes move forward in a nearly rudderless way. Humans watch, almost as spectators, while these processes produce one inadvertent consequence after another. Arthur C. Clarke sensed the semiautonomous nature of communications development when he wrote, in 1963, "When we have true global communications, our way of life will adapt to them, not *vice versa*" (1980, p. 156). The mix of technological innovation and social innovation, joined with processes of aggregation and combination, guarantees the production of a rich supply of inadvertent consequences.

It took the printing press centuries to work its changes on the world via apurposive processes, but contemporary information and communications revolutions do their work in a few years. Before one wave of technological developments and its associated problems can be absorbed, another wave and still another rolls forward. We virtually guarantee that the consequences will surprise us because we make no serious collective effort to anticipate them ahead of time. Little attention is given to technology assessment. No time is taken to inquire into the impact a new technology is likely to have on existing technologies and political, social, and economic structures. Instead, new technologies are turned loose on the world as quickly as they can be developed and users for them can be found. Humans and their institutions are left with no alternative but to cope with them as best they can. Issues that had not been thought of a few years earlier suddenly emerge and become critical. They, in turn, are soon shoved aside by the next set of issues thrusting themselves upward.

The consequences sought through directed diffusion processes may well be benign, as suggested in this passage by Arthur C. Clarke:

> What we are building now is the nervous system of mankind. . . .
> The communications network, of which the satellites will be nodal
> points, will enable the consciousness of our grandchildren to flicker like
> lightning back and forth across the face of this planet. They will be able
> to go anywhere and meet anyone at any time, without stirring from their
> homes. All knowledge will be open to them, all the museums and li-
> braries of the world will be extensions of their living rooms. Marvelous
> machines, with unlimited information-handling capacity, will be able to
> speak directly into their minds. [1961, p. 142]

The consequences that are not planned, those that derive from apurposive processes, may not be benign, however. Change is seldom cost-free. Floods of information will be available, but will societies and the international system as a whole be able to utilize that information effectively? Will communication produce a brave new world, or create new and baffling problems?

The growth of diffusion creates the possibility of the emergence of a global macroculture, a culture that cuts across national lines. Whether that will actually occur is uncertain and whether it would be beneficent is also uncertain. If hundreds of millions of individuals in countries around the world are exposed to the same political appeals and influences at the same time via direct broadcast satellites, might not that introduce a new volatility into international politics? Since ideologies can move with ease across national borders, may not loyalty to nation-states be increasingly affected?

The idea of a macroculture is attractive to many, but nothing says that the items diffused would always be benign, as witness the diffusion of drugs and various forms of terrorism. Diffusion implies an increase in the frequency of behavioral epidemics; it implies nothing about their attractiveness. The rapid flow of information allows for a speedy updating of stereotypes, but it may, just as easily, facilitate the spread of new passions and militantly intolerant ideologies.

What about the impact of diffusion on custom? Diffusion is a powerful solvent. Under the pressure of a continuing flow of new cultural imports, custom dissolves. Societies currently undergoing "modernization" offer examples of this phenomenon. Politics, cultural life, religion, the economy, family life and man/woman relationships, the bases of status and prestige—all are changed or, at least, challenged. The latest thing this week is ripe for replacement by the newest thing next week. It follows logically that as the rate of diffusion of the new increases, the rate of obsolescence and replacement of the old must increase in step.

Humankind has relied on custom to guide much of its behavior. It has been an anchor, a stabilizing force in societies. In traditional societies, to be sure, custom has often been so powerful a force that needed change could not take place. But what happens in such societies and, indeed, in all societies, as custom is eroded? Are people prepared to march bravely into a new future each week, free of the encumbrances of the past? One need not be a Burkean conservative but only an observer of the contemporary scene to have misgivings about the perpetual dissolution of custom.

One may hope that increases in international communication will promote better relations between developed and developing nations, but they may not. What will be the consequences of forced-draft Westernization? What new dependencies are likely to emerge and what new discontents and frustrations are likely to be produced? Diffusion will doubtless have a powerful impact on language, a point made clear by Arthur Koestler's dictum: "Man's deadliest weapon is *language*. He is as susceptible to being hypnotized by slogans as he is to infectious diseases" (1979, p. 15).

Might the further development of communications undermine some of the bases of the city? Arthur Clarke suggests that it will: "The traditional role of the city as a meeting-place is coming to an end; Megapolis may soon go the way of the dinosaurs it now resembles in so many respects. This century may see the beginnings of a slow but irresistible dispersion and decentralization of mankind—a physical dispersion which will take place, paradoxically enough, at the same time as a cultural unification" (Clarke, 1963, p. 157). Since cities have traditionally been the birthplaces of civilizations, might there be complicating inadvertent consequences from that quarter?

With great elan, engineers and administrators solve one communications problem after another. By their successes, are they contributing to what will ultimately be an unmanageable acceleration of change within societies and throughout the global system as a whole? Are they hurrying the global system along the interaction/technology continuum toward the zone of hyperinteractivity?

Part IV.
The Management of
Global Change

13. Planning and Intervention

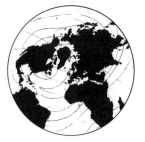

If the collective good is to be satisfied, a community must provide for parks, trash collection, traffic control, and clean water. In the same way, at the global level, requisites must be provided for and threats to them must be forestalled. If the collective good is to be satisfied, a stream of deliberate and effective interventions in global affairs will henceforth be needed, interventions concerned both with avoidance of difficulties and the achievement of positive goals. Since the global system continues to move out along the interaction/technology continuum, its management needs continue to evolve and to become more demanding. Inadvertently, actors have created a system dependent on a consciously created and consciously maintained management apparatus, the scope of which must be progressively enlarged.

When problems emerge in the global system that cannot be dealt with by individual actors, they must be dealt with by constraint systems or not at all. In an earlier era, constraint systems dealt primarily with a range of political/military problems. Now they must try to cope with an increasing number of global problems.

A collective effort to deal with a global problem usually takes the form of an attempt to guide a process that was previously undirected or inadequately directed. If the effort is successful, the process in question ceases to be undirected. The larger the number of such processes under guidance, the smaller the number that remain free to produce inadvertent consequences. For example, if guidelines for the exploitation of the seas could be agreed upon and enforced, the likelihood of a sudden drop in the yield of food from the seas would be much diminished.[1]

Problem Recognition

Before a problem can be dealt with, it must first be recognized. Unfortunately, the fact that something is happening provides no assurance that its happening will be perceived. It also provides no assurance that it will be perceived as a "problem," for that involves additional judgments about trends and the possible significance of the happening. The significance of much that happens from day to day goes unrecognized.

There are many reasons why problem recognition is difficult. Change only becomes change to an observer when it is caught in the act. It never steps forward and announces itself. If change is sufficiently slow or is unlooked for, it will not be discovered. Even exponential change moves slowly, in absolute terms, when it is just getting under way. If a given variable doubles every twenty years, in forty years it will have moved only from one to four. An observer not monitoring the process carefully might fail to note that the process was exponential.

There is a second difficulty, which is that a rate of change may accelerate to the point at which it runs ahead of solutions devised for it. If, a few decades later, we look back at the variable referred to above, we might find that doubling time has dropped to five years and that increments of change are now running 128, 256, and 1,024. That means that the status of a variable such as energy consumption can change quickly from not being recognized as constituting a problem to being regarded as a major crisis. In the same way, the capacity to pollute the seas or to have an impact on environment, after growing slowly for most of human history, now comes on with a rush. Global problems associated with exponential growth rates will have that characteristic. While observers are identifying a problem and arguing about whether it is real, whether it is serious, and what should be done about it, the problem itself may go on evolving and generating new consequences. By the time a problem has been recognized and a solution found, the problem itself may have so grown or changed that it requires a different solution.

There are barriers to problem recognition that have to do with attention bias. The observing mind filters reality and, in so doing, inevitably distorts it to some degree. For example, the attention of government officials may focus easily on the dramatic passing event or the immediate crisis and may not look for consequences that could be twenty or thirty years in unfolding. In practice, "importance" is often viewed as inversely related to distance in the future. This time bias leads to exaggeration of the importance of near problems and events and to a systematic underestimation of the significance of future problems. If a development will not start to produce grave consequences for some years, it is presumed not to be a truly serious problem. Although wisdom dictates that problems should be taken hold of early before they escalate and perhaps become unmanageable, the fact that the problem is not yet producing grave consequences makes it difficult for a government to address it in a serious way. A society that is oriented toward the present, such as the United States, finds it difficult to act on problems that may not become critical for some years to come. The same thing is true of the global system as a whole.

Another feature of attention bias is that familiar problems are perceived more easily than unfamiliar ones. To put it another way, we tend not to find those things we do not expect to find. Minds run along established lines and the novel is easily overlooked. Warnings are likely to be ignored, therefore, when they fall outside the range of past experience. The point is important, for emergent global issues tend to be of unfamiliar kinds. In the late 1940s, for instance, the geologist King Hubbert projected oil and natural gas shortages beginning in the 1970s, but his warnings were not taken seriously. Since observers also prefer problems with readily apparent solutions, they are apt to diagnose a problem in such a way that it will be amenable to their preferred solutions. In a backward way, then, the repertoire of solutions traditionally available influences the problems that will be perceived and the way they will be perceived. It also means that when a genuinely novel problem is perceived, the inclination will be to deal with it in traditional ways.

As noted in an earlier chapter, constraint-system problems are more easily identified by decision makers and analysts than are global problems. Attention is also normally biased in favor of obvious problems rather than subtle ones. Further, the immediate consequences of an action are more likely to be anticipated than are distant consequences. In addition, observers find it easier to identify problems when they stand alone rather than when they are intertwined with others.

Specialists tend to perceive the world in terms of their specialities and are likely to overlook problems that do not fit nicely into established disciplines. There may be a political form of attention bias. Decision makers may be slow to perceive a threat if such perception, and the consequent need to give warning and advocate appropriate action, might be politically dangerous. Similarly, officials are often slow to perceive or acknowledge the existence of a problem if they fear they might be held responsible for its existence.

The perceptual screens that individuals utilize are often helpful since they organize information and, by screening it, assist in avoiding information over-load. They may exact a heavy price for those services, however, in terms of information loss and the narrowing of attention. Although we cannot dispense with such screens, individuals can, through systematic consciousness-raising, become aware of some of their biases, modify them, and reduce their impact.

Time and Management

Individuals know that time is a constant on earth, moving always at a steady pace, yet they lament that it is speeding up in world affairs. Why?

If a driver moves his car along an interstate highway at forty miles per hour, travel will seem leisurely. He can see a long way ahead, and, since his speed is moderate, there is plenty of time for the decisions he has to make. There is a low density of events in a given unit of time, and, therefore, few decisions are called for. He directs the car off the interstate and onto a highway leading through the outskirts of town, but the accelerator has jammed and so the car still moves at forty miles per hour. The density of events per unit of time is now much greater and the driver must work at the wheel as quickly as he can to avoid cars, trucks, and dogs. With the accelerator still stuck, he comes to the downtown area. The density of events per unit of time is now so great, the decisional demands so heavy, that a pileup is inevitable.

Through it all the speed of the car remained constant; it was external cir-cumstances that changed and made time seem to speed up. In the final mo-ments before the crash, events would have seemed to hurtle toward the driver and even frantic corrections would not have been fast enough, yet time moved at the same pace as before.

To say that the global system moves out along the interaction/technology continuum is a shorthand way of saying that the density of developments, including technological changes, increases with successive time periods. As density increases, the global system, like the driver of the car, will find that time seems to accelerate. There will seem to be so much to do and so little time in which to do it. An approach to the zone of hyperinteractivity would be equivalent to arriving at the downtown area.

If a social system is to function well as the density of events increases, it must try: (1) to see and plan further ahead, (2) to shorten response time, and (3) to develop the capacity to handle many problems simultaneously. These are not requirements the global system can easily satisfy. How can it see ahead when so many variables are interacting in such complicated ways and producing rapid and radical change? How can it shorten response time when its institutions and procedures inhibit rapid response and when the very basis on which the system is organized, that of sovereign nation-states, seems to stand in the way? How can it learn to process multiple problems simultaneously when the decision-making system is pluralistic and actors have different values and priorities and perceive problems in quite different ways?

Time and management are intimately connected. For managers, how rapidly time moves depends on how much they have to do in a given time period. At the outset, then, it will be helpful to distinguish the tempo at which a threat develops from the time it takes actors to organize to deal with that threat. "Problem development time" is the period from the point at which informed public figures first become alert to the existence of a threat to the point at which the consequences of the threat first become critical. The length of problem development time depends on the rate at which a problem develops and the success of observers in recognizing it at an early date. If late recognition combines with a rapid development, as in the case of the global petroleum crisis, problem development time may be short.

"Response time" has two components:

(a) Decision time—the length of time from the point at which informed public figures become alert to the possible existence of a threat to the point at which significant remedial action, of a preventive or adaptive nature, is taken.

(b) Implementation time—the length of time from the point at which significant remedial action is taken to the point at which those actions begin to have a significant effect on the problem.

Because of the accelerating evolution of the global system, problem development time for global problems as a group is getting shorter. Response time varies from problem to problem, but, in general, it is getting longer. The increase in interdependence means that a multitude of actors must now be involved in most problems, including minor ones, and that increase necessarily lengthens decision time. Furthermore, because global problems are becoming more complex, the search for acceptable solutions is likely to be more time-consuming than it has been (Alexis and Wilson, 1967). In addition, since the risk element is substantial with many global problems, it may no longer be safe to merely "satisfice," that is, to settle for a minimally attractive solution. Additional time may have to be expended to help assure a better decisional outcome. Implementation time may also tend to become longer the larger the number of interlocking subsystems involved. Each subsystem may have its own structures, procedures, resistances, and delays, and before one can have a desired impact on subsystem D, one may first have to go through subsystems A, B, and C.

Observation as well as logic suggest that response time tends to increase as the global system evolves out along the interaction/technology continuum. For example, the importance of establishing an international regime for the seas began to be recognized in the 1950s and was widely recognized in the 1960s, yet not until late in 1980 was the negotiating logjam broken. Response time for that problem, therefore, has been approximately a quarter of a century, and all the while the problem itself has continued to evolve and take new forms. The area of arms control provides another example. Technology in that field moves so rapidly that new sets of problems are produced before slow-moving discussion at the technical and political levels have dealt with previous sets of problems. Or, again, the evolution of transnational corporations has moved with extraordinary rapidity since World War II. The response to those developments has held to a much more leisurely tempo. Multinationals began to be studied seriously in the 1960s and became a major focus of attention in the 1970s. However, there is not yet international agreement that they constitute a problem, let alone agreement on the nature and purposes of any regulation. It seems unlikely that effective collective action could be taken, in the U.N. or elsewhere, that would have an appreciable effect before 1990. Response time, in that case, would be approximately forty years. Development of the Euromoney problem offers another example. It had emerged as a matter of concern by 1970, but the actors involved still seem to be many years away from agreement on just what the problem is, how serious it might be, and what, if anything, should be done about it. All the while, of course, the problem continues to evolve and take new forms.

Since problem development time and response time vary independently, the two may easily get out of phase. In the field of international communications, response time has been relatively short, but technological developments and associated social infrastructure developments have advanced at such a pace that, even so, response lags well behind the evolution of the problem. In the case of multinational enterprises, the problem may be evolving at, say, twice the rate of the solution. This has important implications. First, if problem development time for a given problem is five years, that problem will, by definition, be invisible as long as it is more than five years away. Regardless of how long it takes to organize a response, there can never be more than a five-year warning of the problem's approach. Therefore, if the normal response time for that kind of problem is, say, eight years, there will be a time deficit of three years. That is, the problem will become critical three years before remedial action can have a significant effect. By the time the problem becomes salient it will already be insoluble.

Second, if anticipation time and response time are out of phase, by the time a solution is agreed upon and begins to take effect the problem is no longer what it was at the outset. The multinationals do not constitute the same problem now that they did in 1960 or 1970 and are likely to be a quite different problem by 1990. When response time is long, and the problem to be dealt with evolves rapidly, planned interventions may prove to be inappropriate or even counterproductive.

A third implication is even more troubling. If there is not a satisfactory fit between the rate at which a system generates problems and the rate at which it recognizes and disposes of those problems, unresolved problems will begin to accumulate. When they do, they will not stay nicely separated and organized like freight in a warehouse but will, instead, form alliances and create new and still more involved problems. If we have a dozen problems and turn our backs on them for a time, we shall soon have more than a dozen. If the carry-over of problems from one period to another is too great, with some of those problems increasing in severity, the control capabilities of the global system must surely be overtaxed at some point.

What can be done to improve the fit between problem development time and response time? It seems unlikely that decision time and implementation time, which are the components of response time, can be shortened substantially. The best hope appears to lie in trying to lengthen problem development time. The earlier the date at which a horizon problem is identified, the more numerous available options are likely to be and the better the prospects of shaping events. Furthermore, a threat that may be dealt with quite easily, if identified early, may require more effort if not identified until later, or may even cease to be manageable.

Actors on the global scene should, therefore, make an effort to lengthen planning horizons. If response time cannot be much shortened, then an effort should be made to begin the response process at an earlier date. For example, in the hypothetical instance referred to above, the time deficit was three years. However, if problem development time could be lengthened from five to eight years, the time deficit would be erased and the problem would not become critical before remedial action could begin to take effect.

Global Monitoring

Developments that surprise have often been en route to the present for a long time, but if their approach is not observed they can still surprise. The most useful thing that could be done to lengthen problem development time would be to establish a global monitoring system designed to maintain watch on potentially dangerous variables and to sound an alarm when one threatened to stray beyond its proper boundaries (Snyder, Hermann, and Lasswell, 1976; Andriole and Young, 1977).

What should be monitored? Where should one look for horizon problems? What would constitute an effective search strategy? Since each requisite is a point of vulnerability, global requisites and constraint-system requisites should be systematically monitored. The task would have the following components:

— identification of key requisites;
— identification of variables that might place those requisites in jeopardy;
— establishment of boundaries for those variables;
— identification of indicators for the movement of those variables;
— continued observation of those indicators;
— assessment of findings.

The most ambitious international monitoring effort to date is the Global Environmental Monitoring System. Earthwatch was proposed in 1973 as a part of the United Nations Environmental Program, and GEMS was a component part of it. The general purpose of GEMS is to provide early warning of impending natural or man-induced environmental changes that threaten direct or indirect harm to humans. There are seven GEMS categories adopted by UNEP:

— expanded warning systems of threats to human health;
— assessment of global atmospheric pollution and its impact on climate;
— assessment of the extent and distribution of contaminants in biological systems, particularly food chains;
— improved systems for international disaster warning;
— assessment of the state of ocean pollution and its impact on marine ecosystems;
— assessment of the response of terrestrial ecosystems to environmental stress;

— assessment of critical problems arising from agricultural and land practices.

The concept of GEMS is splendid, but the gap between theory and practice remains substantial. It does not yet do effectively what it set out to do.[2] Furthermore, GEMS focuses only on environmental variables and, therefore, does not deal with other requisites that require attention such as:

— the adequacy of global transportation and communications systems;
— the availability of a variety of natural resources including, especially, common pool resources;
— the functioning and stability of the international economic system;
— aggregate activities of transnational corporations;
— amounts and kinds of interaction in the global system;
— the capacity of the global system to dispose of global problems.

It is obvious that the number of requisites that should be monitored is large and increasing, but precisely which variables should be monitored is not always self-evident. That determination depends on circumstances and the insight into global processes that has been achieved. Therefore, the inventory of monitored variables needs to be reviewed and updated periodically, as would the danger points established for each variable. If thresholds are set too high or too low, the monitoring system would not sound the alarm when it should.[3]

Since the variables to be monitored change at widely varying rates, the time intervals at which they should be sampled would also vary. Slower-moving variables could be sampled relatively infrequently and would have to be monitored over a long period before significant variation would have a chance to emerge. Variables capable of rapid change would have to be sampled at more frequent intervals.

The utility of a monitoring system could be expected to increase with time as understanding of global system dynamics improved. An early-warning system is only as good as the theory on which it is based, however, so it would be wise not to place reliance on any single body of theory but to pursue the monitoring implications of several theories simultaneously.

Nevertheless, there is no way to guarantee complete success. A monitoring system might keep watch over a number of familiar requisites but overlook a new one because it had occurred to no one that it had become a requisite. We may learn of some requisites only when they fail to be satisfied and the failure creates a system crisis. A systematic effort at identifying and monitoring requisites would certainly reduce risk, however, even if it did not eliminate it.

Intervention

Genuine human choice exists only if events can be shaped at least to some degree. Ideally, it would be the collective task of managers of the global system to maintain existing global controls, as necessary, and to expand the realm of control so that threatening, uncontrolled processes were given direction. To do this, they would need to produce a continuing stream of carefully timed and coordinated interventions into global processes.

If an intervention is too early, it will be unnecessary, and, if too late, ineffective. In Figure 5 below, Variable A is dropping toward its minimum. It passes that threshold at $Time_3$ and continues downward. With the passage of time the gap between the variable and the minimum widens and the emergency, presumably, would become more serious. After $Time_4$ the situation would have become so advanced that intervention would be futile. Actions must, therefore, be taken while the "window" is open, so to speak, that is, between $Time_2$ and $Time_4$. The same analysis holds for Figure 6 except that Variable B is shown exceeding a maximum.

The length of time a window is open will depend on the angle at which a variable crosses a minimum or maximum. If an exponentially changing variable is far along its growth curve and moving toward the vertical, a window will be open only briefly. It might, then, close before actors could get organized for action. If the angle of intersection is slight, however, as in Figure 7, time would be a less critical factor. The window opens at $Time_1$ and does not close until $Time_6$. In practice, to be sure, making accurate determinations about the opening and closing of windows would be extremely difficult.

The planning of interventions will seldom be easy. Before one can even begin the process, there will be the difficulty of getting agreement that there is a problem and that something must be done about it. Much will also depend on whether one is trying to act early in order to forestall the emergence of a problem, or whether the problem has already emerged and one is trying to adapt to its existence. An action planned in connection with one subsystem must, of course, be considered with an eye to its impact on other subsystems. To deal with one without considering the others might only make the situation worse. On the other hand, planners cannot consider the entire universe before

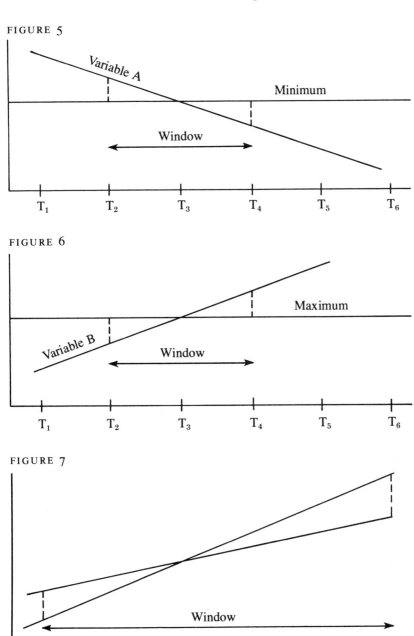

FIGURE 5

FIGURE 6

FIGURE 7

acting on the problem at hand. Managers must, therefore, confine their attention to matters significantly connected with the problem under consideration.

Planning would be made difficult by other factors. At the same time that officials were trying to design a program of actions to forestall future problems they would also have to consider actions to be taken in connection with the continuing consequences of past crises and responses. When multiple threats were involved, as would often be the case, analysis would be difficult and so would the establishment of priorities among conflicting objectives and programs. An intervention that might make sense in terms of a particular constraint system might only exacerbate a global threat.

It is also easy to confuse basic global needs, on the one hand, with the particular constraint-system arrangements by which those needs are being satisfied. Those accustomed to a particular set of arrangements may find it hard to remain aware that a given global requisite can perhaps be satisfied by alternative means. For example, while there needs to be international machinery for dealing with trade and payments problems, that machinery need not include GATT and the IMF. Although it is a global requisite at present that large quantities of petroleum be refined, transported, and made available for consumption, that requisite can be satisfied by a number of different organizational means, as was made clear when OPEC decision making replaced that of an oil company consortium. The prospective collapse of a given set of control arrangements should not, therefore, be greeted as if a global disaster were automatically in the offing.

Those concerned with planning interventions in the global system should be sensitive to questions of timing and be prepared to shift from one time frame to another. Some interventions must be designed for quick results to cope with a present threat. Others must be aimed at forestalling threats that, in the absence of intervention, might not become critical for decades. Managers do not find it easy to move from one time frame to another, however. Instead, they tend, like most other humans, to gravitate toward a time frame that is congenial, usually a short one, and to remain there. The necessities of our situation and the habits of our minds do not always go well together.

Improvement of Management Tools

The burden on those who tried to manage the system would be substantial. There would be requisites and interlocked problems to be aware of, variables to monitor, calculations to be made about windows, and interventions to be planned and coordinated. The analytic tools required for the job do not yet exist.

Measures are needed that would be international equivalents of the national income accounts used by economists, measures, for example, of change in the rate of interaction, the cumulative risk that exists at a given time, the extent to which a given process is under control, and the rate of drift of the global system as a whole.

It would also be useful if means could be developed for assessing the costs and benefits of different levels of global system interaction. One of the costs that would have to be incorporated into the calculus would be that having to do with obsolescence. A highly interactive system will have a high rate of change and innovation, and it must necessarily, therefore, be characterized by a high rate of obsolescence. Taking the global system as a whole, the new cannot be brought in without displacing the old. As we put new cars on the road, we propel older cars into the junkyard, so to speak. Obsolescence is the handmaiden of change, and the more rapidly the global system changes the more rapid is the rate of obsolescence, and obsolescence involves costs.

The obsolescence that rapid change entails may take many forms. Knowledge becomes obsolete. Actors find themselves continually moving out of situations they have begun to understand into those that are unfamiliar. Treaties are abrogated or ignored and informal rules cease to be observed. Alliances and blocs dissolve and institutions lose their vitality. Yesterday's technologies are replaced by today's, and those who think in terms of the older technology may be made obsolete by the change. Yesterday's ideologies are replaced by today's, and values that were once functional become dysfunctional.

Comparative Risk Assessment
Decisions made by system managers would concern risks. What, if anything, should be done about the CO_2 problem, pollution of the seas, and deforestation? Judgments should be based on a capacity to compare the severity of risks across cases. In the absence of such a capacity the tendency is to assume that all hazards are born equal because each contains *some* elements of risk. Comparative risk assessment should be a normal part of decision making. Without it, priorities cannot be established in a realistic way, trade-offs cannot be calculated with precision, and the analyst is left with a stack of variables and risks that may be important but are incommensurable.

At present, comparative risk assessment is in a primitive state. No way yet exists to translate climatic, technological, environmental, economic, and resource hazards into a common language. The unit of measure—say, of mortality—used for one purpose would not be appropriate for another. It would not be easy to fashion a yardstick (or perhaps several, for different purposes), but its development should be pushed since the need is urgent. Existing measures such as the Richter Scale, the Palmer Drought Index, and Gross National Product could perhaps be intercalibrated with one another and with the common yardstick.

Efforts should also be made to improve skills at technology assessment. Under the best of circumstances the capacity for foresight will be limited and imperfect, but that does not remove the responsibility for trying. If humankind does not accept responsibility for its actions, who will? If an attempt to foresee technological consequences is not made, then we will continue to stumble on each new consequence with amazement. And, since we plunge ahead from year to year devising ever more powerful technologies, it is virtually certain that one day we must stumble, amazed, of course, into disaster.

Aggregate Challenge

Research on individual hazards needs to be carried forward so that ways of dealing with them can be learned. At the same time, however, individual problems must be considered together. What would be the total burden to the global system when problems A, B, C, and N are taken together? Analysts need to be able to estimate the probable aggregate challenge deriving from the totality of hazards the system may encounter at some point in the future. Without that capacity it will not be possible to estimate what the system will be coming up against and how much leeway it will have.

Since the hazards that will be operative at $Time_1$ will not be the same as those that come on line at $Time_2$ or $Time_3$, it is apparent that the aggregate of challenges is not a fixed quantity but a variable. What would a curve of Anticipated Aggregate Challenge look like if projected over the next five, ten, or fifteen years? What additional capabilities would be required to deal with challenges of the magnitude indicated by such a curve?

System Resilience

How resilient will the global system be when it encounters a given level of challenge?

The impact of a perturbation will be as much influenced by the social organization of the system and its adaptive capacities as by the nature and magnitude of the perturbation itself. Resilience, that is, depends on the total array of constraints and opportunities that exist and on the context of the times. It will be affected by the amount of redundancy in the system and the resulting ability of backup systems to absorb crises and dampen their consequences.

Resilience will also be affected by the extent to which the global system has infrastructure and procedures enabling it to make use of warnings. The system might be quite sensitive to one form of perturbation and respond quickly, while remaining relatively insensitive to other kinds of perturbations.

The learning capacity of the global system will also affect resilience. Individual societies clearly have the capacity to learn from one another. For instance, technology can be transferred: the wheel does not always have to be reinvented. If an individual society had a substantial influence on collective decision making for the global system, its learning might then constitute system learning. Learning is rarely easy for complex social systems, however, for the crisis this time is not exactly what it was last time. Collective learning is particularly difficult since institutions, attitudes, and entrenched interests often stand in the way, and that which a system most needs to learn it may be least able to learn.

It will obviously be difficult to determine the resilience of the global system ahead of time save in the most general terms. The social consequences of a perturbation will not always be proportional to its magnitude. If a threshold is involved, a small additional input might produce a quite disproportionate output. International tension may increase with little visible result, until war erupts. Alterations in the chemical composition of the atmosphere might have few consequences, until a small additional increment of change had major consequences.

Linearity or nonlinearity of response might be associated with the extent to which the initial sector of impact was integrated into, or isolated from, the rest of the system. If that sector were tightly integrated, the consequences might spread in such a way as to suggest the existence in the system of something akin to the so-called Griffith length. When a material is under continuing tension, it takes more energy initially to get a tear started than is released by the tear. After a certain point, however, associated with the Griffith length for that material, the tear will sustain itself. Similarly, a crisis emerging in sector A might easily and quickly migrate into sectors B, C, and D. There is evidence in the literature on natural hazards that a disaster—an earthquake, a flood, a volcano—is likely to speed up social changes that are already taking place. That is to say, synergisms may come into play. For these reasons, analysts trying to calculate the resilience of the global system if it should encounter challenge will not be able to count on linearity. The consequences deriving from the simultaneous arrival of challenges A, B, and C may not be A plus B plus C but, perhaps, $A \times B \times C$, or even $A \times B^2 \times C^3$.

The Utility of IGOs

IGOs usually represent a collective effort on the part of national governments to deal with problems that cut across the boundaries of a number of nations. As long as the evolution of the global system continues to produce such problems, therefore, there will probably be a demand for the creation of additional IGOs.

The number of IGOs has increased rapidly since the end of World War II, and most observers regard that growth as beneficial. But what of the future? Are IGOs always good, regardless of size and number? Are twenty IGOs twice as good as ten? More realistically, would six hundred be twice as good as the present three hundred? How many would be enough? How can estimates of the worth of an individual IGO be related to efforts to assess the overall effectiveness of IGOs as a group? When nations are considering the creation of a new IGO, would it not be helpful if they could calculate probable costs and benefits?

In an interdependent world, nothing is free of consequences. Interaction, therefore, will always involve costs, and they should not be overlooked. As the number of IGOs continues to climb, for example, so will the total of interaction costs associated with them. At some point, might not the curve of rising total costs cross the curve of declining total benefits? The creation of a host of IGOs is bound to produce important unintended consequences. Organizations seldom do only those things their founders want them to do. Just as problems interweave with one another and create unexpected new problems, so, too, organizations set up to deal with those problems interact with one another and create new layers of consequences. Solutions to microproblems often add up to macroproblems. Efficiency at the microlevel does not necessarily aggregate into efficiency at the macrolevel.

The marginal returns on a prospective IGO should be calculated ahead of time, if possible. Returns on investment were high with the first generation of post–World War II IGOs. However, since IGOs compete with one another for funds, attention, and operating room, does it not seem likely that the yield

per organization will decline as the number of IGOs at play in the global
arena continues to climb? (This assumes, for immediate purposes, that IGOs
are standard units and are therefore interchangeable with one another.) Following this line of thought, planners might conclude that while a prospective
IGO would improve the situation with regard to a particular problem, it would
add still more to the overall control problem because of the increase in numbers, and therefore governments should not be urged to bring that IGO into
existence.

Coordination costs will scale upward rapidly as the number of IGOs rises,
and these will have to be borne not only by the global system as a whole but
by individual governments. When an IGO is established the idea usually is
that direction will be provided, collectively, by the governments involved.
Many of the issues that IGOs deal with will seem somewhat peripheral to
national governments, however, in comparison with domestic issues and those
involving familiar state-centered interests. In consequence, governments find
it difficult to give IGOs the attention and direction that they should, in principle, receive. Almost inevitably, in such circumstances, an organization will
begin to acquire a good deal of operating autonomy. That may be helpful in
the immediate instance, but it raises questions about the viability of the IGO
principle for an era in which IGOs may be quite numerous. Given their other
responsibilities, which are likely to be increasing, is it not asking a lot to
expect that governments will be able to monitor the purposes and activities
of hundreds of IGOs, sort out priorities in numerous conflict situations, and
achieve sufficient collective agreement to provide continuing policy guidance
to each of those organizations?

Conclusion

The task facing international managers would be formidable under
the best of circumstances, and circumstances will seldom be of the best.
Managers will operate under a heavy time pressure and will encounter frequent frustrations in trying to get sensible recommendations agreed upon.
Knowledge will always be imperfect and, sometimes, staggeringly so. Managers will not learn of impending threats as early as they might wish. They
will probably not understand the character of those threats or interconnections
between them as well as they would like, nor will they understand the full implications of the interventions they recommend. Calculate as they may, they

will still find themselves outwitted by mindless processes of aggregation and combination. To say that the global system evolves according to unplanned dynamics and has the capacity to produce novelty is to say that there will be an upper limit to the predictability that can be achieved.

Because of their limited foresight, planners must inevitably make errors of omission and commission, and the damage will sometimes be serious. Indeed, given the vulnerability of the global system and the undeveloped state of the planning arts, we should be prepared for the possibility that, with the best of intentions, planners might nevertheless do irrevocable damage.[4] Knowledge is growing rapidly but that which we *need* to know to survive the unforeseen may be growing more rapidly still.

Managerial efforts will help, but if there is an answer to the disorder crisis, it will probably have to be found somewhere other than in attempts to improve managerial capabilities.

14. Prospects and Perspectives

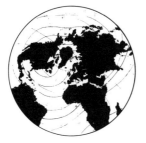

By easy stages humans have created a highly complex, highly interactive, high-technology world—now they must try to understand it and learn to live in it.

Their own creation now constrains them. No attractive alternative remains for the solution of the disorder crisis, and alternatives differ only in their degree of unattractiveness. Although options are limited and uninviting, they must nevertheless be clearly understood, for the lesser of evils may be far superior to the greater.

Option 1: Disregard the Problem—
Suffer the Consequences

One response to the disorder crisis would be to disregard it. Problems would then continue to mount, and, at some point, spasmodic limiting processes would automatically come into play. For example, prior to the Great Depression of the 1930s, a level of international economic activity had been achieved that could not be sustained. Nations lacked the collective ability to manage the global economy that had been created incrementally, and so, following the crash in the United States, a sharp, unplanned reduction in international economic activity took place.

Since there are now many global requisites, potential sources of contraction are numerous. In the economic realm there might be an energy crisis, a crisis deriving from long-continued inflation, a collapse of the international banking system deriving from the default of a major debtor nation, or some other precipitant of a global financial panic. A contraction might also be set off by a war, a global political crisis of some kind, or by an accumulation of medium-sized problems, no one of which would be critical by itself.

Spasmodic contractions are unplanned, and, therefore, neither their scope nor their costs can be limited effectively. Such corrections are harsh and their costs in human terms may be appalling. The costs associated with the Great Depression were immense, and yet, if a comparable contraction came during the present era, its consequences would be far more painful. The reach of the global economy is greater than it was in the 1930s.

A spasmodic reduction in the level of global interaction, although extremely serious, would not mean the end of everything. Many individuals and communities would find the crisis survivable just as they did during the downfall of the Roman Empire. A "phoenix" response might also appear: national societies that did little to stave off system-wide disruption might respond well to an emergency once the crisis was upon them.

Option 2: Deliberate Slowing of Movement
Out Along the Interaction/Technology Continuum

The global system is having more difficulty dealing with its problems in the twentieth century than it did in the nineteenth, and the situation is likely to be still more demanding in the twenty-first century. An attentive observer will be aware of increasing system drift and the declining efficacy of individual nation-states. This holds for both major and minor actors, for, although the former may be able to command lesser nations, they too are victims of apurposive processes. The observer may also be aware of agenda changes for individual nations. Options are increasingly restricted and choices forced. Goal-seeking behavior is giving way to scrambling efforts to survive problems that appear unbidden one after another. The operational goals of nations are defined increasingly in terms of efforts to avoid catastrophe and to adapt to the latest outcomes of undirected processes. It cannot be otherwise.

The global control crisis derives from the tendency of interaction and technology to outrun management capabilities. In the preceding chapter it was pointed out that the problem could not be dealt with by a reliance on improved management capabilities alone. A different kind of approach is needed, one that would seek to alter the character of the problem itself. Might it be possible to attack the problem from the other end, that is, by slowing down the rate of movement out along the interaction/technology continuum? Policymakers in developed countries sometimes seek to cool off a national economy that is overheating by resorting to deliberate efforts at a slowdown; might the same logic be applied to the global system itself?

Clearly, there would be advantages if the evolution of the system could be slowed. It would make sense in terms of environmental and resource imperatives.[1] The emergence of new processes of aggregation and combination would slow as would the rate of production of inadvertent consequences. The rate of increase in the number of global requisites would be slowed and so, therefore, would be the rate of growth in system vulnerability. A slowdown would buy time and provide additional years during which efforts could be made to improve management capabilities. A slowdown would also slow the drift toward undirectedness, slow the movement toward hyperinteractivity, and, in general, improve the "life expectancy" of the global system.

What are some of the ways in which the evolution of the global system along the continuum might be slowed? Since numerous global system requisites now exist, there must necessarily be scores of ways in which a deliberate slowdown could be engineered. For example, international trade might be intentionally reduced. Increases in trade require continuing improvements in payments and currency arrangements: a calculated failure to sustain the tempo of such improvements would, therefore, serve as a brake on the growth of international trade. A decision on the part of trading nations not to press so hard for additional tariff reductions would serve the same purpose. To put it another way, if there had been no GATT and IMF, or if those institutions had been markedly less effective, global economic growth since the end of World War II would have been markedly less impressive.

Efforts are normally made to reduce congestion in the global system so as to ease the growth of interaction. Instead, consideration could be given to utilizing friction as a means of slowing interaction. Governments might, for example, agree to increase the length of time required for the issuance of an export license. Since international commerce requires the communication of vast amounts of information, decisions could be made to constrain the flow of such information.

Since interaction consists of actors taking actions, the rate of increase in the number of transnational actors could be deliberately slowed. Considering the aggregate impact of transnational enterprises on the global economy, might it not make sense that their numbers, size, and operations should be subject to regulation?

If a number of nations sought a limited disengagement from the global economy, that, too, would contribute to a slowing in the rate of growth of interaction. For example, by partially decoupling the Soviet Union and eastern European nations from the global exchange system, Soviet leaders have held the rate of global economic growth below what it otherwise would have been.

Conversely, the increased involvement of those nations in the global economic system during recent years has tended to speed the movement of the system along the interaction/technology continuum.

It would ease the control problem if an international agency for technology assessment were set up to establish guidelines for the development of science and technology. Different forms of technological development are not equally costly in terms of consequences, and an agency could seek to take that into account. Efforts could be directed away from technologies that seemed likely to have a Pandora's box quality about them. Such an agency could also encourage resource-efficient technologies while discouraging the less efficient. It could encourage technologies that advanced the flow of information, perhaps, while discouraging those that would further the flow of commodities.

With all such questions, close attention should be paid to considerations of equity. Any one of the policies noted above might bear more heavily on some societies than on others. Since a high proportion of global interaction and technological development is associated with the developed nations, equity and efficacy might both point toward policies that would weigh more heavily on them than on developing societies.

The idea of deliberately slowing the rate of increase in global interaction may seem startling because interaction is usually thought of as something to be encouraged not constrained. The same thing holds for the advance of technology. Normally, the assumption has been that technology must go whither it will and as fast as it will and that societies must adjust as best they can. Opposition to the slowdown option would be based on short-term definitions of interests. Leaders in developed societies might be troubled by the economic consequences of such an approach while those in developing nations might fear that a slowdown in interaction would slow economic development and freeze existing structural arrangements to their disadvantage. Spokesmen for transnational enterprises are likely to resist arguments for an economic slowdown as well as suggestions that transnational enterprises be subjected to international guidance.

There is no question but that a deliberate slowdown would be costly, but the cost of *not* controlling global processes—of not limiting population growth, not slowing technological development, not slowing the rate of global interaction, not slowing resource use—would be far greater. The argument for a deliberate slowdown is not a conservative plea for the avoidance of change; change will remain rapid no matter what is done. It is, rather, an argument for an option that, if coupled with strenuous efforts to improve management capabilities, would hold some promise of allowing the global system to survive a worsening disorder crisis.

Option 3: National Autarchy

Dependency theorists have pointed out in recent years that when an undeveloped nation becomes involved with more developed nations, relationships are likely to be asymmetrical and it may find itself assigned a role that hampers its development. In addition, if it is tied in with the global system, it will be vulnerable to any major disruption in that system. Policymakers in countries not already irretrievably tied in with the global system might, therefore, wonder whether the national interest did not point toward a degree of disengagement from that system.

It is difficult to consider autarchy with a measure of objectivity because it has had a bad name ever since its association with the Nazi regime in Germany. In addition, it is heretical from the point of view of liberal economics, which emphasizes free trade and comparative advantage. The net result is that the contemporary implications of the idea of autarchy have been little examined.[2]

Is a policy of limited autarchy feasible and, if so, for what kinds of actors? From 1949 until the death of Chairman Mao in 1976, the People's Republic of China pursued a policy of limited involvement with Western nations. The Soviet Union has long pursued a policy of limited involvement, closely controlling foreign trade and all forms of cultural interchange. For those nations it proved feasible—but costly. In the case of the PRC the costs of the policy, in terms of slowed development, were deemed to be greater than the benefits derived from it, and, after Mao's death, the new leadership wasted little time in reversing autarchic policies in favor of substantially increased interaction with other nations. The Soviet leadership, although doubtless acutely aware of the political advantages of insulation from the West, must also be aware of the economic costs of that insulation, for it has been making strenuous efforts to import Western technology.[3]

For a nation attempting it, disengagement might represent an effort to re-achieve a sense of mastery over its own destiny. It would be saying, in effect, "As long as we are heavily involved in world affairs, we will be at the mercy of forces and events beyond our control. On the other hand, if we disengage to a degree and become less involved in global interdependence, we will bear some costs for so doing but will also be less the pawn of events." Alternatively, disengagement might be selected as a survival strategy. A nation might say, "At this late date there is not much hope that nations will find collective solutions to emergent global issues. This nation, therefore, should position itself so as to minimize the impact upon it of the system-based troubles in the offing." Autarchy, or limited disengagement, does not represent an effort to solve global problems but is, rather, an act of resignation in the face of them.

It is a shortcoming of limited autarchy as a policy option that it is not available to nations that are highly resource dependent. A nation such as Japan, for example, which must import 95 percent of its energy, cannot drive toward self-sufficiency unless it is prepared to accept a catastrophic reduction in living standards. It is also not a real option for nations already deeply involved in the global system. For them, numberless small decisions, made over decades, add up to an irreversible commitment. For the United States and some members of the European community, for instance, it is too late to think of disengagement. They have no alternative but to do their best to make the system work and to stand or fall with their success.

Prospects

The global system can continue to operate only if there is an increasing amount of cooperation and coordination between major actors. Not only must actors cooperate more than they have in the past, they must continue that cooperation into the indefinite future—which is quite a requirement, considering their track record. Which of the major nations is prepared to lead the way?

The United States has made some progress in achieving an understanding of the importance of key global processes, but state-centered interests have strong emotional appeal and the support of articulate constituencies while system-centered interests usually lack supportive constituencies. Furthermore, although Americans have developed a variety of useful managerial skills, the governmental system in the United States is ill adapted to long-term planning. Its capacity to offer leadership is also affected by the fact that it is a complex society and is, therefore, moving rapidly out along its own interaction/ technology continuum and is encountering some of the early problems associated with an approach to the zone of hyperinteractivity. It is also handicapped by the fact that, at the same time it is trying to understand and cope with global problems, it must also try to cope with the tactics of the Soviet Union and the suspicion and dislike felt by many developing countries.

The Soviet Union has a better capacity to plan ahead, but, because of its political and managerial arrangements, it is apt to be too inflexible to plan wisely. It has been slow to recognize global issues and tends not to give them high priority. Will Soviet leaders adapt Marxist-Leninist theory so that it is hospitable to emergent global issues, or will they remain irretrievably locked into a set of parochial power concerns? Can they learn to recognize mounting global problems, or will they continue, as now, rarely able to resist the temptation represented by passing politico-military targets of opportunity?

The fact that actors share problems in common does not mean, unfortunately, that they will be able to agree on a common course of action. Even if they could agree to work together, there might still be disagreements concerning the nature, magnitude, and proximity of a threat, its urgency, the need for remedial action, and priorities. There might also be differences concerning the likely efficacy of alternative lines of action. If all these difficulties were overcome, and institutions were set up to meet needs, could the skill and wisdom to manage those institutions be found?

As the global system moves out along the continuum, the concerns of actors should change and global issues should move front and center. Can peoples learn to treasure the earth, and care for it, and pass it on in good condition to generations yet unborn? The world no longer has the tolerance it once had for bold dreams of conquest and domination. If the Soviet Union continues to be preoccupied with the power game, global prospects will be grim indeed. That preoccupation will lead the great powers to devote more attention to conflicting interests than shared interests and to neglect global issues in favor of more parochial ones.

Community and the National Spirit

If nations are to live together in this interdependent world, they will need to focus less on state-centered interests and more on system-centered interests. Even if nations were to define their interests more broadly, however, a problem would remain. In communities it has long been recognized that the pursuit of individual self-interest does not add up to the common good. By itself, self-interest will not produce the necessary amount of cooperative communal behavior.

So it is in global affairs. The exclusive pursuit of the national interest does not create community nor does it produce sufficient cooperative behavior. In conditions of interdependence, even enlightened national interest is an inadequate guide to national behavior. Living with interdependence requires a sense of obligation to the community as a whole. The "global interest" must become of concern, and officials must learn to ask what good citizenship implies for a nation wishing to be responsive to the global interest.

Nations find it hard to be generous with one another. Indeed, so long as "national interest" is the ultimate criterion for all national behavior, there can be no independent justification for generosity. Therefore, those who would provide food for the hungry or relief for the afflicted are easily forced onto the defensive. Support for the service programs of the United Nations is miniscule, for example, because such support cannot persuasively be justified in terms of a narrow conception of the national interest. If nations could agree that something is owed to the global interest as well as to the national interest, doing good might not make them so anxious. In time, national leaders might then feel free to suggest that a nation behave in a responsible and neighborly way, not because of calculations that it would pay to do so, but because that was the way members of a community behave toward one another.

We must begin to develop an ethic of responsibility that will encourage actors of all kinds to consider the consequences of their actions and take responsibility for them. Acting in accord with such an ethic, nations would seek to settle differences without war, not only because it was in their interest to do so, but because they felt an obligation not to risk doing harm, perhaps irreparable, to the broader community. Such an ethic would suggest that damaging the environment, wasting resources, failing to curb population, or introducing dangerous or ill-considered technologies endangers community values and is therefore antisocial. Such an ethic would also entail an obligation to consider the likely consequences of a prospective action if it were to be aggregated with the actions of others.

An ethic of responsibility would be forward-looking. Actors, including transnational enterprises, should feel it part of their duty to leave the planet in at least as good a condition as they found it. The capacity to despoil the globe, which each generation will henceforth possess, should carry with it a special responsibility not to do so. Earth is the home of the human race, the only one it will ever have. Humankind cannot say with E. E. Cummings,

> . . . listen: there's a hell
> of a good universe next door; let's go.

The national interest points toward cooperative action to solve common problems, for, as interdependence increases, the effectiveness of the foreign policy of an individual nation will decline. To achieve enough thrust to overcome the apurposive inertia of the global system, a nation must combine with others. The larger the coalition the more effective it can be, other things being equal.

Movement of the global system along the interaction/technology continuum has increased the need for coordination among actors but has done little to make it easier to achieve. The key decisional units continue to be nation-states, as they have been since the seventeenth century, and national sovereignty and the primacy of the national interest continue to be the key operational values of the system. At the same time that the coordination requirements of the system have been escalating, the structure of the system has continued to impede the achievement of that coordination and has, therefore, contributed to the severity of the disorder crisis.

As a consequence, the global system is markedly undercoordinated and undergoverned. It has difficulty producing badly needed collective goods such as an international regime for the seas, an international energy regime, an international agreement on the use of nuclear energy, and so on. Since the need for collective goods will increase as the global system continues its evolution, the cost of this structural feature will continue to mount.

Conditions of interdependence make essential a sense of community but do not automatically engender that sense. Actors find it easy to operate without a concern for the global interest. They often prefer to enjoy benefits in the present while transferring costs to the future. One thinks of the casual way in which nuclear wastes are produced without assurance of adequate storage, the easy way in which nonrenewable resources are consumed, the relaxed manner in which carcinogens are released into the environment, and the rapid proliferation of nuclear weapons. They apparently see no answer to the kind of question that Robert Heilbroner asks:

> By the year 2075, I shall probably have been dead for three-quarters
> of a century. My children will also likely be dead, and my grandchildren,
> if I have any, will be in their dotage. What does it matter to me, then,
> what life will be like in 2075, much less 3075? Why should I lift a finger
> to affect events that will have no more meaning for me seventy-five years
> after my death than those that happened seventy-five years before I was
> born?

There is no rational answer to that terrible question. No argument based on reason will lead me to care for posterity or to lift a finger in its behalf. Indeed, by every rational consideration, precisely the opposite answer is thrust upon us with irresistible force. [1980, p. 180]

During the course of a few decades an evolutionary process has led to the emergence of a host of global problems and has created a need for worldwide organizations and global loyalties. Has this process done anything to improve the capacity of individuals to become attached to such organizations and to be motivated by such loyalties? Are the psychological implications of interdependence congruent with the psychological predilections of individuals? Individuals often seem most comfortable in social groupings of a modest size. In many nations a separatist spirit is growing, suggesting that in some cases the nation may be too large a unit for individuals to identify with easily.

What percentage of the population in any society is psychologically ready to live under conditions of interdependence? Is it perhaps one of the unanticipated consequences of the evolution of the global system that humankind is busily fashioning for itself socioeconomic conditions that it may find psychologically unacceptable? Is it building a world in which it is destined to feel alien and lost? The answer is not yet clear.

History and the Apurposive

Earlier chapters noted that the number of apurposive processes in a complex social system will increase with the advance of technology and the growth of interaction. Since the term "complex system" refers not only to the global system itself but to many subsystems within it such as the economies of developed countries, vast metropolitan areas, and western Europe, the application of the principle is wide. How, then, should it affect our understanding of history and the unfolding of human affairs?

— Humankind is no longer contesting with forces of nature so much as with forces of its own making. These forces, however, because they are apurposive and undirected, seem external to mankind and as impersonal as if they were forces of nature.
— As a consequence of time and processes of aggregation and combination, new bits of reality are continually coagulating and emerging into existence, and the tempo of such creation is picking up.

— Historical accounts, therefore, should increasingly look to apurposive processes and the way they interact with purposeful behavior.
— Such accounts should also recognize that if humans are creative so,
too, is the historical process. Novelty is being created from day to
day quite apart from deliberate human intent.
— There has been the hope, implicit perhaps in the concept of
"progress," that humankind would bring its destiny progressively
more under its own control. However, since apurposive processes
are becoming relatively more important in complex social systems
and purposeful processes relatively less significant, that hope is
likely to be disappointed. The prospects for a neat, orderly, con-
trollable world are poor. As humans move forward, learning more
and becoming more powerful in an absolute sense, their capacity to
control their own destiny is weakening. From month to month they
are fashioning a world they are less and less able to shape.
— Because of the increasingly prominent role of apurposive processes,
history is becoming less determinate, in some respects, with the
passage of time. It will be both harder to shape and harder to
anticipate.

There are indications that the global disorder crisis may mature rather
rapidly. On the one hand, interaction and technological advances show little
sign of slackening their pace. On the other, the political structure of the global
system is likely to change only slowly. Governments are usually supportive of
existing arrangements and efforts at major institutional innovation must always
encounter the single most powerful political emotion at work in the world
today—nationalism. As long as rapid movement out along the interaction/
technology continuum continues, system disorder will increase and the possibility of breakdown will cast a dark shadow over the future. The way is
already perilous, and, with each additional decade, the mountains become
higher and the rivers harder to cross. Can humans continue to manage the
high-speed, flame-lit world they have created, or are they already in the
process of surrendering their collective destinies to unfathomed apurposive
processes?

If they have chosen, unknowingly, to acclerate the evolution of the global
system, might they not choose, deliberately, to slow it down? The idea of
bringing apurposive global processes under control is a challenging one, and
mankind has every incentive to try. After all, we are not observers indiffer-

ently watching a windup toy scurry across a tabletop toward the edge. With
Dylan Thomas we can say:

> Do not go gentle into that good night,
> Rage, rage against the dying of the light.

Perhaps, with effort and luck, we will find a way to deal with emergent problems. Perhaps a new and fair prospect will open and there will yet be time to
visit the stars.

Appendixes

Appendix 1
The Growth of Interaction and Technology—
Illustrative Examples

TABLE I. World Trade (in billions of U.S. dollars)

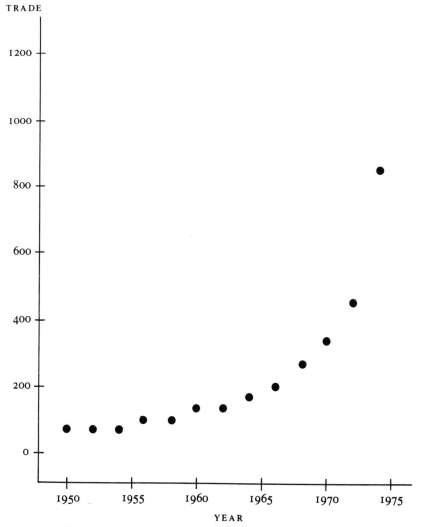

Source: *United Nations Statistical Yearbook, 1950–1975.*

TABLE 2. Number of NGOs in the World System, 1905–1980

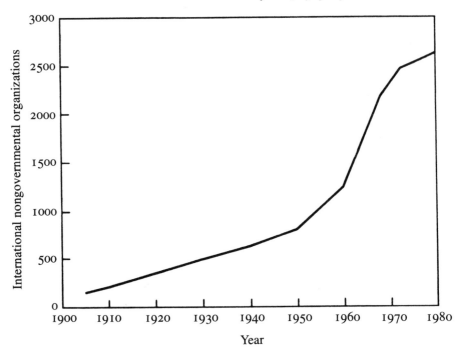

Source: Bruce Russett and Harvey Starr, *World Politics: The Menu for Choice* (San Francisco: W. H. Freeman, 1981), p. 53.

TABLE 3. Growth of IGOs and States in the World System, 1815–1975

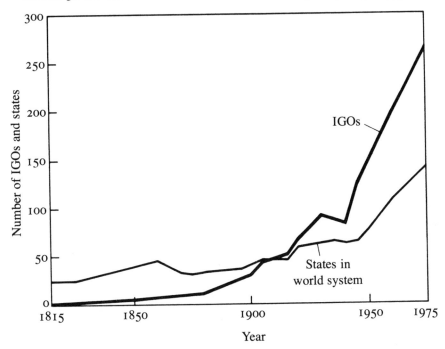

Source: Bruce Russett and Harvey Starr, *World Politics: The Menu for Choice* (San Francisco: W. H. Freeman, 1981), p. 52.

Appendix 2
Classifying Constraint Systems

If one is interested in classifying constraint systems, as distinct from profiling them, the two most useful variables appear to be actor capabilities and degree of perceived legitimacy. Figure A then emerges:

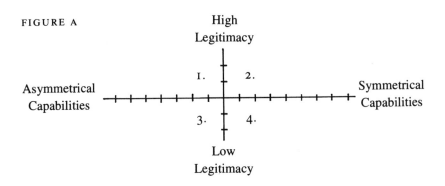

FIGURE A

High
Legitimacy

I.   2.

Asymmetrical Capabilities   Symmetrical Capabilities

3.   4.

Low
Legitimacy

In Quadrant 1 would be located those systems characterized by asymmetrical member capabilities and high legitimacy. Imperial systems that have not yet been challenged would fit here, such as the Spanish Empire in the New World and England's rule in the American colonies before 1776.

In Quadrant 2 would be placed those systems in which capabilities are relatively symmetrical and legitimacy is high. One thinks of systems such as the Concert of Europe or the European Economic Community.

In Quadrant 3 would be located those systems in which capabilities are asymmetrical and legitimacy is low. Examples would be the Western Hemisphere system, the Warsaw Pact, and French colonial rule in Indochina and Algeria after World War II.

Quadrant 4 would include any system in which capabilities are symmetrical and legitimacy is low. It is hard to find examples of this mix, for, if legitimacy is low and capabilities are symmetrical, dissatisfied members can easily withdraw from the system. This combination might, however, be found in systems that have not yet dissolved but are on their way to dissolution.

Since the two variables are scalar, there is room for variations within each quadrant as well as movement from one quadrant to another. For example, the legitimacy of a system located in Quadrant 1 might decline, and its position on the vertical axis would therefore drop. If subordinate actors came to reject its legitimacy, it might even migrate from Quadrant 1 to Quadrant 3. Or, it might move into Quadrant 2 if the degree of asymmetry in the distribution of capabilities changed markedly.

When the characteristics usually associated with these two variables are combined, the picture that emerges is as follows:

Quadrant 1 (high legitimacy, asymmetrical capabilities)
    — payoffs probably asymmetrical although not necessarily so
    — rule-making is asymmetrical
    — obedience enforced by dominant actor(s)
    — little deep dissatisfaction
    — little effort to change basic rules
    — little violent resistance
    — low level of victimization and official violence

Quadrant 2 (symmetrical capabilities, high legitimacy)
    — payoffs symmetrical
    — rule-making is symmetrical
    — rule-enforcement based on voluntarism
    — few deep dissatisfactions
    — little effort to change basic rules
    — little violent resistance
    — low level of victimization and official violence

Quadrant 3 (capabilities asymmetrical, legitimacy low)
    — payoffs probably asymmetrical
    — rule-making asymmetrical
    — obedience enforced by dominant actor
    — serious discontents and differences exist
    — pressure for changing basic rules
    — amount of violent resistance may be substantial
    — level of victimization and official violence high
    — high cost system to maintain for dominant actor

Constraint-System Payoffs

Asymmetry of payoffs tends to be associated with asymmetry of capabilities, but the relation between the two is not invariable. A dominant actor may be able to extract more from a system than an examination of relative capabilities would suggest. Imperial systems in decline have sometimes been able to do that when subordinate actors underestimated the extent and rapidity of the decline in dominant actor capabilities. Alternatively, a dominant actor may fail to extract a payoff proportionate to its capabilities. This might be explained by a lag in its perceptions of its capabilities, by inefficiency, by a lack of experience and bargaining skill, or by an unwillingness to press its advantage. The last instance might derive from a sense of restraint and decency or from an awareness that a short-term effort to maximize payoff might jeopardize the system in the long run. Historically, Great Britain's economic exploitation of the American colonies and Canada was mild, and, in the twentieth century, the United States has not sought to maximize returns from the Western Hemisphere system despite an overwhelming preponderance of capabilities.[1]

If system payoff is treated as an independent variable, then Figure A would be replaced by a box with each of the three variables representing one of its dimensions. Constraint systems could then be located in a three-dimensional space instead of on a two-dimensional surface. In Figure B the horizontal dimension represents capabilities, the vertical dimension represents legitimacy, and the depth dimension represents payoff. The eight corners represent extreme points for each of the three variables and the space within the box, away from the surfaces, would represent less extreme values.

Constraint systems can be located within the box in accordance with their characteristics, although some corners may be null in practice. Thus, for example, one could locate the EEC by noting that the asymmetry of capabilities is high, that the legitimacy of the system is also high, and that the payoff from the system is relatively symmetrical. That would locate it near corner 5. As a system's characteristics change over time, its position within the box would shift. If the payoffs in EEC were perceived as becoming less symmetrical, then the legitimacy of the system would probably decline and the EEC could be conceived of as migrating toward corner 7.

FIGURE B

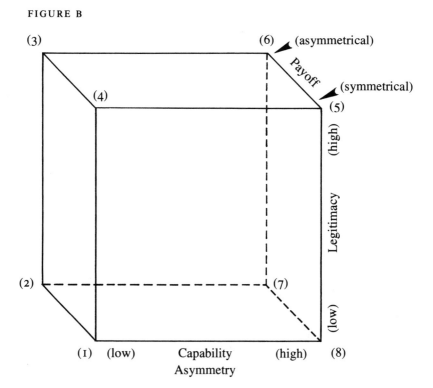

FIGURE C

Corner	Capability Asymmetry	Legitimacy	Payoff
No. 1	low	low	symmetrical
No. 2	low	low	asymmetrical
No. 3	low	high	asymmetrical
No. 4	low	high	symmetrical
No. 5	high	high	symmetrical
No. 6	high	high	asymmetrical
No. 7	high	low	asymmetrical
No. 8	high	low	symmetrical

Appendix 3
Styles of Domination

Differences between the various types of domination are indicated schematically in Figure D. The dominant actor is A and the subordinate is B:

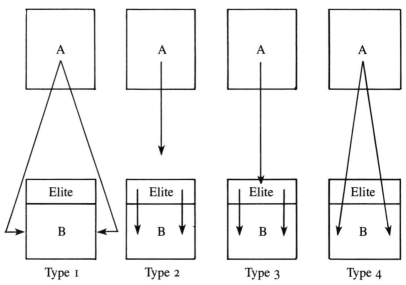

Since these different types of domination are located along a continuum extending from elite independence at one extreme (Type 1) to thoroughgoing elite control at the other (Types 3 and 4), it is to be expected that one type might evolve into another as circumstances change. Rumania, for example, has evolved from a Type 3 form of control (direct political and administrative penetration) toward a Type 1 situation. The Soviet Union will probably not be able to reestablish Type 3 control unless it is prepared to use the Red army to do so. Because the different types of domination are located along a continuum, it is not always easy to fit a given arrangement into one or another of these categories. For instance, it could be argued that political and administrative controls serve to guide the nations of eastern Europe only because units of the Soviet army are a few hours away. Therefore, while the Warsaw Pact system does not fall nicely into category 3, neither is it simply a category 4 example. Perhaps it is 3 1/2?

Dominant actors tend to develop characteristic styles. Generally speaking, the Soviet Union appears to be more comfortable with Type 2 domination than Type 1 and more comfortable with Type 3 (or 3 1/2) than Type 2. In its view, the benefits from more complete control outweigh costs. In Afghanistan, not content with working through a co-opted elite (Type 2), the Soviet Union invaded in December 1979 to consolidate its position and establish a Type 3 or Type 4 form of control.

U.S. domination, on the other hand, is almost always Type 1. The United States has shown itself inept in co-opting foreign elites and in establishing direct controls. The case of South Vietnam has already been mentioned. The United States has a great economic stake in Canada but has not sought to co-opt Canadian decision-making elites nor to establish direct controls. After invading the Dominican Republic, during the administration of Lyndon Johnson, American forces were quickly withdrawn and no effort was made to establish a puppet regime. Puerto Rico is a dependency of the United States, but, even there, the United States does not have Type 2 or Type 3 control. The United States, after overseeing the drafting of a new Japanese constitution, ended its military occupation on schedule and was content to try to exercise Type 1 influence after that time.

The American style of domination, unusually benign for a great power, is congruent with the American democratic tradition, which denies legitimacy to efforts to co-opt foreign elites or to use direct controls over other societies save in the case of a military occupation following a war. If it appears that a foreign elite, or part of it, has been working closely with the CIA, for example, that elite, however much it may or may not be discredited abroad, is certain to be discredited with a segment of the American people. During the late 1960s and early 1970s the CIA fell into disfavor with Congress and many Americans precisely because of evidence that, among other things, it was seeking to co-opt members of foreign elites. It would be out of character for the United States, for instance, to organize and sponsor a network of political parties abroad functionally equivalent to Communist parties the Soviet Union has guided. The United States did, however, go as far as to provide covert financial support to western European political parties in the years immediately after World War II.

Appendix 4
The Warsaw Pact System: Ideology and Euphemism

The Warsaw Pact system exemplifies a constraint system based on direct controls over elites in subordinate countries and, through them, control over important processes in those countries. Each type of constraint system will have its own set of advantages and disadvantages from the point of view of a dominant actor, and, for this system, they would include the following:

— The more extensive the system of controls (over armed forces, police, the economy, labor, peasantry, media, science, education, cultural life, etc.), the more frequent will be the reminders to the population that much of the life of the nation is directed from abroad through an elite imposed by a foreign master.
— Extensive controls allow a dominant society to exert great leverage on the life of a subordinate society. On the other hand, the more extensive the controls, the greater the administrative burden for both Soviet and local elites. An administrative task that would be burdensome under the best of circumstances is made more difficult by the need for ideological and programmatic conformity and by the unwillingness of those involved to admit error openly.
— Direct controls over a foreign elite will do much to assure its reliability but will, at the same time, undermine its credibility in its own country. Elite reliability and elite legitimacy pull in opposite directions.
— Extensive controls make it easier to bottle up or channel expressions of discontent but, at the same time, make it harder to estimate the depth of the discontents that do exist.
— Direct controls make it possible to coordinate efforts within each society and, to a degree, within the entire Warsaw Pact system. On the other hand, this control inhibits initiative and guarantees that the system as a whole, and in its parts, will have a low level of responsiveness and adaptability.
— Direct controls make it possible for the Soviet Union to insulate subordinate societies, to a degree, from contact with societies outside the system. This reduces the contagion of foreign ideas and makes it harder to compare the merits of life within the system with life outside.[1] On the other hand, insulation is always imperfect, is

administratively cumbersome and costly, is an irritant to subject populations, and is economically disadvantageous. On this matter, political control and economic efficiency point in opposite directions. An easing of superpower tensions makes this problem more difficult. Just as an easing of East-West tensions led to increasing dissension within NATO, so it led in eastern Europe to demands for increased intercourse with western Europe.

— Imposition of the Warsaw Pact system means that the nationalist passions of the peoples of eastern Europe are no longer directed against one another—but, instead, are directed toward a single object, the USSR. Despite intense and prolonged efforts by the Soviet Union at ideological manipulation, nationalism and anti-Soviet sentiment have become virtually the same thing.

Ideological aspects of the Warsaw Pact system deserve special attention. One of the rules of the game of the system is that no policy shall be deemed legitimate until it has been properly squared with Marxist-Leninist theory. A second, and crucial, rule is that the Soviet leadership is always the final authority on all matters of "theory." Soviet leaders are, therefore, in a position to legitimize those policies they favor and to set aside as bad "theory" the arguments for policies they oppose. Because the Soviet leadership is alone capable of recognizing true Marxist-Leninist doctrine, members of the governing elites in Warsaw Pact countries are doomed always to be wrong when they disagree with Soviet leaders no matter how right they may be. They are involved in a game they cannot win because Soviet officials make up the rules as they go along.

One of the functions a system ideology often performs, as noted earlier, is that of presenting system arrangements in the best possible light. The seamy side of reality must be obscured or denied. Individuals must be encouraged to see reality only through the lens offered by the ideology. If they do so, then there can be no gap between ideology and reality, for they will see only the formulations of theory when looking at reality. Ideology, that is, tries to teach adherents to substitute theory for reality.

In his essay, "Politics and the English Language," George Orwell noted the special role that euphemism can play in political communication:

In our time, political speech and writing are largely the defence of the indefensible. Things like the continuance of British rule in India, the Russian purges and deportations, the dropping of the atom bombs on

Japan, can indeed be defended, but only by arguments which are too brutal for most people to face, and which do not square with the professed aims of political parties. Thus political language has to consist largely of euphemism, question-begging and sheer cloudy vagueness. Defenseless villages are bombarded from the air, the inhabitants driven out into the countryside, the cattle machine-gunned, the huts set on fire with incendiary bullets: this is call *pacification*. Millions of peasants are robbed of their farms and sent trudging along the roads with no more than they can carry: this is called *transfer of population* or *rectification of frontiers*. People are imprisoned for years without trial, or shot in the back of the neck or sent to die of scurvy in Arctic lumber camps: this is called *elimination of unreliable elements*. Such phraseology is needed if one wants to name things without calling up mental pictures of them. [1950, p. 88]

A euphemism involves the use of a term that is innocuous, or that has attractive associations, to refer to an unattractive reality. Euphemisms allow users to talk about things while directing attention away from their essential elements, particularly their meaning in human terms. No regime has a monopoly on the use of euphemisms, for resort to them is likely to appear whenever an actor wishes to obscure the gap between pretensions and a less attractive reality.

Euphemisms may be used in a narrow zone or much more extensively if the gap between pretension and reality extends through virtually the entire society. If the operational principles of a constraint system, and the results those principles lead to, are out of keeping with the *avowed* code of the system and the realities that code is *supposed* to produce, then wholesale use of euphemism is almost inevitable. A special language will have to be developed that will enable those communicating to understand one another without having to make explicit reference to realities that are embarrassing or repugnant.

The process will be thoroughly familiar to those who follow internal Soviet affairs. There are scores of realities that cannot be referred to openly because they are not supposed to exist and, therefore, must be designated by code words, by euphemism. Forced labor camps become "correctional colonies." The mass murder in the countryside associated with forced collectivization is alluded to as a period in which officials were "dizzy with success." Stalin's excesses are referred to under the general rubric of the "cult of personality." The terror of the 1930s is alluded to as "violations of Leninist party norms."

Crop failures are translated into "non-fulfillment of the agricultural plan." Opposition to Soviet rule by national minorities becomes "acts of bourgeois nationalism," and so on.

The Soviet Union has carried the use of euphemism further than it has ever been taken before. For scores of procedures, relationships, and conditions, euphemisms have been devised. Established euphemisms must be used in all public rhetoric, and to assist individuals in using the correct terminology the Communist party publishes a *Political Dictionary*. Official pronouncements are sometimes little more than a series of such euphemisms carefully strung together. As long as Soviet officialdom professes one set of values and lives by another, euphemisms will be indispensable. They constitute the language of official hypocrisy.

A language of euphemism has been created, and communication can be carried on in that language as in any learned tongue. Communication in that tongue is inescapably monotonous, however, for the language is designed to inhibit spontaneity. Freshness of expression might lead an individual to hint at those things that must not be spoken of. Under such conditions, if there is to be good literature, it will have to be underground. As George Orwell remarked in the essay referred to above, "Orthodoxy, of whatever color, seems to demand a lifeless, imitative style."

In the internal communication of the Warsaw Pact system, there is the same heavy reliance on euphemism. It could hardly be otherwise, for the gap between theory and reality is great and must, therefore, be systematically obscured. Always, there are two levels—the level of theory and ideology, on the one hand, and the level of operational reality on the other:

— In theory, the governments of the eastern European members are freely chosen. In fact, they are imposed by the Soviet Union.
— In theory, these countries are completely independent. In fact, they are subject to Soviet rule.
— In theory, relations among system members are those of socialist brotherliness. In fact, frustrated nationalism has generated a great deal of anti-Soviet sentiment.
— In theory, adherence to the system is purely voluntary. In fact, it is enforced by Soviet armed might.
— In theory, there are no conflicts of national interest between the USSR and other members of the system. In fact, there are serious interest conflicts.

— In theory, relations among system members are those of equals. In
fact, the relationship is that of domination and subordination.
— In theory, decisions are made jointly. In fact, Soviet preferences are
likely to be controlling.
— In theory, the only military threat to eastern European system
members is from the capitalist camp. In fact, as the record shows, if
a system member gets too far out of line, it will be punished
militarily by the Soviet Union.

The language of euphemism must be used in public discourse within the
constraint system even if it has ceased to carry much conviction. The thinking
processes of individuals are heavily influenced by the terms in which they
state their thoughts, and a public that is permitted only the language of euphemism will be, to some extent, intellectually crippled and will have difficulty
analyzing its problems. Only when that language is set aside can serious
analysis begin. For that reason, a failure to use the language of euphemism
is treated as a deliberate challenge to authority. It is as if officialdom recognizes the lesson in the parable of the Emperor's New Clothes: truth may be
contagious when spoken aloud in a time of pretense.

To speak the truth when authority is determined to falsify reality is a profoundly revolutionary activity. In 1956 Hungarian dissidents insisted on setting
aside the language of euphemism and speaking the truth, and, for them, it was
a thrilling and energizing experience. Officialdom quickly labeled the practice
as anticlass, antistate, unpatriotic, and counterrevolutionary (Molnar, 1971).

Appendix 5
Capability Ratios

The implications of the capability-ratio argument are worth spelling out:

— If the capabilities of dominant and subordinate actors increase equally, in absolute terms, the relative position of the dominant actor will have deteriorated.

— If the capabilities of the dominant actor increase more than those of the subordinate, but not in keeping with the ratio of their capabilities, then the change will have brought about an overall weakening in the position of the dominant actor. In Figure E the difference between dominant actor A and actor B is 7,500 units at Time 1. At Time 2 the absolute difference has climbed to 8,000 units, and traditional analysis might suggest that A's coercive power has increased. More significantly, however, the ratio of capabilities has declined from 4/1 to 3/1. B's capacity to inflict costs on A has improved and so, therefore, has its capacity to extract concessions from A.

— When capability ratios are high, small changes in the absolute capabilities of the weaker may have a pronounced effect on those ratios. In Figure F, although actor A still has a healthy margin in absolute capabilities at Time 4, and although B's capabilities have increased by only 150 units, that change is enough to shift capability ratios from 20/1 to 5/1. The United States was overwhelmingly preponderant in western Europe after World War II, but, as the European economies began to recover, capability ratios quickly changed and the United States soon found itself engaged in hard, and sometimes unsuccessful, bargaining with its NATO allies.

FIGURE E

	Time 1	Time 2
Actor A	10,000	12,000
Actor B	2,500	4,000
Absolute Difference in Capabilities	7,500	8,000
Ratio of Capabilities	4/1	3/1

FIGURE F

	Time 1	Time 2	Time 3	Time 4
Actor A	1,000	1,000	1,000	1,000
Actor B	50	100	150	200
Difference in Absolute Capabilities	950	900	850	800
Capability Ratios	20/1	10/1	20/3	5/1

— If the capabilities of a dominant actor should decline, in absolute terms, at the same time that the capabilities of the subordinate were increasing, ratio change would be marked.

— The logic of coalition formation is made evident by a consideration of capability ratios. The capabilities of actor A, relative to each subordinate actor B, C, D, E, and F, are in the ratio of 10/1, as indicated in Figure G. If the subordinate actors were to form a coalition, assuming that capabilities are additive but not multiplicative, the capability ratio immediately changes to 2/1.

FIGURE G

	Time 1	Time 2
Actor A (Dominant Actor)	1,000	1,000
Actor B	100	
Actor C	100	
Actor D	100	500
Actor E	100	
Actor F	100	
Capability Ratio	10/1	2/1

Marginal improvements in the position of a subordinate actor may therefore have a pronounced impact on the capacity of a dominant actor to make and enforce the rules of the game. As the costs of punishments climb, arguments in favor of negotiation, concessions, and the overlooking of disobedience to rules will rapidly gain in attractiveness. By the time capability ratios are, say, 4/1 or 3/1, the capacity of a subordinate actor to inflict costs on the dominant actor will be so great that the latter would opt for a trial of strength only as a last resort. For certain purposes, then, the subordinate actor will have achieved operational equality even though its capabilities are heavily outweighed in absolute terms. Some British strategists, for example, believe that Britain's strategic nuclear forces, although quite small in comparison to those of the Soviet Union, might, nevertheless, serve as an effective deterrent (Smart, 1978, p. 22).

Appendix 6
Constraints on Diffusion

The following are some of the constraints on diffusion processes.

The Source May Constrain Diffusion

An item may not move from one society to another because the source may deliberately prevent that movement. For example, the United States seeks to constrain the sale of certain nuclear technologies, and it does not license the export of a number of advanced weapons. The Soviet Union, for its part, does not encourage the travel of Soviet citizens abroad and is very proprietary about many kinds of information concerning internal affairs that other countries would not consider to be national security matters.

Constraints on the Part of the Recipient

National borders are often unimportant in transnational diffusion, yet they can be extremely important. Decision makers may virtually close borders, restricting diffusion and almost ending it. During Mao's life, the People's Republic of China pursued what might be called an enclave policy, seeking to insulate the Chinese people from most contact with the outer world. The Soviet Union has sought to control the inflow of Western political ideas, art, music, journalistic practices, and so on.

In an interactive and interdependent world, in which transnational diffusion is the natural condition, it is both difficult and costly for national governments to seek to insulate their populations from the currents at play in the rest of the world. Leaders in eastern European nations have found it difficult to import Western technology, for example, without at the same time importing Western cultural influences.

Appropriate Networks May Not Be Available

If an elaborate distributional network is needed before an item can move out of one society and into another, then diffusion of that item must wait until such a network exists. For instance, the large-scale movement of Japanese automobiles and color television sets did not begin until sales and service networks were set up in recipient countries. In the same way, the diffusion of advanced medical practices is not possible until a network of hospitals and training facilities is created.

The Absence of Subcultures

As noted before, items often move transnationally from a subculture in one society to its counterpart in another. If, for whatever reason, there is no counterpart in the society in question, the elements that such a subculture would have received may not diffuse. A society that does not have a business community or has only a limited intellectual and artistic community will not absorb many items appropriate to such communities. Student demonstrations take place where students congregate and interact, which usually means around universities. If there are few universities, the formation of a youth subculture will be impeded and that will, in turn, inhibit the reception of items from equivalent subcultures in other societies. When a subculture does exist, it will, of course, have its own reasons for accepting some items and rejecting others.

Cultural Distance

In some diffusion processes the friction of geographical distance is important, but, in others, it is the friction of cultural distance that is central. If the cultural distance between two societies is great, it is unlikely that there will be large-scale diffusion between them. Even when existing subcultures are taken into account, each society may be relatively impervious to the social and political ideas of the other and even to its popular culture. Sharp differences in the level of development of societies, for example, will tend to inhibit diffusion. A traditional society will have little use for advanced computers and sophisticated electronics systems. The wealth of a society will also affect cultural distance. An affluent society can afford passing fads in dress and entertainment, but a really poor society is likely to have other, and more pressing, needs for resources. Societies at different stages of development will also be encountering different problems and will, therefore, have different needs. At present, for instance, the concern of some of the developed nations for environmental issues does not diffuse easily to the less developed countries.

Competition Among Items

Diffusion processes are at work all the time. At a given moment several score items may be diffusing through the subcultures of a given society. Because many diffusion processes are operating simultaneously, it is only reasonable to expect that the success of some must limit the success of others. Item X might be diffusing through a society while item Y, coming along a little later, begins to overtake it. The diffusion of X is, therefore, constrained by Y and vice versa.

Appendix 7
A Market Approach to the
Analysis of Diffusion

Standard approaches to the study of diffusion—the communications approach and spatial geography—are mechanical and inflexible. They do not allow adequately for the variability found in diffusion processes. A different kind of approach is needed, perhaps one based on market analysis.

In a market area there will be products, producers, distributors, distribution systems, buyers, choices, and costs and benefits associated with those choices. "Products," in this analogy, would be cultural items available for diffusion. "Producers" are those who bring the items into being. "Distributors" are those who serve to move the items through a distribution network, across national borders from producers to consumers. "Importers" are distributors who arrange for the movement of an item into a country and who move it along toward the final consumers.

Producers may occasionally develop a product with an export market in mind, but, more often, products are developed for the home market—films, television series, special forms of music and dance, forms of political activism, etc. Distributors may, however, see a potential market abroad and seek to market them more broadly.

In a given market area there will normally be an array of consumer preferences or needs and an array of potentially importable products that might satisfy some of them. Products that do not meet needs—say, equipment for high-energy research in an extremely poor country—will simply not move into the local market. They will not diffuse, that is, because of a poor fit between product and consumer needs. Sometimes a cultural item may be able to move into a market that would otherwise be closed to it if it is adapted or is packaged somewhat differently. For example, as Marxist ideas on colonialism, neocolonialism, and alienation have been developed and elaborated, they have become more attractive in developing countries.

The capacity of a society to absorb items will be limited, which means that the expectations of some importers must be disappointed. A successful importer is likely to be one with access to group leaders or trend-setters, individuals who are in a position to shape consumption patterns for entire organizations or subcultures. As in most markets, importers of cultural items will have imperfect knowledge of the market and the products they are considering. They do not know, for sure, that consumers will "buy" a product until they see it happening. When consumers do "buy" a cultural import, the price they pay may include a financial component, will certainly include alternative choices that could not be pursued, and will include the consequences flowing from the choice made.

Markets for cultural exchange vary in the extent to which they are organized. A well-organized market will have a variety of distribution channels and the potential, therefore, for the movement of many kinds of items simultaneously. Distribution arrangements can take many forms. One company or organization might, for example, gain access to the distribution network of another in return for patents, licenses, loans, or a profit-sharing arrangement.

A market approach of this kind makes it easy to explain why societies vary in the extent to which they are importers or exporters of cultural items. The United States, for instance, is a major exporter of cultural products but is a relatively modest importer. Why, first, is it a major exporter? There are a number of contributing reasons. The United States is a world power and is at the crossroads of a great deal of international interaction, political, economic, military, and cultural. It is a focal point for many distributional networks reaching into other societies. It is an affluent society, which means that it will, in the normal course of events, develop a wide variety of cultural products. The United States is culturally diverse, which means that it has numerous subcultures that can serve as points of origin for the production of cultural items that might be attractive to parallel subcultures in other societies. Furthermore, the United States is a developed, innovative, and technologically advanced society, which means that it is often the source of products that are attractive on the export market. Finally, in some market areas, but not all, its products may be accorded high status because of the country of their origin.

What are likely to be some of the characteristics of a society that is a major cultural importer, given its size? It would be culturally diverse, and its subcultures would tend to regard corresponding subcultures in other societies as having high status and as often providing cues. It must be wealthy enough to be able to afford a variety of cultural imports but not so developed that it can satisfy its own needs. It must have needs and wants that make foreign imports attractive, and it should have a substantial number of distribution networks reaching into it. It should not be rigidly ideological concerning the acceptability of imports because of country of origin.

Considering the size of the United States and its cultural diversity, it is less of an importer of cultural products than might be expected. Part of the explanation for that may lie in those very factors, however. Its continental size may allow it to be relatively self-sufficient culturally. Furthermore, because it is culturally diverse as well as innovative, perhaps it can satisfy its passion for change and novelty with domestically produced items. Chicago and St. Louis do not need to import from London or Paris because they can import from San Francisco, New Orleans, and New York.

This discussion has taken it for granted that markets are open to the free play of competition among cultural products. In fact, of course, distortions of one kind or another or of one degree or another are quite common. A government may seek, with some success, to establish control over imports. When it does so, it asserts, in effect, the right to disallow the importing of any cultural item of which it does not approve. If two societies are in a dependency relationship, the dominant one will be a favored source of cultural imports for the other. Its products need not be fully competitive with the products of other countries because they will have special access to the market of the dependent country.

The analytic approaches that come to be associated with a field in its infancy can have a great impact on the development of that field. Use of the communications approach and spatial geography have led investigators to use analogies from physics, mechanics, and epidemiology, which have made it harder to get a handle on the subject matter. It has affected the way in which research questions were formulated and answered, has slowed the growth of interest in the subject, and has impeded the development of insight. Use of a market approach might prove more fruitful. It would allow analysts of diffusion to utilize an established and highly developed body of literature within economics, and it should make it easier to develop a body of theory on diffusion extending from micro to macro levels with no significant gaps. Furthermore, information can be, and often is, analyzed as an economic good. One can easily think in terms of the supply of information, the demand for it, the structure of the market, production costs, patterns of consumption, marketing strategies, investment policy, and the like (Pronk, 1979).

Notes

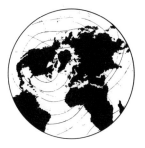

Chapter 1: A World In Transition

1. Immanuel Wallerstein perceives four phases in the evolution of the modern world economy: 1450–1640; 1640–1815; 1815–1917; 1917 to the present. This periodization is useful but he defines periods in terms of economic processes rather than, more generally, in terms of shifts in the rate of growth of global interaction (*The Modern World System*).
2. For a review of the sociological literature dealing with cultural acceleration, see Hornell Hart, "Social Theory and Social Change," in *Symposium on Sociological Theory*, edited by Llewellyn Gross (Evanston, Ill.: Row, Peterson, 1959), particularly pp. 200–219.

Chapter 2: Inadvertent Change

1. Richard K. Betts, addressing issues of national security in "Analysis, War, and Decision," notes that the analyst is faced with "an incoherent environment" and with evidence that is "riddled with ambiguities" (p. 69). In the circumstances, he concludes, "intelligence failures are not only inevitable, they are natural" (p. 88).

Chapter 3: Crises and System Vulnerability

1. There exists a rich and useful literature on "crises" but, unfortunately for our purposes here, it focuses primarily on crises in the political-military realm. Contributors have centered their attention on the threat of war. A crisis exists, as they perceive it, when there is a danger of war, and the crisis is deemed to have been successfully managed when war is averted. The existence of an enemy is taken for granted. By implication, if there were no enemy there would be no crisis. The idea of a crisis without a clearly defined enemy has no place in that literature. By the same token, the crises dealt with are those deriving from deliberate intent. The idea of a crisis developing inadvertently as the result of an apurposive process would be foreign to most of the crisis literature. Accordingly, it does not deal with matters

having to do with resources, food, energy, population, environment, or instabilities in the global economy.

Contributors to this body of literature also focus their attention on nation-states and, to a lesser extent, on alliances. They do not expect crises to originate from the actions of nonstate actors. An economic threat that might be generated by a collection of transnational actors, such as multinational corporations, falls outside the focus of those writing in this tradition.

Crises are usually taken to involve limited time spans, perhaps a few months. This characteristic rules out the development of long-term threats from slow moving continuous processes. Therefore, while this literature might deal with the danger of nuclear war deriving from the actions of a single actor at a particular time, it would not treat as a "crisis" a process of nuclear proliferation that extended over some years. It might be able to focus on a threat of war growing out of an acute petroleum shortage, but it would not examine the long-term origins of the shortage itself.

Those who have contributed to this literature have sometimes studied crises comparatively but they have not been concerned with simultaneous crises, crises linked longitudinally, or with what might be called cumulative or rolling crises, save in the case of the origins of World War I. They have been interested in risk but have not sought to analyze cumulative risk, that is, risk deriving from a multiplicity of sources.

For a useful bibliography and review of the literature, see Richard W. Parker, *Crisis Forecasting and Crisis: A Critical Examination of the Literature*, Defense Advanced Research Projects Agency, Technical Report 72–21 (December 1976).

2. There has been a lively debate in the systems literature concerning whether greater complexity may not increase system stability because of the flexibility provided by back-up systems and alternative ways of meeting needs. For some systems, under favorable circumstances, that might be the case. To take full advantage of such flexibility in the event of a breakdown in one sector, however, would require that there be central direction of the system, that system functioning be fully understood by those directing it, that corrective action be swift and well-conceived, and that all components respond smoothly, swiftly, and in a coordinated way. These conditions may be satisfied if one is dealing with a regional electric power grid, for then the response could be automatic and preprogrammed. These conditions are not met in an international system in which the dominant actors are sovereign nations. In that system, increased complexity means increased vulnerability and instability.

For an alternative view, see Martin Landau, "Redundancy, Rationality, and the Problem of Duplication and Overlap," *Public Administration Review* 29 (1969): 346–58.

Chapter 4: Purpose, Process, and Time

1. There were, of course, a few interesting exceptions such as Henry George, Henry Adams, and Frederick Jackson Turner. See Scott, "Henry George, Henry Adams, and the Dominant American Ideology," pp. 234–51.

2. The economist A. O. Hirschman, in his essay, "The Principle of the Hiding Hand," has also examined the ways in which unintended beneficent consequences may grow out of calculated, purposeful behavior (pp. 9–34).

Theodore White, writing in *In Search of History* about his years covering the Marshall Plan in Europe, was intrigued by unintended consequences. The United States, he notes, was determined to be severe in its administration of aid in Germany:

> Lucius Clay and his advisers decided that Germans must work a forty-eight-hour week, and work they did. The U.S. Army, advised by its experts, said the Germans must rebuild their factories, roads, and bridges first; meanwhile, let them shiver in cellars, ruins and rags; no housing or clothing until they earned their way back. . . . Somehow, the severity with which the Americans policed Germany and directed the flow of aid proved more fruitful than the affection and support we gave the free government of the English people to do as they wished with our billions.

> Neither Clay nor MacArthur nor Hoffman nor Harriman nor George Marshall nor Dean Acheson nor Milton Katz could have envisioned that what they tried to do in the reconstruction of Europe and Asia would result in the rise of Germany and Japan—and that thirty years later, our two former enemies would threaten, like giant pincer claws, America's industrial supremacy in the new trading world we had tried to open to all. [p. 306]

Another economist, Fred Hirsch, in *Social Limits to Growth*, examines the way in which unplanned change takes place because of "the nature of economic growth in advanced societies" (p. 1):

> What precisely is *new* about this situation? The limits have always been there at some point, but they have not until recent times become obtrusive. That is the product, essentially, of past achievements in material growth not subject to social limits. In this sense, the concern with the limits to growth that has been voiced by and through the Club of Rome is strikingly misplaced. It focuses on distant and uncertain physical limits and overlooks the immediate if less apocalyptic presence of social limits to growth. [pp. 3, 4]

Special mention should be made of the stimulating volume by Alfred W. Crosby, Jr., *The Columbian Exchange*. As a historian, Crosby does not try to deal with the general phenomenon of apurposive processes and unintended consequences but, instead, treats a single case, the reciprocal impact of the Old World upon the New and the New upon the Old, following the voyage of Columbus.

For a recent analysis by a political scientist, see Vernon, "Unintended Consequences."

3. Jay Forrester's *World Dynamics* was a path-breaking work and showed the way that macroprocesses might begin to be studied systematically:

> The world system is encountering new pressures. By "world system" we mean man, his social systems, his technology, and the natural environment.

These interact to produce growth, change, and stress. It is not new to have great forces generated from within the socio-technical-natural system. But only recently has mankind become aware of rising forces that cannot be resolved by the historical solutions of migration, expansion, economic growth, and technology.

The manifestations of stress in the world system are excessive population, rising pollution, and disparity in standards of living. But are growing population, pollution, and economic inequality causes or symptoms? Can they be ameliorated directly, or do the causes of stress lie elsewhere in the world system?

There is a growing awareness that past efforts to relieve stress in our social systems have often been, in retrospect, only efforts to suppress symptoms without altering the underlying causes. More and more, the world system is becoming tightly interrelated. An action in one sector of the system can produce consequences in another sector. Often the consequences are unintended and undesirable. We need to understand the ways in which the major factors are influencing one another on a worldwide scale if we are to have confidence that our actions will lead to improvement rather than to making matters worse.

This book sets forth a dynamic model of world scope, a model which interrelates population, capital investment, geographical space, natural resources, pollution, and food production. From these major sectors and their interactions appear to come the dynamics of change in the world system. Rising population creates pressures to increase industrialization, grow more food, and occupy more land. But more food, material goods, and land tend to encourage and permit larger populations. The growth in population, with its attendant industrialization and pollution, comes from circular processes in which each sector both enhances and feeds on other sectors. But in time, growth encounters limits set by nature. Land and natural resources become exhausted, and the pollution-dissipation capacity of the earth becomes overloaded. [pp. 1–2]

4. If we are not starting from zero in thinking about social time, we are at least fairly close to it. See Gurvitch, *The Spectrum of Social Time*.

Chapter 6: Constraint Systems and Rules of the Game

1. One hesitates to propose the use of a new term in a discipline that may already be suffering from terminological overabundance, but no established term appears sufficiently inclusive, including that of "international regime." The most fully elaborated treatment of international regimes is that offered in the useful volume by Robert O. Keohane and Joseph S. Nye, *Power and Interdependence*. The term is used to refer to "sets of governing arrangements that affect relationships of interdependence" (p. 19). A term is needed, however, that applies not only to relation-

ships of international interdependence but to traditional forms of domination, subordination, and cooperation as well. While "regime" would include fisheries conservation, international meteorological coordination, international telecommunications policy, and the like (p. 20), the term would not apply to a regional arrangement such as the European Economic Community, to spheres of influence, to satellite relationships, to imperial systems, or to the kind of relationships covered in dependency theory, for example.

The two terms are not competitive but complementary. "International regime" should be used as it was designed to be and "constraint system" can be used when a more inclusive analytic scheme is needed.

Chapter 7: Constraint System Dynamics

1. In the discussion of maintenance costs and escape costs I am indebted to Benjamin J. Cohen's *The Question of Imperialism*, particularly pp. 215–16.

Chapter 8: Contemporary Constraint Systems

1. For a full and perceptive treatment of the rise and decline of the Bretton Woods system, see Block, *The Origins of International Economic Disorder*.
2. The ambitious nature of the undertaking is illustrated by the statement of purposes in Article I of the Fund Agreement:

> (1) To promote international monetary cooperation through a permanent institution which provides the machinery for consultation and collaboration on international monetary problems.
>
> (2) To facilitate the expansion and balanced growth of international trade, and to contribute thereby to the promotion and maintenance of high levels of employment and real income and to the development of the productive resources of all members as primary objectives of economic policy.
>
> (3) To promote exchange stability, to maintain orderly exchange arrangements among members, and to avoid competitive exchange depreciation.
>
> (4) To assist in the establishment of a multilateral system of payments in respect of current transactions between members and in the elimination of foreign exchange restrictions.
>
> (5) To give confidence to members by making the Fund's resources available to them under adequate safeguards, thus providing them with the opportunity to correct maladjustments in their balance of payments without resorting to measures destructive of national or international prosperity.
>
> (6) In accordance with the above, to shorten the duration and lessen the degree of disequilibrium in the international balances of payments of members. [Horsefield, *The International Monetary Fund, 1945–1965*, 3:187–88]

3. For an excellent account of the intellectual and organizational origins of the

demands for a New International Economic Order, see Murphy, "The Emergence of the New International Economic Order Ideology."

4. For a discussion of this convergence, see Cees Hamelink, *The New International Economic Order and the New International Information Order*, Document 34, prepared for the International Commission for the Study of Communications Problems (Paris: UNESCO, 1979).

5. The PRC is familiar with the Soviet use of the slow probe. For some years there has been a dispute concerning the border between the USSR and the PRC's Xinjiang Uygur Autonomous Region. On 30 September 1979 the *New York Times* reported an interview with Abdulla Rehmin, deputy director of foreign affairs in Utumqui, in which he gave details of the Soviet encroachment. "In some disputed areas, the Russians are intruding into Chinese territory bit by bit. They are using tractors to plow the land and each year they penetrate further." He goes on to explain how they consolidate their gains by the erection of barbed wire fences. They are moving into Chinese territory, he said, like "a silkworm devouring a mulberry tree leaf by leaf."

Chapter 9: Interdependence and National Interests

1. System-centered interests may involve "collective goods" but need not. The aspiration to universalize human rights is not a collective good. It is not a good, such as clean air, which, once supplied (1) can be consumed by anyone irrespective of his or her contribution to its provision and (2) the use of which by one actor does not diminish the amount available to another. In the case of human rights, your not achieving them does not prevent me from achieving them, and my achieving them does not automatically make them available to you. Human rights would be a collective good only in the sense that they can be achieved broadly only if they are pursued collectively. For a discussion of collective goods, see Olson, *The Logic of Collective Action*, and Ruggie, "Collective Goods and Future International Collaboration."

2. See, for example, Rapoport, *Fights, Games, and Debates*, pp. 173–74, and Schelling, *Micromotives and Macrobehavior*, pp. 218 ff.

Chapter 10: Power and Impact in an Interactive World

1. "The Vietnam war may be seen as having been fought on two fronts—one bloody and indecisive in the forests and mountains of Indochina, the other essentially nonviolent—but ultimately more decisive—within the political and social institutions of the United States" (Mack, "Why Big Nations Lose Small Wars," p. 177).

2. See also Lasswell and Kaplan, *Power and Society*, Cox and Jacobson, *The Anatomy of Influence*, Knorr, *The Power of Nations*, Nagel, *The Descriptive Analysis of Power*, Bell, *Power, Influence, and Authority*, and Dahl, *Modern Political Analysis*.

Chapter 11: Transnational Actors and the Global System

1. "The fact is, the big banks are now so deeply enmeshed in the whole deficit financing process that they cannot afford to say 'no,' either to their major depositors or to their major borrowers" (U.S. Congress, Senate, Foreign Relations Committee, "International Debt, the Banks, and U.S. Foreign Policy," p. 174).

2. "Increasingly the power of the nation-state is being shared with supranational institutions and multinational corporations. Neither traditional economic nor political theory is capable of analyzing and describing this process" (Brown, *World Without Borders*, p. 186).

Chapter 12: Communication and Diffusion

1. Donald A. Schon cites the following in *Beyond the Stable State*:

> Curves showing the length of time required for technological innovations to spread broadly throughout populations of users, suggest an exponential rate of shrinkage.
>
> | Invention | Time required for diffusion in years |
> |---|---|
> | steam engine | 150–200 |
> | automobile | 40–50 |
> | vacuum tube | 25–30 |
> | transistor | about 15 |
>
> The time required for the diffusion of major technological innovations would appear to be approaching zero as a limit! [p. 24]

2. In some instances diffusion patterns can also be usefully examined in terms of class, race, and ethnic groups.

3. According to Schiller, *Communication Accompanies Capital Flows*:

> The salient feature in the worldwide growth of advertising expenditures is the overwhelming predominance of U.S. advertising agencies and their overseas affiliates. "International advertising," writes one analyst, "is almost entirely a U.S. industry." . . . Of the 25 largest agencies in the world in 1975, 22 are U.S.-owned or closely associated with U.S. capital. "In each European country," one account reveals, "about half of the top ten billing agencies are U.S.-owned; for example, in Belgium it is six, Britain eight, Netherlands five, Sweden three, Switzerland two and West Germany six." . . .
>
> In the underdeveloped world, United States control is even more pronounced. A study of the presence of foreign advertising affiliates among the five largest agencies of 46 developing countries in 1973 revealed that "in all countries, and for each of the 135 agencies on which data were available, foreign ownership—whether majority or minority—means (with one exception) that the parent agency is either entirely North American or has strong

U.S. participation. More specifically, in 29 of these 46 countries, the largest advertising agency is foreign majority-owned and in an additional four countries foreigners have acquired an often substantial minority interest. . . . in only 13 (or 28 percent of the 46 countries), the biggest agency is entirely owned by nationals. . . . In terms of the 135 agencies, nearly two-thirds are foreign majority-owned, 9 percent have foreign minority participation and less than 30 percent are entirely in national hands." . . . Additionally, the concentration of the foreign (U.S.) control is extreme. Five foreign (U.S.) agencies control two-thirds of all the firms in the 46-country survey. [p. 7]

Chapter 13: Planning and Intervention

1. To be sure, in trying to direct a process that had been previously undirected, a constraint system will quite likely produce consequences that were not intended. That is, in trying to achieve guidance over an undirected system in order to reduce its capacity to produce inadvertent consequences, the purposeful effort will generate inadvertent consequences of its own. Presumably, however, there will be a sharp *net* reduction in such consequences. The surprises produced by imperfect knowledge and control should be fewer than those deriving from the complete absence of control.

2. "Despite recent activity, there is disappointment in certain quarters that the idea of a comprehensive monitoring system is not being translated into reality. The delay in implementation may be connected with the fact that deficiencies exist in our basic understanding of how to go about monitoring and hence how to build a comprehensive global monitoring system. The initial generalized planning is much easier than its subsequent practical implementation" (Holdgate and White, *Environmental Issues*, pp. 102–4).

3. Individual actors may wish to monitor the requisites of particular constraint systems, asking such questions as the following:

—What changes, if any, are taking place in the means of constraint used by the dominant actor?

— Are the maintenance costs of a system climbing? Are benefits changing?

— Is there an evolution in the issues being raised by subordinate actors? Are they challenging rules central to the control system?

— Is the legitimacy of the control system declining in the eyes of subordinate members? Are subordinate members actively engaged in undermining the ideology that justifies the system? Are serious ideological strains emerging?

— What are the means being used by subordinate actors in trying to change the rules of the game? Are increasingly militant techniques being used? Less militant? Is there a widening in the range of techniques being utilized?

— Is discontent rising and, if so, how rapidly?

— How rapidly are the capabilities of subordinate actors changing? Is that change roughly in step with changing demands?

— Are system rules and payoffs changing approximately in step with changing actor capabilities or are they lagging badly?

— Are costs to the subordinate actor from remaining in the system beginning to approach the costs of escape from the system?

— Is the basis for a coalition among subordinate actors improving? Are efforts at coalition-formation discernible?

— Is the behavior being exchanged by actors within the system becoming more conflictual, less so, or is it remaining unchanged?

— Do exogenous or endogenous factors appear to be undermining key control procedures within the constraint system?

4. "My survey of the intractability of the inadequacy of intelligence, and its inseparability from mistakes in decision, suggests one final conclusion that is perhaps most outrageously fatalistic: tolerance for disaster" (Betts, "Analysis, War, and Decision," p. 89).

Chapter 14: Prospects and Perspectives

1. The arguments of steady-state economists, though powerful, have been little regarded. See, for example, Olson and Landsberg, *The No-growth Society*; Daly, *Toward a Steady-State Economy* and *Steady-State Economics*; and, in a different vein, Pirages, *The Sustainable Society*.

2. For an exception, see the thoughtful piece by Holsti, "Underdevelopment and the 'Gap' Theory of International Conflict." Wallerstein discusses the "strategy of self-reliance" in *The Modern World System*, pp. 67–84.

3. In their monograph, *Multiple Vulnerabilities: The Context of Environmental Repair and Protection*, the Sprouts noted the difficulty of the choice: ". . . national communities, especially those dependent on a technologically advanced industrialized economy, face increasingly the unwelcome *choice between high-cost autarky and high-risk interdependence*" (p. 20).

   Klaus Knorr has also posed the issue succinctly. "The critical question relates to sacrificing what may be moderate income gains from foreign trade and investment in order to diminish national vulnerability to externally produced disruptions" ("Economic Interdependence and National Security," p. 9).

Appendix 2

1. Olson and Zeckhauser have noted that in the case of a system established for purposes of a collective good, the dominant actor may not only choose not to exploit the system but may contribute disproportionately to the maintenance of a collective good. See "An Economic Theory of Alliances," pp. 175–98.

Appendix 4

1. "A crafty autocrat will seek to separate his people from the outside world so far as he can—by checking trade and travel and improving self-sufficiency, by reducing the flow of information not useful to his regime, by generating suspicion and hostility. It is politic to hold up foreigners as enemies and to persuade one's own people of the superiority or special virtue of their culture and social order. Foreign contacts and respect for foreign ideas tend to check domestic authority and to increase freedoms in numerous ways. . . . Contrariwise, if the world without is of small importance, the ruler can much better think of himself as a demigod and behave as one" (Wesson, *The Imperial Order*, p. 460).

Bibliography

Adams, Henry
1918   *The Education of Henry Adams.* Boston: Houghton-Mifflin.
Alexis, Marcus, and Wilson, Charles Z.
1967   *Organizational Decision-Making.* Englewood Cliffs, N.J.: Prentice-
            Hall.
Allison, Graham
1971   *The Essence of Decision: Explaining the Cuban Missile Crisis.* Boston:
            Little, Brown.
Andriole, Stephen J., and Young, Robert A.
1977   "Toward the Development of an Integrated Crisis Warning System."
            International Studies Quarterly 21, no. 1 (March): 107–50.
Aronson, Jonathan David
1977   *Money and Power: Banks and the World Monetary System.* Beverly
            Hills, Calif.: Sage Publications.
Baldwin, David A.
1979   "Power Analysis and World Politics: New Trends versus Old Ten-
            dencies." *World Politics* 31, no. 2 (January): 161–94.
Barnet, Richard J., and Muller, Ronald E.
1974   *Global Reach: The Power of the Multinational Corporation.* New York:
            Simon and Schuster.
Bath, C. Richard, and James, Dilmus D.
1976   "Dependency Analysis of Latin America." *Latin American Research
            Review* II, no. 3, pp. 3–54.
Behrman, Jack N.
1970   *National Interests and the Multinational Enterprise.* Englewood Cliffs,
            N.J.: Prentice-Hall.
1974   *Conflicting Constraints on the Multinational Enterprise.* New York:
            Council of the Americas.
Bell, David V. J.
1975   *Power, Influence, and Authority.* New York: Oxford University Press.
Betts, Richard K.
1978   "Analysis, War, and Decision: Why Intelligence Failures Are Inevi-
            table." *World Politics* 31 (October): 61–89.

Block, Fred L.
1977   *The Origins of International Economic Disorder: A Study of United
          States International Monetary Policy from World War II to the Present.*
          Berkeley: University of California Press.
Braudel, Fernand
1966, 1972 *The Mediterranean and the Mediterranean World in the Age of
          Philip II.* 2 vols. New York: Harper and Row.
Brown, Lester R.
1972   *World Without Borders.* New York: Random House.
Cardoso, Fernando H.
1974   "Dependent Capitalist Development in Latin America." *New Left
          Review*, no. 74 (July–August): 83–96.
Cardoso, Fernando H., and Faletto, Enzo
1979   *Dependency and Development in Latin America.* Berkeley: University of
          California Press.
Choucri, Nazli, and North, Robert
1975   *Nations in Conflict: National Growth and International Violence.* San
          Francisco: W. H. Freeman.
Christensen, Cheryl
1977   "Structural Power and National Security." In *Economic Issues and
          National Security*, edited by Klaus Knorr and Frank Trager, pp. 127–59.
          Lawrence, Kans.: Regents Press of Kansas.
Clarke, Arthur C.
1945   *Voices from the Sky.* Reprint. New York: Pocket Books, 1980.
1961   "The Social Consequences of Satellites." Reprinted in *Voices from the
          Sky*, pp. 132–43. New York: Pocket Books, 1980.
1963   "The World of the Communications Satellite." Reprinted in *Voices from
          the Sky*, pp. 148–58. New York: Pocket Books, 1980.
Cohen, Benjamin
1973   *The Question of Imperialism: The Political Economy of Dominance and
          Dependence.* New York: Basic Books.
Cohen, Raymond
1980   "Rules of the Game in International Politics." *International Studies
          Quarterly* 24, no. 1 (March): 129–50.
Cooper, Richard N.
1968   *The Economics of Interdependence: Economic Policy in the Atlantic
          Community.* New York: McGraw-Hill.
Cox, Robert W., and Jacobson, H. K.
1973   *The Anatomy of Influence.* New Haven: Yale University Press.
Crosby, Alfred W.
1972   *The Columbian Exchange: Biological and Cultural Consequences of
          1492.* Westport, Conn.: Greenwood.
Dahl, Robert A.
1976   *Modern Political Analysis.* 3d ed. Englewood Cliffs, N.J.: Prentice-Hall.

Daly, Herman E.
1977   *Steady-State Economics: The Economics of Biophysical Equilibrium and Moral Growth*. San Francisco: W. H. Freeman.
1973, ed.   *Toward a Steady-State Economy*. San Francisco: W. H. Freeman.
Deutsch, Karl W.
1966   *The Nerves of Government*. 2d ed. New York: Free Press.
Deutsch, Karl W., et al.
1968   *Political Community and the North Atlantic Area*. Princeton: Princeton University Press.
Dougherty, James E.
1979   "The Soviet Strategy of Finlandization of Western Europe—the External Process." In *The Atlantic Community in Crisis*, edited by Walter F. Hahn and Robert L. Pfaltzgraff, Jr., pp. 193–212. Elmsford, N.Y.: Pergamon Press.
Eiseley, Loren
1958   *Darwin's Century: Evolution and the Men Who Discovered It*. Garden City, N.Y.: Doubleday.
Engels, Friedrich
1942   "Letter to Joseph Bloch: 21 September 1890." In *Selected Correspondence, 1846–1895: Karl Marx and Friedrich Engels*, pp. 476–77. New York: International Publishers.
Falk, Richard A.
1975   *A Study of Future Worlds*. New York: Free Press.
Feld, Werner J.
1972   *Nongovernmental Forces and World Politics*. New York: Praeger.
Forrester, Jay W.
1971   *World Dynamics*. Cambridge, Mass.: Wright-Allen Press.
Frank, André Gunder
1969   *Capitalism and Underdevelopment in Latin America*. New York: Monthly Review Press.
Frohlich, Norman; Oppenheimer, Joe A.; and Young, Oran R.
1971   *Political Leadership and Collective Goods*. Princeton: Princeton University Press.
Galtung, Johan
1971   "A Structural Theory of Imperialism." *Journal of Peace Research* 8, no. 2, pp. 81–117.
George, Henry
1884, 1912 *Progress and Poverty*. Garden City, N.Y.: Doubleday. 1st and 2d eds.
Gerth, H. H., and Mills, C. Wright, eds.
1946   *From Max Weber: Essays in Sociology*. New York: Oxford University Press.
Gilpin, Robert
1975   *United States Power and the Multinational Corporation: The Political Economy of Foreign Direct Investment*. New York: Basic Books.

1977   "Economic Interdependence and National Security in Historical Perspective." In *Economic Issues and National Security*, edited by Klaus Knorr and Frank N. Trager, pp. 19–66. Lawrence, Kans.: Regents Press of Kansas.

Gosovic, Branislaw

1972   *UNCTAD Conflict and Compromise: The Third World's Search for an Equitable World Economic Order Through the U.N.* Leyden: A. W. Sijthoff.

Gurvitch, Georges

1964   *The Spectrum of Social Time*. Translated by Myrtle Korenbaum. Dordrecht, Holland: R. Riedel.

Haas, Ernest R.

1968a   *Beyond the Nation-State: Functionalism and International Organization.* Stanford, Calif.: Stanford University Press.

1968b   *The Uniting of Europe: Political, Social, and Economic Forces, 1950–1957.* Stanford, Calif.: Stanford University Press.

Hamilton, Alexander

1934   *Papers on Public Credit, Commerce, and Finance.* Edited by Samuel McKee. New York: Columbia University Press.

Hardin, Garrett

1970   "To Trouble A Star: The Cost of Intervention in Nature." *Science and Public Affairs: Bulletin of the Atomic Scientists* 26 (January): 17–20.

Hasner, Pierre

1972   "Sphere of What?: An Exchange." *Foreign Policy*, no. 6 (Spring): 142–49.

Heilbroner, Robert L.

1978   *Beyond Boom and Crash.* New York: W. W. Norton.

1980   *An Inquiry into the Human Prospect.* New York: W. W. Norton.

Hirsch, Fred

1976   *Social Limits to Growth.* Cambridge, Mass.: Harvard University Press.

Hirsch, Fred; Doyle, Michael D.; and Morse, Edward L.

1977   *Alternatives to Monetary Disorder.* New York: McGraw-Hill.

Hirsch, Fred, and Goldthorpe, John A.

1978   *The Political Economy of Inflation.* Cambridge, Mass.: Harvard University Press.

Hirschman, Albert O.

1967   "The Principle of the Hiding Hand." In *Development Projects Observed*, pp. 9–34. Washington, D.C.: Brookings Institution.

Hoffmann, Stanley

1978   *Primacy or World Order.* New York: McGraw-Hill.

Holdgate, Martin W., and White, Gilbert F.

1977   *Environmental Issues.* Report 10, published on behalf of the Scientific Committee on Problems of the Environment (SCOPE) of the ICSU (International Council of Scientific Unions). New York: Wiley.

Holsti, K. J.
1975   "Underdevelopment and the 'Gap' Theory of International Conflict."
          American Political Science Review 69 (September): 827–39.
Horsefield, John Keith
1969   *The International Monetary Fund, 1945–1965.* 3 vols. Washing-
          ton, D.C.: International Monetary Fund.
Inkeles, Alex
1975   "The Emerging Social Structure of the World." *World Politics* 27 (July):
          467–95.
Johansen, Robert C.
1980   *The National Interest and the Human Interest: An Analysis of U.S.
          Foreign Policy.* Princeton: Princeton University Press.
Kaplan, Morton A.
1957   *System and Process in International Politics.* New York: Wiley.
Kaufman, Edy
1976   *The Superpowers and Their Spheres of Influence.* New York:
          St. Martin's Press.
Keohane, Robert O., and Nye, Joseph S.
1974   "Transgovernmental Relations and International Organizations." *World
          Politics* 27 (October): 39–62.
1977   *Power and Interdependence: World Politics in Transition.* Boston: Little,
          Brown.
1972, eds.   *Transnational Relations and World Politics.* Cambridge: Harvard
          University Press.
Keynes, John Maynard
1920   *The Economic Consequences of the Peace.* New York: Harcourt, Brace
          and Howe.
Kindleberger, Charles P.
1973   *The World in Depression, 1929–1939.* Berkeley and Los Angeles:
          University of California Press.
Knorr, Klaus
1975   *The Power of Nations: The Political Economy of International Relations.*
          New York: Basic Books.
1977   "Economic Interdependence and National Security." In *Economic Issues
          and National Security*, edited by Klaus Knorr and Frank Trager,
          pp. 1–18. Lawrence, Kans.: Regents Press of Kansas.
Koestler, Arthur
1979   *Janus: A Summing Up.* New York: Random House.
Kothari, Rajni
1974   *Footsteps into the Future.* New York: Free Press.
Kuhn, Thomas S.
1962   *The Structure of Scientific Revolutions.* Chicago: University of Chicago
          Press.

La Porte, Todd R., ed.
1975   *Organized Social Complexity: Challenge to Politics and Policy.* Princeton, N.J.: Princeton University Press.
Lasswell, Harold D., and Kaplan, Abraham
1950   *Power and Society.* New Haven: Yale University Press.
Lindblom, Charles E.
1977   *Politics and Markets: The World's Political-Economic Systems.* New York: Basic Books.
McClelland, Charles A.
1955   "Applications of General Systems Theory in International Relations." *Main Currents in Modern Thought* 12, no. 2 (November): 27–34.
1966   *Theory and the International System.* New York: Macmillan.
Mack, Andrew J. R.
1975   "Why Big Nations Lose Small Wars: The Politics of Asymmetric Conflict." *World Politics* 27 (January): 175–200.
Mackinder, Halford J.
1919, 1942 *Democratic Ideals and Reality.* New York: Henry Holt.
Mahan, Alfred Thayer
1893   *The Influence of Sea Power upon History, 1660–1783.* Boston: Little, Brown.
Marx, Karl, and Engels, Friedrich
1959   *Basic Writings on Politics and Philosophy.* Edited by Lewis S. Feuer. Garden City, N.Y.: Doubleday.
Meadows, Donnella; Meadows, Dennis L.; Rander, Jorgen; and Behrens, William W.
1972, 1974 *The Limits to Growth.* 1st and 2d eds. New York: Universe Books.
Mendlovitz, Saul H.
1975   *On the Creation of a Just World Order.* New York: Free Press.
Merton, Robert
1936   "The Unanticipated Consequences of Purposive Social Action." *American Sociological Review* 1, no. 6 (December): 894–904.
Mesarovic, Mijalo, and Pestel, Eduard
1972   *Mankind at the Turning Point.* New York: E. P. Dutton.
Molnar, Miklos
1971   *Budapest 1956: A History of the Hungarian Revolution.* London: Allen and Unwin.
Murphy, Craig N.
1980   "The Emergence of the New International Economic Order Ideology." Ph.D. dissertation, University of North Carolina at Chapel Hill.
Nagel, Jack H.
1975   *The Descriptive Analysis of Power.* New Haven: Yale University Press.
Olson, Mancur, Jr.
1965   *The Logic of Collective Action: Public Goods and the Theory of Groups.* Cambridge, Mass.: Harvard University Press.
Olson, Mancur, Jr., and Landsberg, Hans J., eds.
1974   *The No-growth Society.* New York: W. W. Norton.

Olson, Mancur, Jr., and Zeckhauser, Richard
1970   "An Economic Theory of Alliances." In *Alliances in International Politics*, edited by Julian Friedman, Christopher Bladen, and Steven Rosen, pp. 175–98. Boston: Allyn and Bacon.

Orr, David W.
1979   "Catastrophe and Social Order." *Human Ecology* 7, no. 1, pp. 41–52.

Orwell, George
1950   "Politics and the English Language." In *Shooting an Elephant and Other Essays*, pp. 77–92. New York: Harcourt, Brace.

Ostrum, Vincent, and Ostrum, Eleanor
1977   "A Theory for Institutional Analysis of Common Pool Problems." In *Managing the Commons*, edited by Garrett Hardin and John Baden, pp. 157–72. San Francisco: W. H. Freeman.

Pirages, Dennis C.
1977   *The Sustainable Society: Implications for Limited Growth*. New York: Praeger.

Popper, Karl R.
1957   *The Poverty of Historicism*. London: Routledge and Kegan Paul.

Rapoport, Anatol
1960   *Fights, Games, and Debates*. Ann Arbor: University of Michigan Press.

Rosenau, James N.
1979   "The Concept of Aggregation and Third World Demands: An Analytic Opportunity and an Empirical Challenge." Paper read at the Conference on Constancy and Change, November 14–17, Ojai, California.

1964, ed. *International Aspects of Civil Strife*. Princeton: Princeton University Press.

1969, ed. *Linkage Politics: Essays on the Convergence of National and International Systems*. New York: Free Press.

Ruggie, John Gerard
1972   "Collective Goods and Future International Collaboration." *American Political Science Review* 66, no. 3 (September): 874–93.

Russell, Bertrand
1938   *Power: A New Social Analysis*. New York: W. W. Norton.

Russett, Bruce M., and Sullivan, John D.
1971   "Collective Goods and International Organization." *International Organization* 25, no. 4 (Autumn): 845–65.

Schelling, Thomas C.
1978   *Micromotives and Macrobehavior*. New York: W. W. Norton.

Schiller, Herbert I.
1979   *Communication Accompanies Capital Flows*. Document 74 prepared for the International Commission for the Study of Communication Problems. Paris: UNESCO.

Schon, Donald
1971   *Beyond the Stable State*. New York: Random House.

Schumacher, E. F.
1977   *A Guide for the Perplexed*. New York: Harper and Row.
Scott, Andrew M.
1951   *The Anatomy of Communism*. New York: Philosophical Library.
1965   *The Revolution in Statecraft: Informal Penetration*. New York: Random
            House.
1967   *The Functioning of the International Political System*. New York:
            Macmillan.
1977   "Henry George, Henry Adams, and the Dominant American Ideology."
            South Atlantic Quarterly 76, no. 2 (Spring): 234–51.
Scott, Andrew M., et al.
1970   *Insurgency*. Chapel Hill: University of North Carolina Press.
Singh, Jyoti S.
1977   *A New International Economic Order: Toward a Fair Redistribution of
            the World's Resources*. New York: Praeger.
Smart, Ian
1978   "The Future of the British Nuclear Deterrent." *Survival* 20 (January–
            February).
Snyder, Richard C.; Hermann, Charles F.; and Lasswell, Harold D.
1976   "A Global Monitoring System: Appraising the Effects of Government on
            Human Dignity." *International Studies Quarterly* 20 (June): 221–60.
Sprout, Harold, and Sprout, Margaret
1962   *Foundations of International Politics*. New York: Van Nostrand.
1971   *Toward a Politics of the Planet Earth*. New York: Van Nostrand.
1974   *Multiple Vulnerabilities: The Context of Environmental Repair and
            Protection*. Princeton: Princeton University Center of International
            Studies.
Starr, Harvey, and Ostrum, Charles W.
1976   *A Collective Goods Approach to Understanding Transnational Action*.
            New York: Learning Resources in International Studies.
Steel, Ronald
1971–72   "A Spheres-of-Influence Policy." *Foreign Policy*, no. 5 (Winter):
            107–18.
Stein, Stanley J., and Stein, Barbara H.
1970   *The Colonial Heritage of Latin America*. New York: Oxford University
            Press.
Sterling, Richard W.
1974   *Macropolitics: International Relations in a Global Society*. New York:
            Alfred Knopf.
Tawney, R. H.
1926   *Religion and the Rise of Capitalism*. New York: Harcourt, Brace.
Thompson, William Irwin
1976   *Evil and World Order*. New York: Harper and Row.
Toulmin, Stephen, and Goodfield, June
1965   *The Discovery of Time*. New York: Harper and Row.

Turner, Frederick Jackson
1893, 1962   *The Frontier in American History.* New York: Holt, Rinehart, and
              Winston.
U.S. Congress, Senate, Foreign Relations Committee, Subcommittee on Foreign
Economic Policy
1977   *International Debt, the Banks, and U.S. Foreign Policy,* by Karin
              Lissakers. 95th Cong., 1st sess., 1977.
Vernon, Raymond
1971   *Sovereignty at Bay.* New York: Basic Books.
Vernon, Richard
1979   "Unintended Consequences." *Political Theory* 7, no. 1 (February):
              47–73.
Wagner, R. Harrison
1974   "Dissolving the State: Three Recent Perspectives on International
              Relations." *International Organization* 28 (Summer): 435–66.
Wallerstein, Immanuel M.
1974   *The Modern World System: Capitalist Agriculture and the Origins of the
              European World Economy in the Sixteenth Century.* New York:
              Academic Press.
1979   *The Capitalist World Economy.* Cambridge and New York: Cambridge
              University Press.
Waltz, Kenneth N.
1979   *Theory of International Relations.* Reading, Mass.: Addison-Wesley.
Watt, Kenneth
1974   *The Titanic Effect.* New York: E. P. Dutton.
Weber, Max
1930   *The Protestant Ethic and the Spirit of Capitalism.* London: George Allen
              and Unwin.
1968   *Economy and Society.* 3 vols. Edited by Guenther Roth and Claus
              Wittich. New York: Bedminster Press.
Wesson, Robert G.
1967   *The Imperial Order.* Berkeley: University of California Press.
White, Theodore H.
1978   *In Search of History: A Personal Adventure.* New York: Harper and
              Row.
Whitehead, Alfred North
1933   *Adventures of Ideas.* New York: Macmillan.
Wolf, Eric
1959   *Sons of the Shaking Earth.* Chicago: University of Chicago Press.
Young, Oran R.
1969   "Interdependence in World Politics." *International Journal* 24
              (Autumn): 726–50.

Index

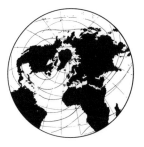